METROPOLIS
75TH ANNIVERSARY EDITION
THEA VON HARBOU

METROPOLIS

Thea von Harbou

75th Anniversary Edition

**Introduction by
Forrest J Ackerman**

Sense of Wonder Press
JAMES A. ROCK & COMPANY, PUBLISHERS
ROCKVILLE • MARYLAND

Metropolis, 75th Anniversary Edition
With an introduction by Forrest J Ackerman
Illustrations and Stillustrations selected by Forrest J Ackerman

is an imprint of *JAMES A. ROCK & CO., PUBLISHERS*

Address comments and inquiries to:
SENSE OF WONDER PRESS
James A. Rock & Company, Publishers
113 N. Washington Street, Box 347
Rockville, MD 20850

E-mail:
jrock@rockpublishing.com   lrock@senseofwonderpress.com
Internet URL: www.SenseOfWonderPress.com

Paperbound ISBN: 0-918736-35-8
Limited Edition Hardbound ISBN: 0-918736-34-x

Printed in the United States of America
First Sense of Wonder Press Edition: January 2002

METROPOLIS BOOK FOTO CREDITS
Profound Gratitude for the provision by or copyright acknowledgement of Individual Stills:
Academy of Motion Picture Arts & Sciences, Ackermuseum Imagi-Movie Still Archives,
Berlin Film Museum Still Archives, Bill Malone, Ron Borst, David Bradley,
British Film Institute, Cinematheque Belgique, Cinematheque Francais,
Walt Daugherty, Oscar G. Estes, Jr., Karl Freund, Rolf Giesen, Joe Green,
Wolfgang Jacobsen, Irving Klaw, Joe Kucera, Fritz Lang, Peter Latta, Eddie Lichtig,
Paramount Studios, Phil Riley, Walter Schulze-Mittendorf, Bob Short,
Werner Sundendorf, Universum Film Aktiengesellschaft (UFA), Horst von Harbou,
Anne Hardin, Wardour Films Ltd., Geo. H. Wyman.

METROPOLIS
DEDICATED TO THE MEMORIES OF

FRITZ LANG
BRIGITTE HELM
KARL FREUND
RUDOLF KLEIN-ROGGE
ALFRED ABEL
GUSTAV FREULICH
THEA VON HARBOU (OF 1926)
FAN AITAM BAR-SAGI
AND TO
TODAY'S SUPER METROPOLIS FAN
DOUGLAS AIKEN

GRAPHICS, ART AND STILLUSTRATIONS

GRAPHICS, ART AND STILLUSTRATIONS, CONT.

GRAPHICS, ART AND STILLUSTRATIONS, CONT.

Forrest J Ackerman with Fritz Lang at a "Count Dracula" Banquet in the 1960's.

METROPOLIS

FJA "Reaches for the Moon" in his home town of METROPOLIS!

Introduction

BY FORREST J ACKERMAN

"Mr. Science Fiction" and Metropolis Fan #1.

Welcome to Metropolis, My Home Town.

Population—estimated by my slan-friend A. E. van Vogt—approximately 40 million.

I've lived here since I was 10 years old. It's the most exciting, fabulous city on the face of the earth—and under it. London, Los Angeles, New York, Paris, Berlin, Tokyo ... all rolled and roiled into one.

Just imagine!

When I say the magic name—*Metropolis*—it is as tho I combine the skyscraping dominance of the Empire State Building with the elegance of the Taj Mahal, the fame of the Eiffel Tower and the eternal mystery of the Sphinx of Egypt. *Metropolis*—The New Babel, architectural masterpiece of monolithic magnificence. The skyscrapers of the 20th century dwarfed by the towering stratoscrapers of the 21st.

And far beneath, in man-made caverns below, the monster-machines of Moloch: the incredible, inhuman Geyser Machine, the Heart Machine, that must be forever tended by the Human Clocks, the subterranean sub-humans, the helpless workers of the mole-world who slave their hopeless lives away, serfs for the surface people, blind puppets to the will of the Master of Metropolis.

The Master of Metropolis: *Joh Fredersen*, a man forged of ten-point steel, cold as the surface of Pluto—and as distant. A ruler as ruthless and imperious as ancient Caesar.

Hidden somewhere amidst the futuristic superstructures of Metropolis is an anachronistic dwelling, a baroque and gothic survival housing a laboratory wherein alchemical marvels are performed. With the Seal of Solomon on its door, the legendary Golem might have been born here hundreds of years before. Today a wild-eyed white-haired albino spider spins within, a sinister genius who has sacrificed one hand to his supramundane science. It is the eerie abode of *Rotwang*, the evil Ralph 124C41+ of his day.

And Rotwang has created *Futura*—sometimes also called *Parody*—a simulucrum in sentient metal of artificial female flesh. A robotrix of which Rossum might have dreamt.

Metropolis—the book—has been compared to Karel Capek's play *RUR*, to Samuel Butler's Utopian novel *Erewhon*, "of a future period when machinery would develop a soul and become man's master", to *The Time Machine*, in which "the restless far-seeing mind of H.G.Wells conceived an unforgettable picture of the development of social and economic conditions under his Eloi, the epicurean and effete aristocrats of the future world, and their underground and uncanny slaves, the Morlocks." *When the Sleeper Wakes* (Wells), *Land Under England* (O'Neill), *Looking Backward* (Bellamy) and *Summer in 3000* (Martin)—two of which came later—are reminiscent in some respects of the book.

When I speak of *Metropolis* the film there is nothing with which to compare it: it remains the science-fantasy classic incomparable, the single greatest scientifilm I ever saw.

This masterpiece originally sold in book form in the late 20's in a chain of Ten Cent Stores! A wretched piece of book-making, the first edition nevertheless has become a cornerstone item in the collections of film adaptation collectors and a work particularly coveted by aficionados of fantasy filmdom. The lastime I had a spare copy it was snapped up for $25. It is undoubtedly going for more now.

Today, in its 75th year and at the birth of the new Millenium is hightime, and over time, that a new edition of this unique book be made available. Thea von Harbou, its gifted authoress, now dead, in her lifetime exhibited a literary mind that leapt ahead of reality. When rocketry was in its infancy, long before it was in its launching cradle, she authored the world-famous *Woman in the Moon*, both book and screenplay. "The Indian Tomb", "The Isle of the Immortals", "Destiny", "Spies"; "Siegfried" in film form and a cinemadaptation of "Dr. Mabuse"; were among Frau von Harbou's literary and motion picture legacy. She was married to the celebrated director Fritz Lang, who so masterfully materialized her masterpiece *Metropolis* on the screen.

"*Metropolis* is unlike any other novel as yet written," enthused an observer at the time. "It is distinct, unique and original. It has a tremendous drama of conflicting forces and an idyllic love theme."

The language of the novel is sometimes as thesauric as Shiel, as kaleidoscopic as Merritt in "The Metal Emperor", as bone-spare as Bradbury in "The Skeleton", as poetic as Poe, as macabre as Machen. The title belongs on your Hugo Award shelf along with *The World Below, The House on the Borderland, The Demolished Man, The Forever War, Childhood's End, Last Men in London, Stranger In A Strange Land, 1984.*

Science and Fantasy, Horror and Beauty; Mystery, Menace, Madness, Magnificence, Significance—Once in a Lifetime all the Elements were Magically Combined to Create the Imaginative Classic, the Filmasterpiece Supreme:

METROPOLIS!

This is the book on which the film was based.

The book has been called a work of genius.

I agree. In the next few hours you will have an experience in reading that will last you all the rest of your life.

—FORREST J ACKERMAN
Apt. 4sJ, Rotwang Towers
Lang Level and Harbou Skyway
METROPOLIS
24 Novembro 2027

---

6 April 2027

I've lost track (remember, I'm 111 years old), I think I've now seen METROPOLIS 119 times. And MEGALOPOLIS, the scientifilm first projected in 2001, numerous times. I remember 1918's World War was described as "the war to end war." Then I devoted 3 years 4 months and 29 days to WW2 and my brother lost his life. H. G. Wells said, "If we don't end war, war will end us." I never thought I'd live to see WW3—The Terrorist War—but it pearlharbored us, a surprise attack, alas.

A quarter century ago in 2001, Anne Hardin was proofreading this 75th Anniversary Edition of *METROPOLIS* during the 2 weeks following September 11. She's my collaborator on *RAINBOW FANTASIA, MARTIANTHOLOGY* and many other Sense of Wonder Press publications of the last 5 lustrums. Her reaction: "I think in many ways I could have inserted the text on the destruction of Metropolis into the *NY Times* any day of the past 2 weeks and the vivid picture of a city's destruction would have been the same: the images of fire, heat and being trapped by water, the trains crashing in and preventing Maria's escape with the children—all too real. The resemblance between Manhattan and the Metropolis of the film is chilling; the imagination of the set builders was remarkably prescient." She continues: "There are stories and there are STORIES. Only once in a blue moon does someone's mind create a novel concept. Just think of all the books that Shelley's book influenced. Seems to me the same incredible creativeness that you see in *Frankenstein* is present in *Metropolis*. And the translation has a rhythm to it that is hypnotic. I also wonder if von Harbou was influenced by Meyrink's *Der Golem*: I think bringing

Futura to life as Maria is a bit akin to the infusion of life in the man of clay, eh?"

Judge for yourself!

In the meantime, on a happier note, in my original introduction I noted that A. E. van Vogt, whom we lost 27 years ago, estimated the population of Metropolis to be 40 million; for purists I have since learned that the correct figure is 60 million.

Read, now, Thea von Harbou's coruscating classic; it will give you a rush like an evening in Yoshiwara!

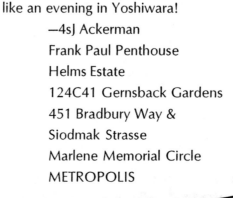

—4sJ Ackerman
Frank Paul Penthouse
Helms Estate
124C41 Gernsback Gardens
451 Bradbury Way &
Siodmak Strasse
Marlene Memorial Circle
METROPOLIS

Cover of first Edition (German) of Thea von Harbou's METROPOLIS.

A. Scherl Berlin, 1926, 273 pages. Cover based on an original design by Walter Reimann.

"Rotwang menaces Maria—"
"Rudolf Klein-Rogge in METROPOLIS (1927)
"Artist: Oscar G. Estes, Jr., personal gift to Forrest J Ackerman, 1963

German Movie Poster depicting (left to right): Joh Fredersen, Master of Metropolis, Rotwang, the crazed but brilliant man of science, and the mechanical robot, "Futura".

Forrest J Ackerman with his encyclopedic collection of METROPOLIS Stills, Artwork, Books, and assorted items of interest to movie and book fans.

METROPOLIS

The year is 2026, a Dickensian "best of times, worst of times," where total oppression and manipulation of the masses is wielded by the unquestionable power of the few. Far below the City of Metropolis is the Underground City where machines are operated by the workers who live even further below. Day after day, in mechanical routine, they are forced to the limits of human endurance.

Fritz Lang made this film in 1926. Against his wishes the film was subsequently shortened for its American release which left the story disjointed, difficult to comprehend and caused the loss of many scenes, most of which have disappeared forever.

By following the original script, the novel of the film, recently discovered missing pieces of the film and photographs, Metropolis has been restored as close to its original conception as possible.

Metropolis is now presented with a contemporary score, sound effects and color tinting.

Lang once said: "To begin with I should say that I am a visual person. I experience with my eyes and never, or only rarely, with my ears—to my constant regret."

EXCLUSIVE ENGAGEMENT BEGINS
FRIDAY, AUGUST 10, 1984

57ᵀᴴ PLAYHOUSE
Avenue of the Americas on 57th Street 581-7360

Reverse side of handbill reads "Academy Award winner Giorgio Moroder presents Fritz Lang's classic vision of the future, now beautifully restored and with a contemporary musical score."

CHAPTER I
THESE ARE YOUR BROTHERS

NOW THE rumbling of the great organ swelled to a roar, pressing, like a rising giant, against the vaulted ceiling, to burst through it.

Freder bent his head backwards, his wide-open, burning eyes stared unseeingly upward. His hands formed music from the chaos of the notes; struggling with the vibration of the sound and stirring him to his innermost depths.

He was never so near tears in his life and, blissfully helpless, he yielded himself up to the glowing moisture which dazzled him.

Above him, the vault of heaven in *lapis lazuli*; hovering therein, the twelve-fold mystery, the Signs of the Zodiac in gold. Set higher above them, the seven crowned ones: the planets. High above all a silver-shining bevy of stars: the universe.

Before the bedewed eyes of the organ-player, to his music, the stars of heavens began the solemn mighty dance. The breakers of the notes dissolved the room into nothing. The organ, which Freder played, stood in the middle of the sea.

It was a reef upon which the waves foamed. Carrying crests of froth, they dashed violently onward, and the seventh was always the mightiest. But high above the sea, which bellowed in the uproar of the waves, the stars of heaven danced the solemn, mighty dance.

Shaken to her core, the old earth started from her sleep. Her torrents dried up; her mountains fell to ruin. From the ripped open depths the fire welled up; The earth burnt with all she bore. The waves of the sea became waves of fire. The organ flared up, a roaring torch of music. The earth, the sea and the hymn-blazing organ crashed in and became ashes.

1

But high above the deserts and the spaces, to which creation was burnt, the stars of heaven danced the solemn mighty dance.

Then, from the grey, scattered ashes, on trembling wings unspeakably beautiful and solitary, rose a bird with jewelled feathers. It uttered a mournful cry. No bird which ever lived could have mourned so agonisingly.

It hovered above the ashes of the completely ruined earth. It hovered hither and thither, not knowing where to settle. It hovered above the grave of the sea and above the corpse of the earth. Never, since the sinning angel fell from heaven to hell, had the air heard such a cry of despair.

Then, from the solemn mighty dance of the stars, one freed itself and neared the dead earth. Its light was gentler than moonlight and more imperious than the light of the sun. Among the music of the spheres it was the most heavenly note. It enveloped the mourning bird in its dear light; it was as strong as a deity, crying: "To me . . . to me!"

Then the jewelled bird left the grave of the sea and earth and gave its sinking wings up to the powerful voice which bore it. Moving in a cradle of light, it swept upwards and sang, becoming a note of the spheres, vanishing into Eternity . . .

Freder let his fingers slip from the keys. He bent forward and buried his face in his hands. He pressed his eyes until he saw the fiery dance of the stars behind his eyelids. Nothing could help him—nothing. Everywhere, everywhere, in an agonising, blissful omnipresence, stood, in his vision, the one one countenance.

The austere countenance of the virgin, the sweet countenance of the mother—the agony and the desire with which he called and called for the one single vision for which his racked heart had not even a name, except the one, eternal, you . . . you . . . you . . .!

He let his hands sink and raised his eyes to the heights of the beautifully vaulted room, in which his organ stood. From the sea-deep blue of the heavens, from the flawless gold of the heavenly bodies, from the mysterious twilight around him, the girl looked at him with the deadly severity of purity, quite maid and mistress, inviolability, graciousness itself, her beautiful brow in the diadem of goodness, her voice, pity, every word a song. Then to turn, and to go, and to vanish—no more to be found. Nowhere, nowhere.

"You—!" cried the man. The captive note struck against the walls, finding no way out.

Now the loneliness was no longer bearable. Freder stood up and opened the windows. The works lay, in quivering brightness, before him. He pressed his eyes closed, standing still, hardly breathing. He felt the proximity of the servants, standing silently, waiting for the command which would permit them to come to life.

There was one among them—Slim, with his courteous face, the expression of which never changed—Freder knew of him: one word to him, and, if the girl still walked on earth with her silent step, then Slim would find her. But one does not set a blood-hound on the track of a sacred, white hind, if one does not want to be cursed, and to be, all his life long, a miserable, miserable man.

Freder saw, without looking at him, how Slim's eyes were taking stock of him. He knew that the silent creature, ordained, by his father, to be his all-powerful protector, was, at the same time, his keeper. During the fever of nights, bereft of sleep, during the fever of his work, in his work-shop, during the fever when playing his organ, calling upon God, there would be Slim measuring the pulse of the son of his great master. He gave no reports; they were not required of him. But, if the hour should come in which they were demanded of him, be would certainly have a diary of faultless perfection to produce, from the number of steps with which one in torment treads out his loneliness with heavy foot, from minute to minute, to the dropping of a brow into propped up hands, tired with longing.

Could it be possible that this man, who knew everything, knew nothing of her?

Nothing about him betrayed that he was aware of the upheaval in the well-being and disposition of his young master, since that day in the "Club of the Sons." But it was one of the slim, silent one's greatest secrets never to give himself away, and, although he had no entrance to the "Club of the Sons" Freder was by no means sure that the money-backed agent of his father would be turned back by the rules of the club.

He felt himself exposed, unclothed. A cruel brightness, which left nothing concealed, bathed him and everything in his workshop which was almost the most highly situated room in Metropolis.

"I wish to be quite alone," he said softly.

Silently the servants vanished, Slim went . . . But all these doors, which closed without the least sound, could also, without the least sound, be opened again to the narrowest chink.

His eyes aching, Freder fingered all the doors of his work-room.

A smile, a rather bitter smile, drew down the corners of his mouth. He was a treasure which must be guarded as crown jewels are guarded. The son of a great father, and the only son.

Really the only one—?

Really the only one—?

His thoughts stopped again at the exit of the circuit and the vision was there again and the scene and the event . . .

The "Club of the Sons" was, perhaps, one of the most beautiful buildings of Metropolis, and that was not so very remarkable. For fathers, for whom every revolution of a machine-wheel spelt gold, had presented this house to their sons. It was more a district than a house. It embraced theatres, picture-palaces, lecture-rooms and a library—in which, every book, printed in all the five continents, was to be found—race tracks and stadium and the famous "Eternal Gardens."

It contained very extensive dwellings for the young sons of indulgent fathers and it contained the dwellings of faultless male servants and handsome, well-trained female servants for whose training more time was requisite than for the development of new species of orchids.

Their chief task consisted in nothing but, at all times, to appear delightful and to be incapriciously cheerful; and, with their bewildering costume, their painted faces, and their eye-masks, surmounted by snow-white wigs and fragrant as flowers, they resembled delicate dolls of porcelain and brocade, devised by a master-hand, not purchaseable but rather delightful presents.

Freder was but a rare visitant to the "Club of the Sons." He preferred his work-shop and the starry chapel in which this organ stood. But when once the desire took him to fling himself into the radiant joyousness of the stadium competitions he was the most radiant and joyous of all, playing on from victory to victory with the laugh of a young god.

On that day too . . . on that day too.

Still tingling from the icy coolness of falling water, every muscle still quivering in the intoxication of victory he had lain, stretched out, slender, panting, smiling, drunken, beside himself, almost insane with joy. The milk-coloured glass ceiling above the Eternal Gardens was an opal in the light which bathed it. Loving little women attended him, waiting roguishly and jealously, from whose white hands, from whose fine finger-tips he would eat the fruits he desired.

One was standing aside, mixing him a drink. From hip to knee billowed sparkling brocade. Slender, bare legs held proudly together, she stood, like ivory, in purple, peaked shoes. Her gleaming body rose, delicately, from her hips and—she was not aware of it—quivered in the same rhythm as did the man's chest in exhaling his sweet-rising breath. Carefully did the little painted face under the eye-mask watch the work of her careful hands.

4

Freder was but a rare visitant to the "Club of the Sons." He preferred his work-shop and the starry chapel in which this organ stood. But when once the desire took him to fling himself into the radiant joyousness of the stadium competitions he was the most radiant and joyous of all, playing on from victory to victory with the laugh of a young god.

Her mouth was not rouged, but yet was pomegranate red. And she smiled so unselfconsciously down at the beverage that it caused the other girls to laugh aloud.

Infected, Freder also began to laugh. But the glee of the maidens swelled to a storm as she who was mixing the drink, not knowing why they were laughing, became suffused with a blush of confusion, from her pomegranate-hued mouth to her lustrous hips. The laughter induced the friends, for no reason, only because they were young and care-free, to join in the cheerful sound. Like a joyously ringing rainbow, peal upon peal of laughter arched itself gaily above the young people.

Then suddenly—suddenly—Freder turned his head. His hands, which were resting on the hips of the drink-mixer, lost hold of her, dropping down by his sides as if dead. The laughter ceased, not one of the friends moved. Not one of the little, brocaded, bare-limbed women moved hand or foot. They stood and looked.

The door of the Eternal Gardens had opened and through the door came a procession of children. They were all holding hands. They had dwarves' faces, grey and ancient. They were little ghost-like skeletons, covered with faded rags and smocks. They had colourless hair and colourless eyes. They walked on emaciated bare feet. Noiselessly they followed their leader.

Their leader was a girl. The austere countenance of the Virgin. The sweet countenance of the mother. She held a skinny child by each hand. Now she stood still, regarding the young men and women one after another, with the deadly severity of purity. She was quite maid and mistress, inviolability—and was, too, graciousness itself, her beautiful brow in the diadem of goodness; her voice, pity; every word a song.

She released the children and stretched forward her hand, motioning towards the friends and saying to the children:

"Look, these are your brothers!"

And, motioning towards the children, she said to the friends:

"Look, these are your brothers!"

She waited. She stood still and her gaze rested upon Freder.

Then the servants came, the door-keepers came. Between these walls of marble and glass, under the opal dome of the Eternal Gardens, there reigned, for a short time, an unprecedented confusion of noise, indignation and embarrassment. The girl appeared still to be waiting. Nobody dared to touch her, though she stood so defenceless, among the grey infant-phantoms, Her eyes rested perpetually on Freder.

Then she took her eyes from his and, stooping a little, took the children's hands again, turned and led the procession out. The door swung to behind her; the servants disappeared with many apologies for not having been able to prevent the occurrence. All was emptiness and silence. Had not each of those before whom the girl had appeared, with her grey procession of children, so large a number of witnesses to the event they would have been inclined to put it down to hallucination.

Near Freder, upon the illuminated mosaic floor, cowered the little drink-mixer, sobbing uncontrolledly.

With a leisurely movement, Freder bent towards her and suddenly twitched the mask, the narrow black mask, from her eyes.

The drink-mixer shrieked out as though overtaken in stark nudity. Her hands flew up, clutching, and remained hanging stiffly in the air.

A little painted face stared, horror-stricken at the man. The eyes, thus exposed, were senseless, quite empty. The little face from which the charm of the mask had been taken away, was quite weird.

Freder dropped the black piece of stuff. The drink-mixer pounced quickly upon it, hiding her face. Freder looked around him.

The Eternal Gardens scintillated. The beautiful beings in it, even if, temporarily, thrown out of balance, shone in their well-cared-for-ness, their cleanly abundance. The odour of freshness, which pervaded everywhere, was like the breath of a dewy garden.

Freder looked down at himself. He wore, as all the youths in the "House of the Sons," the white silk, which they wore but once—the soft, supple shoes, with the noiseless soles,

He looked at his friends. He saw these beings who never wearied, unless from sport—who never sweated, unless from sport—who were never out of breath, unless from sport. Beings requiring their joyous games in order that their food and drink might agree with them, in order to be able to sleep well and digest easily.

The tables, at which they had all eaten, were laid, as before-hand, with untouched dishes. Wine, golden and purple, embedded in ice or warmth, was there, proffering itself, like the loving little women. Now the music was playing again. It had been silenced when the girlish voice spoke the five soft words:

"Look, these are your brothers!"

And once more, with her eyes resting on Freder:

"Look, these are your brothers!"

As one suffocating, Freder sprang up. The masked women stared at

Their leader was a girl. The austere countenance of the Virgin. The sweet countenance of the mother. She held a skinny child by each hand. Now she stood still, regarding the young men and women one after another, with the deadly severity of purity . . . And, motioning towards the children, she said to the friends: "Look, these are your brothers!" [Brigitte Helm (Maria)]

him. He dashed to the door. He ran along passages and down steps. He came to the entrance.

"Who was that girl?"

Perplexed shrugs. Apologies. The occurrence was inexcusable, the servants knew it. Dismissals, in plenty, would be distributed.

The Major Domo was pale with anger.

"I do not wish," said Freder, gazing into space, "that anyone should suffer for what has happened. Nobody is to be dismissed . . . I do not wish it . . ."

The Major Domo bowed in silence. He was accustomed to whims in the "Club of the Sons."

"Who is the girl . . . can nobody tell me?"

No. Nobody. But if an inquiry is to be made . . .?

Freder remained silent. He thought of Slim. He shook his head. First slowly, then violently. "No—

One does not set a bloodhound on the track of a sacred, white hind.

"Nobody is to inquire about her," he said, tonelessly.

He felt the soulless glance of the strange, hired person upon his face. He felt himself poor and besmirched. In an ill-temper which rendered him as wretched as though he had poison in his veins, he left the club. He walked home as though going into exile. He shut himself up in his workroom and worked. At nights he clung to his instrument and forced the monstrous solitude of Jupiter and Saturn down to him.

Nothing could help him—nothing! In an agonising blissful omnipresence stood, before his vision the one, one countenance; the austere countenance of the virgin, the sweet countenance of the mother.

A voice spoke:

"Look, these are your brothers."

And the glory of the heavens was nothing, and the intoxication of work was nothing. And the conflagration which wiped out the sea could not wipe out the soft voice of the girl:

"Look, these are your brothers!" My God, my God—

* * * * * *

With a painful, violent jerk, Freder turned around and walked up to his machine. Something like deliverance passed across his face as he considered this shining creation, waiting only for him, of which there was not a steel link, not a rivet, not a spring which he had not calculated and created.

9

The creature was not large, appearing still more fragile by reason of the huge room and flood of sunlight in which it stood. But the soft lustre of its metal and the proud swing with which the foremost body seemed to raise itself to leap, even when not in motion, gave it something of the fair godliness of a faultlessly beautiful animal, which is quite fearless, because it knows itself to be invincible.

Freder caressed his creation. He pressed his head gently against the machine. With ineffable affection he felt its cool, flexible members.

"To-night," he said, "I shall be with you. I shall be entirely enwrapped by you. I shall pour out my life into you and shall fathom whether or not I can bring you to life. I shall, perhaps, feel your throb and the commencement of movement in your controlled body. I shall, perhaps, feel the giddiness with which you throw yourself out into your boundless element, carrying me—me, the man who made—through the huge sea of midnight. The seven stars will be above us and the sad beauty of the moon. Mount Everest will remain, a hill, below us. You shall carry me and I shall know: You carry me as high as I wish . . ."

He stopped, closing his eyes. The shudder which ran through him was imparted, a thrill, to the silent machine. "But perhaps," he continued, without raising his voice, "perhaps you notice, you, my beloved creation, that you are no longer my only love. Nothing on earth is more vengeful than the jealousy of a machine which believes itself to be neglected. Yes, I know that . . . You are imperious mistresses . . . Thou shalt have none other Gods but me." . . . Am I right? A thought apart from you—you feel it at once and become perverse. How could I keep it hidden from you that all my thoughts are not with you. I can't help it, my creation. I was bewitched, machine. I press my forehead upon you and my forehead longs for the knees of the girl of whom I do not even know the name . . ."

He ceased and held his breath. He raised his head and listened.

Hundreds and thousands of times had he heard that same sound in the city. But hundreds and thousands of time, it seemed to him, he had not comprehended it.

It was an immeasurably glorious and transporting sound. As deep and rumbling as, and more powerful than, any sound on earth. The voice of the ocean when it is angry, the voice of falling torrents, the voice of very close thunderstorms would be miserably drowned in this Behemoth-din. Without being shrill it penetrated all walls, and, as long as it lasted, all things seemed to swing in it. It was omnipresent, coming from the heights and from the depths, being beautiful and horrible, being an irresistible command.

It was high above the town. It was the voice of the town.

Their chief task consisted in nothing but, at all times, to appear delightful and to be incapriciously cheerful; and, with their bewildering costume, their painted faces, and their eye-masks, surmounted by snow-white wigs and fragrant as flowers, they resembled delicate dolls of porcelain and brocade, devised by a master-hand, not purchaseable but rather delightful presents. [Center, Heinrich Gotho]

Metropolis raised her voice. The machines of Metropolis roared; they wanted to be fed.

Freder pushed open the glass doors. He felt them tremble like strings under strokes of the bow. He stepped out on to the narrow gallery which ran around this, almost the highest house of Metropolis. The roaring sound received him, enveloped him, never coming to an end.

Great as Metropolis was: at all four corners of the city, this roared command was equally perceptible.

Freder looked across the city at the building known to the world as the "New Tower of Babel."

In the brain-pan of this New Tower of Babel lived the man who was himself the Brain of Metropolis.

As long as the man over there, who was nothing but work, despising sleep, eating and drinking mechanically, pressed his fingers on the blue metal plate, which apart from himself, no man had ever touched, so long would the voice of the machine-city of Metropolis roar for food, for food, for food . . .

She wanted living men for food.

Then the living food came pushing along in masses. Along the street it came, along its own street which never crossed with other people's streets. It rolled on, a broad, an endless stream. The stream was twelve files deep. They walked in even step. Men, men, men—all in the same uniform, from throat to ankle in dark blue linen, bare feet in the same hard shoes, hair tightly pressed down by the same black caps.

And they all had the same faces. And they all appeared to be of the same age. They held themselves straightened up, but not straight. They did not raise their heads, they pushed them forward. They planted their feet forward, but they did not walk. The open gates of the New Tower of Babel, the machine center of Metropolis, gulped the masses down.

Towards them, but past them, another procession dragged itself along, the shift just used. It rolled on, a broad, an endless stream. The stream was twelve files deep. They walked in even step. Men, men, men—all in the same uniform, from throat to ankle in dark blue linen, bare feet in the same hard shoes, hair tightly pressed down by the same black caps.

And they all had the same faces. And they all seemed one thousand years old. They walked with hanging fists, they walked with hanging heads. No, they planted their feet forward but they did not walk. The open gates of the New Tower of Babel, the machine centre of Metropolis, threw the masses up as it gulped them down.

When the fresh living food had disappeared through the gates the roaring voice was silent at last. And the never ceasing, throbbing hum of the great Metropolis became perceptible again, producing the effect of silence, a deep relief. The man who was the great brain in the brain-pan of Metropolis had ceased to press his fingers on the blue metal plate.

In ten hours he would let the machine brute roar anew. And in another ten hours, again. And always the same, and always the same, without ever loosening the ten-hour clamp.

Metropolis did not know what Sunday was. Metropolis knew neither high days nor holidays. Metropolis had the most saintly cathedral in the world, richly adorned with Gothic decoration. In times of which only the chronicles could tell, the star-crowned Virgin on its tower used to smile, as a mother, from out her golden mantle, deep, deep down upon the pious red rooves and the only companions of her graciousness were the doves which used to nest in the gargoyles of the water-spouts and the bells which were called after the four archangels and of which Saint Michael was the most magnificent.

It was said that the Master who cast it turned villain for its sake, for he stole consecrated and unconsecrated silver, like a raven, casting it into the metal body of the bell. As a reward for his deed he suffered, on the place of execution, the dreadful death on the wheel. But, it was said, be died exceedingly happy, for the Archangel Michael rang him on his way to death so wonderfully, touchingly, that all agreed the saints must have forgiven the sinner already, to ring the heavenly bells, thus, to receive him.

The bells still rang with their old, golden voices but when Metropolis roared, then Saint Michael itself was hoarse. The New Tower of Babel and its fellow houses stretched their somber heights high above the cathedral spire, that the young girls in the work-rooms and wireless stations gazed down just as deep from the thirtieth story windows on the star-crowned virgin as she, in earlier days, had looked down on the pious red rooves. In place of doves, flying machines swarmed over the cathedral roof and over the city, resting on the rooves, from which, at night glaring pillars and circles indicated the course of flight and landing points.

The Master of Metropolis had already considered, more than once, having the cathedral pulled down, as being pointless and an obstruction to the traffic in the town of fifty million inhabitants.

But the small, eager sect of Gothics, whose leader was Desertus, half monk, half one enraptured, had sworn the solemn oath: If one hand from the wicked city of Metropolis were to dare to touch just one stone of the cathedral, then they would neither repose nor rest until the wicked city of Metropolis should lie, a heap of ruins, at the foot of her cathedral.

The Master of Metropolis used to avenge the threats which constituted one sixth of his daily mail. But he did not care to fight with opponents to whom he rendered a service by destroying them for their belief. The great brain of Metropolis, a stranger to the sacrifice of a desire, estimated the incalculable power which the sacrificed ones and martyrs showered upon their followers too high rather than too low. Too, the demolition of the cathedral was not yet so burning a question as to have been the object of an estimate of expenses. But when the moment should come, the cost of its pulling down would exceed that of the construction of Metropolis. The Gothics were ascetics; the Master of Metropolis knew by experience that a multi-milliardaire was more cheaply bought over than an ascetic.

Freder wondered, not without a foreign feeling of bitterness, how many more times the great Master of Metropolis would permit him to look on at the scene which the cathedral would present to him on every rainless day: When the sun sank at the back of Metropolis, the houses turning to mountains and the streets to valleys; when the stream of light, which seemed to crackle with coldness, broke forth from all windows, from the walls of the houses, from the rooves and from the heart of the town; when the silent quiver of electric advertisments began; when the searchlights, in all colours of the rainbow, began to play around the New Tower of Babel; when the omnibuses turned to chains of light-spitting monsters, the little motor cars to scurrying, luminous fishes in a waterless deep-sea, while from the invisible harbour of the underground railway, an ever equal, magical shimmer pressed on to be swallowed by the hurrying shadows—then the cathedral would stand there, in this boundless ocean of light, which dissolved all forms by outshining them, the only dark object, black and persistent, seeming, in its lightlessness, to free itself from the earth, to rise higher and ever higher, and appearing in this maelstrom of tumultuous light, the only reposeful and masterful object.

But the Virgin on the top of the tower seemed to have her own gentle starlight, and hovered, set free from the blackness of the stone, on the sickle of the silver moon, above the cathedral.

Freder had never seen the countenance of the Virgin and yet he knew it so well he could have drawn it: the austere countenance of the Virgin, the sweet countenance of the mother.

He stooped, clasping the burning palms of his hands around the iron railing.

"Look at me, Virgin," he begged, "Mother, look at me!"

The spear of a searchlight flew into his eyes causing him to close them angrily. A whistling rocket hissed through the air, dropping down into the pale twilight of the afternoon, the word : Yoshiwara . . .

Remarkably white, and with penetrating beams, there hovered, towering up, over a house which was not to be seen, the word: Cinema.

All the seven colours of the rainbow flared, cold and ghostlike in silently swinging circles. The enormous face of the clock on the New Tower of Babel was bathed in the glaring cross-fire of the searchlights. And over and over again from the pale, unreal-looking sky, dripped the word: Yoshiwara.

Freder's eyes hung on the clock of the New Tower of Babel, where the seconds flashed off as sparks of breathing lightning, continuous in their coming as in their going. He calculated the time which had passed since the voice of Metropolis had roared for food, for food, for food. He knew that behind the throbbing second flashes on the New Tower of Babel there was a wide, bare room with narrow windows, the height of the walls, switch-boards on all sides, right in the centre, the table, the most ingenious instrument which the Master of Metropolis had created, on which to play, alone, as solitary master.

On the plain chair before it, the embodiment of the great brain: the Master of Metropolis. Near his right hand the sensitive blue metal plate, to which he would stretch out his right hand, with the infallible certainty of a healthy machine, when seconds enough had flicked off into eternity, to let Metropolis roar once more—"for food, for food, for food—"

In this moment Freder was seized with the persistent idea that he would lose his reason if he had, once more, to hear the voice of Metropolis thus roaring to be fed. And, already convinced of the pointlessness of his quest, he turned from the spectacle of the light crazy city and went to seek the Master of Metropolis, whose name was Joh Fredersen and who was his father.

Carpenters work on the construction of the skyscrapers for the movie set of METROPOLIS. Note parts of the city in the background of the photo.

CHAPTER II

DOESN'T IT FILL YOU WITH HORROR?

THE BRAIN-PAN of the New Tower of Babel was peopled with numbers.

From an invisible source the numbers dropped rhythmically down through the cooled air of the room, being collected, as in a water-basin, at the table at which the great brain of Metropolis worked, becoming objective under the pencils of his secretaries. These eight young men resembled each other as brothers, which they were not. Although sitting as immovable as statues, of which only the writing fingers of the right hand stirred, yet each single one, with sweat-bedewed brow and parted lips, seemed the personification of Breathlessness.

No head was raised on Freder's entering, Not even his father's.

The lamp under the third loud-speaker glowed white-red.

New York spoke.

Joh Fredersen was comparing the figures of the evening exchange report with the lists which lay before him. Once his voice sounded, vibrationless:

"Mistake. Further inquiry."

The first secretary quivered, stooped lower, rose and retired on soundless soles. Joh Fredersen's left eyebrow rose a trifle as he watched the retreating figure—only as long as was possible without turning his head.

A thin, concise penal-line crossed out a name.

The white-red light glowed. The voice spoke. The numbers dropped down through the great room. In the brain-pan of Metropolis.

Freder remained standing, motionless, by the door. He was not sure as to whether or not his father had noticed him. Whenever he entered this room he was once more a boy of ten years old, his chief characteristic uncertainty,

17

before the great concentrated, almighty certainty, which was called Joh Fredersen, and was his father.

The first secretary walked past him, greeting him silently, respectfully. He resembled a competitor leaving the course, beaten. The chalky face of the young man hovered for one moment before Freder's eyes like a big, white, lacquer mask. Then it was blotted out.

Numbers dropped down through the room.

One chair was empty. On seven others sat seven men, pursuing the numbers which sprang unceasingly from the invisible.

A lamp glowed white-red.

New York spoke.

A lamp sparkled up: white-green.

London began to speak.

Freder looked up at the clock opposite the door, commanding the whole wall like a gigantic wheel. It was the same clock, which, from the heights of the New Tower of Babel, flooded by searchlights, flicked off its second-sparks over the great Metropolis.

Joh Fredersen's head stood out against it. It was a crushing yet accepted halo above the brain of Metropolis.

The searchlights raved in a delirium of colour upon the narrow windows which ran from floor to ceiling. Cascades of light frothed against the panes. Outside, deep down, at the foot of the New Tower of Babel boiled the Metropolis. But in this room not a sound was to be heard but the incessantly dripping numbers.

The Rotwang-process had rendered the walls and windows sound-proof.

In this room, which was at the same time crowned and subjugated by the mighty time-piece, the clock, indicating numbers, nothing had any significance but numbers. The son of the great Master of Metropolis realised that, as long as numbers came dripping out of the invisible no word, which was not a number, and coming from a visible mouth, could lay claim to the least attention.

Therefore he stood, gazing unceasingly at his father's head, watching the monstrous hand of the clock sweep onward, inevitably, like a sickle, a reaping scythe, pass through the skull of his father, without harming him, climb upwards, up the number-beset ring, creep around the heights and sink again, to repeat the vain blow of the scythe.

At last the white-red light went out. A voice ceased.

Then the white-green light went out, too.

Silence.

Freder crossed to his father, whose glance was sweeping the lists of captured number-drops. . . .

"How did you know it was I?" he asked, softly.

Joh Fredersen did not look up at him. Although his face had gained an expression of patience and pride at the first question which his son put to him he had lost none of his alertness. . . .

"The door opened. Nobody was announced. Nobody comes to me unannounced. Only my son." [Alfred Abel (Joh Frederson)]

The hands of those writing stopped and, for the space of a moment, they sat as though paralysed, relaxed, exhausted. Then Joh Fredersen's voice said with a dry gentleness: "Thank you, to-morrow."

And without looking round:

"What do you want, my boy?"

The seven strangers quitted the now silent room. Freder crossed to his father, whose glance was sweeping the lists of captured number-drops. Freder's eyes clung to the blue metal plate near his father's right hand.

"How did you know it was I?" he asked, softly.

Joh Fredersen did not look up at him. Although his face had gained an expression of patience and pride at the first question which his son put to him he had lost none of his alertness. He glanced at the clock. His fingers glided over the flexible keyboard. Soundlessly were orders flashed out to waiting men.

"The door opened. Nobody was announced. Nobody comes to me unannounced. Only my son."

A light below glass—a question. Joh Fredersen extinguished the light. The first secretary entered and crossed over to the great Master of Metropolis.

"You were right. It was a mistake. It has been rectified," he reported, expressionlessly.

"Thank you." Not a look. Not a gesture. "The G— bank has been notified to pay you your salary. Good evening."

The young man stood motionless. Three, four, five, six seconds flicked off the gigantic time-piece. Two empty eyes burnt in the chalky face of the young man, impressing their brand of fear upon Freder's vision.

One of Joh Fredersen's shoulders made a leisurely movement.

"Good evening," said the young man, in a strangled tone.

He went.

"Why did you dismiss him, father?" the son asked.

"I have no use for him," said Joh Fredersen, still not having looked at his son.

"Why not, father?"

"I have no use for people who start when one speaks to them," said the Master over Metropolis.

"Perhaps he felt ill . . . perhaps he is worrying about somebody who is dear to him."

"Possibly. Perhaps too, he was still under the effects of the too long night in Yoshiwara. Freder, avoid assuming people to be good, innocent and victimized just because they suffer. He who suffers has sinned, against himself and against others."

"You do not suffer, father?"

"No."

"You are quite free from sin?"

"The time of sin and suffering lies behind me, Freder."

"And if this man, now . . . I have never seen such a thing . . . but I believe that men resolved to end their lives go out of a room as he did . . ."

"Perhaps."

"And suppose you were to hear, to-morrow, that he were dead . . . that would leave you untouched . . .?"

"Yes."

Freder was silent.

His father's hand slipped over a lever, and pressed it down. The white lamps in all the rooms surrounding the brain-pan of the New Tower of Babel went out. The Master over Metropolis had informed the circular world around him that he did not wish to be disturbed without urgent cause.

"I cannot tolerate it," he continued, "when a man, working upon Metropolis, at my right hand, in common with me, denies the only great advantage he possesses above the machine."

"And what is that, father?"

"To take delight in work," said the Master over Metropolis.

Freder's hand glided over his hair, then rested on its glorious fairness. He opened his lips, as though he wanted to say something; but he remained silent.

"Do you suppose," Joh Fredersen went on, "that I need my secretaries' pencils to check American stock-exchange reports? The index tables of Rotwang's trans-ocean trumpets are a hundred times more reliable and swift than clerk's brains and hands. But, by the accuracy of the machine I can measure the accuracy of the men, by the breath of the machine, the lungs of the men who compete with her."

"And the man you just dismissed, and who is doomed (for to be dismissed by you, father, means going down! . . . Down! . . . Down! . . .) he lost his breath, didn't he?"

"Yes."

"Because he was a man and not a machine . . ."

"Because he denied his humanity before the machine."

Freder raised his head and his deeply troubled eyes.

"I cannot follow you now, father," he said, as if in pain. The expression of patience on Joh Fredersen's face deepened.

21

"The man," he said quietly, "was my first secretary! The salary he drew was eight times as large as that of the last. That was synonymous with the obligation to perform eight times as much. To me. Not to himself. To-morrow the fifth secretary will be in his place. In a week he will have rendered four of the others superfluous. I have use for that man."

"Because he saves four others."

"No, Freder. Because he takes delight in the work of four others. Because he throws himself entirely into his work—throws himself as desiringly as if it were a woman."

Freder was silent. Joh Fredersen looked at his son. He looked at him carefully.

"You have had some experience?" he asked.

The eyes of the boy, beautiful and sad, slipped past him, out into space. Wild, white light frothed against the windows, and, in going out, left the sky behind, as a black velvet cloth over Metropolis.

"I have had no experience," said Freder, tentatively, "except that I believe for the first time in my life to have comprehended the being of a machine . . ."

"That should mean a great deal," replied the Master over Metropolis. "But you are probably wrong, Freder. If you had really comprehended the being of a machine you would not be so perturbed."

Slowly the son turned his eyes and the helplessness of his incomprehension to his father.

"How can one but be perturbed," he said, "if one comes to you, as I did, through the machine-rooms. Through the glorious rooms of your glorious machines . . . and sees the creatures who are fettered to them by laws of eternal watchfulness . . . lidless eyes . . ."

He paused. His lips were dry as dust.

Joh Fredersen leant back. He had not taken his gaze from his son, and still held it fast.

"Why did you come to me through the machine-rooms?" he asked quietly. "It is neither the best, nor the most convenient way."

"I wished," said the son, picking his words carefully, "just once to look the men in the face—whose little children are my brothers—my sisters . . ."

"H'm," said the other with very tight lips. The pencil which he held between his fingers tapped gently, dryly, once, twice, upon the table's edge. Joh Fredersen's eyes wandered from his son to the twitching flash of the seconds on the clock, then sinking back again to him.

"And what did you find?" he asked.

22

Seconds, seconds, seconds of silence. Then it was as though the son, uprooting and tearing loose his whole ego, threw himself, with a gesture of utter self-exposure, upon his father, yet he stood still, head a little bent, speaking softly, as though every word were smothering between his lips.

"Father! Help the men who live at your machines!"

"I cannot help them," said the brain of Metropolis. "Nobody can help them. They are where they must be. They are what they must be. They are not fitted for anything more or anything different."

"I do not know for what they are fitted," said Freder, expressionlessly: his head fell upon his breast as though almost severed from his neck. "I only know what I saw—and that it was dreadful to look upon . . . I went through the machine-rooms—they were like temples. All the great gods were living in white temples. I saw Baal and Moloch, Huitzilopochtli and Durgha; some frightfully companionable, some terribly solitary. I saw juggernaut's divine car and the Towers of Silence, Mahomet's curved sword, and the crosses of Golgotha. And all machines, machines, machines, which, confined to their pedestals, like deities to their temple thrones, from the resting places which bore them, lived their god-like lives: Eyeless but seeing all, earless but hearing all, without speech, yet, in themselves, a proclaiming mouth—not man, not woman, and yet engendering, receptive, and productive—lifeless, yet shaking the air of their temples with the never-expiring breath of their vitality. And, near the god-machines, the slaves of the god-machines: the men who were as though crushed between machine companionability and machine solitude. They have no loads to carry: the machine carries the loads. They have not to lift and push: the machine lifts and pushes. They have nothing else to do but eternally one and the same thing, each in this place, each at his machine. Divided into periods of brief seconds, always the same clutch at the same second, at the same second. They have eyes, but they are blind but for one thing, the scale of the manometer. They have ears, but they are deaf but for one thing, the hiss of their machine. They watch and watch, having no thought but for one thing: should their watchfulness waver, then the machine awakens from its feigned sleep and begins to race, racing itself to pieces. And the machine, having neither head nor brain, with the tension of its watchfulness, sucks and sucks out the brain from the paralysed skull of its watchman, and does not stay, and sucks, and does not stay until a being is hanging to the sucked-out skull, no longer a man and not yet a machine, pumped dry, hollowed out, used up. And the machine which has sucked out and gulped down the spinal marrow and brain of the man and has wiped out the hollows in his skull with the soft, long tongue of its soft, long hissing, the machine gleams in its silver-velvet radiance, anointed with oil, beautiful, infallible—Baal and Moloch, Huitzilopochtli and Durgha. And you, father, you press your fingers upon the little blue metal plate near your right hand, and your great glorious, dreadful city of Metropolis roars out, proclaiming that she is hungry for fresh human marrow and human brain and then the living food rolls on, like a stream, into the machine-rooms, which are like temples, and that, just used, is thrown up . . ."

His voice failed him. He struck his fists violently together, and looked at his father.

" . . . and they are all human beings!"

"Unfortunately. Yes."

The father's voice sounded to the son's ear as though he were speaking from behind seven closed doors.

"That men are used up so rapidly at the machines, Freder, is no proof of the greed of the machine, but of the deficiency of the human material. Man is the product of change, Freder. A once-and-for-all being. If he is miscast he cannot be sent back to the melting-furnace. One is obliged to use him as he is. Whereby it has been statistically proved that the powers of performance of the non-intellectual worker lessen from month to month."

Freder laughed. The laugh came so dry, so parched, from his lips that Joh Fredersen jerked up his head, looking at his son from out narrowed eyelids. Slowly his eyebrows rose.

"Are you not afraid, father (supposing that the statistics are correct and the consumption of man is progressing increasingly, rapidly) that one fine day there will be no more food there for the man-eating god-machines, and that the Moloch of glass, rubber and steel, the Durgha of aluminium with platinum veins, will have to starve miserably?"

"The case is conceivable," said the brain of Metropolis.

"And then?"

"Then," said the brain of Metropolis, "by then a substitute for man will have to have been found."

"The improved man, you mean—? The machine-man—?"

"Perhaps," said the brain of Metropolis.

Freder brushed the damp hair from his brow. He bent forward, his breath touching his father.

"Then just listen to one thing, father," he breathed, the veins on his temples standing out, blue. "See to it that the machine-man has no head, or, at any rate, no face, or give him a face which always smiles. Or a Harlequin's face, or a closed visor. That it does not horrify one to look at him! For, as I walked through the machine-rooms to-day, I saw the men who watch your machines. And they know me, and I greeted them, one after the other. But not one returned my greeting. The machines were all too eagerly tautening their nerve-strings. And when I looked at them, father, quite closely, as closely as I am now looking at you-I was looking myself in the face . . . Every single man, father, who slaves at your machines, has my face—has the face of your son . . ."

"Then mine too, Freder, for we are very like each other," said the Master over the great Metropolis. He looked at the clock and stretched out his hand. In all the rooms surrounding the brain-pan of the New Tower of Babel the white lamps flared up.

"And doesn't it fill you with horror," asked the son, "to know so many shadows, so many phantoms, to be working at your work?"

"The time of horror lies behind me, Freder."

Then Freder turned and went, like a blind man—first missing the door with groping hand, then finding it. It opened before him. It closed behind him, and he stood still, in a room that seemed to him to be strange and icy.

Forms rose up from the chairs upon which they had sat, waiting, bowing low to the son of Joh Fredersen, the Master of Metropolis.

Freder only recognized one; that was Slim.

He thanked those who greeted him, still standing near the door, seeming not to know his way. Behind him slipped Slim, going to Joh Fredersen, who had sent for him.

The master of Metropolis was standing by the window, his back to the door.

"Wait!" said the dark square back.

Slim did not stir. He breathed inaudibly. His eye-lids lowered, he seemed to sleep while standing. But his mouth, with the remarkable tension of its muscles, made him the personification of concentration.

Joh Fredersen's eyes wandered over Metropolis, a restless roaring sea with a surf of light. In the flashes and waves, the Niagara falls of light, in the colour-play of revolving towers of light and brilliance, Metropolis seemed to have become transparent. The houses, dissected into cones and cubes by the moving scythes of the search-lights gleamed, towering up, hover-ingly, light flowing down their flanks like rain. The streets licked up the shining radiance, themselves shining, and the things gliding upon them, an incessant stream, threw cones of light before them. Only the cathedral, with the star-crowned Virgin on the top of its tower, lay stretched out, massively, down in the city, like a black giant lying in an enchanted sleep.

Joh Fredersen turned around slowly. He saw Slim standing by the door. Slim greeted him. Joh Fredersen came towards him. He crossed the whole width of the room in silence; he walked slowly on until he came up to the man. Standing there before him, he looked at him, as though peeling everything corporal from him, even to his innermost self.

Slim held his ground during this peeling scrutiny.

Joh Fredersen said, speaking rather softly:

"From now on I wish to be informed of my son's every action."

Slim bowed, waited, saluted and went.

But he did not find the son of his great master again where he had left him. Nor was he destined to find him.

CHAPTER III
#11811 & YOSHIWARA

THE MAN WHO had been Joh Fredersen's first secretary stood in a cell of the Pater-noster, the never-stop passenger lift which, like a series of never ceasing well-buckets, trans-sected the New Tower of Babel.—With his back against the wooden wall, he was making the journey through the white, humming house, from the heights of the roof, to the depths of the cellars and up again to the heights of the roof, for the thirtieth time, never moving from the one spot.

Persons, greedy to gain a few seconds, stumbled in with him, and stories higher, or lower, out again. Nobody paid the least attention to him. One or two certainly recognised him. But, as yet, nobody interpreted the drops on his temples as being anything but a similar greed for the gain of a few seconds. All right—he would wait until they knew better, until they took him and threw him out of the cell: What are you taking up space for, you fool, if you've got so much time? Crawl down the stairs, or the first escape . . .

With gasping mouth he leant there and waited . . .

Now emerging from the depths again, he looked with stupefied eyes towards the room which guarded Joh Fredersen's door, and saw Joh Fredersen's son standing before that door. For the fraction of a second they stared into each other's over-shadowed faces, and the glances of both broke out as signals of distress, of very different but of equally deep distress. Then the totally indifferent pump-works carried the man in the cell upwards into the darkness of the roof of the tower, and, when he dipped down again, becoming visible once more on his way downwards, the son of Joh Fredersen was standing before the opening of the cell and was, in a step, standing beside the man whose back seemed to be nailed to the wooden wall.

"What is your name?" he asked gently.

A hesitation in drawing breath, then the answer, which sounded as though he were listening for something: "Josaphat . . ."

"What will you do now, Josaphat?"

They sank. They sank. As they passed through the great hall the enormous windows of which overlooked the street of bridges, broadly and ostentatiously, Freder saw, on turning his head, outlined against the blackness of the sky, already half extinguished, the dripping word: "Yoshiwara . . ."

He spoke as if stretching out both hands, as just if closing his eyes in speaking:

"Will you come to me, Josaphat?"

A hand fluttered up like a scared bird.

"I—?" gasped the stranger.

"Yes, Josaphat."

The young voice so full of kindness . . .

They sank. They sank. Light—darkness—light—darkness again.

"Will you come to me, Josaphat?"

"Yes!" said the strange man with incomparable fervour. "Yes!"

They dropped into light. Freder seized him by the arm and dragged him out with him, out of the great pump-works of the New Tower of Babel, holding him fast as he reeled.

"Where do you live, Josaphat?"

"Ninetieth Block. House seven. Seventh floor."

"Then go home, Josaphat. Perhaps I shall come to you myself; perhaps I shall send a messenger who will bring you to me. I do not know what the next few hours will bring forth . . . But I do not want any man I know, if I can prevent it, to lie a whole night long, staring up at the ceiling until it seems to come crashing down on him . . ."

"What can I do for you?" asked the man.

Freder felt the vice-like pressure of his hand. He smiled. He shook his head. "Nothing. Go home. Wait. Be calm. Tomorrow will bring another day and I hope a fair one . . ."

The man loosened the grip of his hand and went. Freder watched him go. The man stopped and looked back at Freder, and dropped his head with an expression which was so earnest, so unconditional, that the smile died on Freder's lips.

"Yes, man," he said. "I take you at your word!"

The Pater-noster hummed at Freder's back. The cells, like scoop-buckets,

28

gathered men up and poured them out again. But the son of Joh Fredersen did not see them. Among all those tearing along to gain a few seconds, he alone stood still listening how the New Tower of Babel roared in its revolutions. The roaring seemed to him like the ringing of one of the cathedral bells—like the golden voice of the archangel Michael. But a song hovered above it, high and sweet. His whole young heart exulted in this song.

"Have I done your will for the first time, you great mediatress of pity?" he asked in the roar of the bell's voice.

But no answer came.

Then he went the way he wanted to go, to find the answer.

As Slim entered Freder's home to question the servants concerning their master, Joh Fredersen's son was walking down the steps which led to the lower structure of the New Tower of Babel. As the servants shook their heads at Slim saying that their master had not come home, Joh Fredersen's son was walking towards the luminous pillars which indicated his way. As Slim, with a glance at his watch, decided to wait, to wait, at any rate for a while—already alarmed, already conjecturing possibilities and how to meet them—Joh Fredersen's son was entering the room from which the New Tower of Babel drew the energies for its own requirements.

He had hesitated a long time before opening the door. For a weird existence went on behind that door. There was howling. There was panting. There was whistling. The whole building groaned. An incessant trembling ran through the walls and the floor. And amidst it all there was not one human sound. Only the things and the empty air roared. Men in the room on the other side of this door had powerless sealed lips. But for these men's sakes Freder had come.

He pushed the door open and then fell back, suffocated. Boiling air smote him, groping at his eyes that he saw nothing. Gradually he regained his sight.

The room was dimly lighted and the ceiling, which looked as though it could carry the weight of the entire earth, seemed perpetually to be falling down.

A faint howling made breathing almost unbearable. It was as though the breath drank in the howling too.

Air, rammed down to the depths, coming already used from the lungs of the great Metropolis, gushed out of the mouths of pipes. Hurled across the room, it was greedily sucked back by the mouths of pipes on the other side. And its howling light spread a coldness about it which fell into fierce conflict with the sweat-heat of the room.

In the middle of the room crouched the Pater-noster machine. It was like

29

Heat spat from the walls in which the furnaces were roaring. . . . Men glided by like swimming shadows. Their movements, the soundlessness of their inaudible slipping past, had something of the black ghostliness of deep-sea divers. Their eyes stood open as though they never closed them.

Ganesha, the god with the elephant's head. It shone with oil. It had gleaming limbs. Under the crouching body and the head which was sunken on the chest, crooked legs rested, gnome-like, upon the platform. The trunk and legs were motionless. But the short arms pushed and pushed alternately forwards, backwards, forwards. A little pointed light sparkled upon the play of the delicate joints. The floor, which was stone, and seamless, trembled under the pushing of the little machine, which was smaller than a five-year-old child.

Heat spat from the walls in which the furnaces were roaring. The odour of oil, which whistled with heat, hung in thick layers in the room. Even the wild chase of the wandering masses of air did not tear out the suffocating fumes of oil. Even the water which was sprayed through the room fought a hopeless battle against the fury of the heat-spitting walls, evaporating, already saturated with oil-fumes, before it could protect the skins of the men in this hell from being roasted.

Men glided by like swimming shadows. Their movements, the soundlessness of their inaudible slipping past, had something of the black ghostliness of deep-sea divers. Their eyes stood open as though they never closed them.

Near the little machine in the centre of the room stood a man, wearing the uniform of all the workmen of Metropolis: from throat to ankle, the dark blue linen, bare feet in the hard shoes, hair tightly pressed down by the black cap. The hunted stream of wandering air washed around his form, making the folds of the canvas flutter. The man held his hand on the lever and his gaze was fixed on the clock, the hands of which vibrated like magnetic needles.

Freder groped his way across to the man. He stared at him. He could not see his face. How old was the man? A thousand years? Or not yet twenty? He was talking to himself with babbling lips. What was the man muttering about? And had this man, too, the face of Joh Fredersen's son?

"Look at me!" said Freder bending forward.

But the man's gaze did not leave the clock. His hand, also, was unceasingly, feverishly, clutching the lever. His lips babbled and babbled, excitedly.

Freder listened. He caught the words. Shreds of words, tattered by the current of air.

"Pater-noster . . . that means, Our Father! . . . Our Father, which are in heaven! We are in hell. Our Father! . . . What is thy name? Art thou called Pater-noster, Our Father? Or Joh Fredersen? Or machine? . . . Be hallowed by us, machine. Pater-noster! . . . Thy kingdom come . . . Thy kingdom come, machine . . . Thy will be done on earth as it is in heaven . . . What is thy will of us,

31

machine, Pater-noster? Art thou the same in heaven as thou art on earth? . . . Our Father, which art in heaven, when thou callest us into heaven, shall we keep the machines in thy world—the great wheels which break the limbs of thy creatures—the great merry-go-round called the earth? . . . Thy will be done, Pater-noster! . . . Give us this day our daily bread . . . Grind, machine, grind flour for our bread. The bread is baked from the flour of our bones . . . And forgive us our trespasses . . . what trespasses, Pater-noster? The trespass of having a brain and a heart, that thou hast not, machine? And lead us not into temptation . . . Lead us not into temptation to rise against thee, machine, for thou art stronger than we, thou art a thousand times stronger than we, and thou art always in the right and we are always in the wrong, because we are weaker than thou art, machine . . . But deliver us from evil, machine . . . Deliver us from thee, machine . . . For thine is the kingdom, the power and the glory, for ever and ever, Amen . . . Pater-noster, that means: "Our Father . . . Our Father, which are in heaven . . ."

Freder touched the man's arm. The man started, struck dumb.

His hand lost its hold of the lever and leaped into the air like a shot bird. The man's jaws stood gaping open as if locked. For one second the white of the eyes in the stiffened face was terribly visible. Then the man collapsed like a rag and Freder caught him as he fell.

Freder held him fast. He looked around. Nobody was paying any attention, either to him or to the other man. Clouds of steam and fumes surrounded them like a fog. There was a door near by. Freder carried the man to the door and pushed it open. It led to the tool-house. A packing case offered a hard resting place. Freder let the man slip down into it.

Dull eyes looked up at him. The face to which they belonged was little more than that of a boy.

"What is your name?" said Freder.

"11811 . . ."

"I want to know what your mother called you . . ."

"Georgi."

"Georgi, do you know me?"

Consciousness returned to the dull eyes together with recognition.

"Yes, I know you . . . You are the son of Joh Fredersen . . . of Joh Fredersen, who is the father of us all . . ."

"Yes. Therefore I am your brother, Georgi, do you see? I heard your Pater-noster . . ."

The body flung itself up with a heave.

"The machine—" He sprang to his feet. "My machine—!"

"Leave it alone, Georgi, and listen to me . . ."

"Somebody must be at the machine!"

"Somebody will be at the machine; but not you . . ."

"Who will, then?"

"I."

Staring eyes were the answer.

"I," repeated Freder. "Are you fit to listen to me, and will you be able to take good note of what I say? It is very important, Georgi!"

"Yes," said Georgi, paralysed.

"We shall now exchange lives, Georgi. You take mine, I yours. I shall take your place at the machine. You go quietly out in my clothes. Nobody noticed me when I came here. Nobody will notice you when you go. You must only not lose your nerve and keep calm. Keep under cover of where the air is brewing like a mist. When you reach the street take a car. You will find more than enough money in my pockets. Three streets further on change the car. And again after another three streets. Then drive to the Ninetieth Block. At the corner pay off the taxi and wait until the driver is out of sight. Then find your way to the seventh floor of the seventh house. A man called Josaphat lives there. You are to go to him. Tell him I sent you. Wait for me or for a message from me. Do you understand, Georgi?"

"Yes."

But the "Yes" was empty and seemed to reply to something other than Freder's question.

A little while later the son of Joh Fredersen, the Master of the great Metropolis, was standing before the machine which was like Ganesha, the god with the elephant's head.

He wore the uniform of all the workmen of Metropolis: from throat to ankle the dark blue linen, bare feet in the hard shoes, hair firmly pressed down by the black cap.

He held his hand on the lever and his gaze was set on the clock, the hands of which vibrated like magnetic needles. The hunted stream of air washed around him making the folds of the canvas flutter.

Then he felt how, slowly, chokingly, from the incessant trembling of the floor, from the walls in which the furnaces whistled, from the ceiling which seemed eternally to be in the act of falling down, from the pushing of the short arms of the machine, from the steady resistance of the gleaming body, terror welled up in him—terror, even to the certainty of Death.

He felt—and saw, too—how, from out the swathes of vapour, the long soft elephant's trunk of the god Ganesha loosened itself from the head, sunken on the chest, and gently, with unerring finger, felt for his, Freder's forehead. He felt the touch of this sucker, almost cool, not in the least painful, but horrible. Just in the centre, over the bridge of the nose, the ghostly trunk sucked itself fast; it was hardly a pain, yet it bored a fine, dead-sure gimlet, towards the centre of the brain. As though fastened to the clock of an infernal machine the heart began to thump. Pater-noster . . . Pater-noster . . . Pater-noster . . .

"I will not," said Freder, throwing back his head to break the cursed contact: "I will not . . . I will . . . I will not . . ."

He groped for he felt the sweat dropping from his temples like drops of blood in all pockets of the strange uniform which he wore. He felt a rag in one of them and drew it out. He mopped his fore-head and, in doing so, felt the sharp edge of a stiff piece of paper, of which he had taken hold together with the cloth.

He pocketed the cloth and examined the paper.

It was no larger than a man's hand, bearing neither print nor script, being covered over and over with the tracing of a strange symbol and an apparently half-destroyed plan.

Freder tried hard to make something of it but he did not succeed. Of all the signs marked on the plan he did not know one. Ways seemed to be indicated, seeming to be false ways, but they all led to one destination; to a place which was filled with crosses.

A symbol of life? Sense in nonsense?

As Joh Fredersen's son, Freder was accustomed swiftly and correctly to grasp anything called a plan. He pocketed the plan though it remained before his eyes.

The sucker of the elephant's trunk of the god Ganesha glided down to the occupied unsubdued brain which reflected, analysed and sought. The head, not tamed, sank back into the chest. Obediently, eagerly, worked the little machine which drove the Pater-noster of the New Tower of Babel.

A little glimmering light played upon the more delicate joints almost on the top of the machine, like a small malicious eye.

The machine had plenty of time. Many hours would pass before the Master of Metropolis, before Joh Fredersen would tear the food which his machines were chewing up from the teeth of his mighty machines.

Quite softly, almost smilingly, the gleaming eye, the malicious eye, of the delicate machine looked down upon Joh Fredersen's son, who was standing before it . . .

Georgi had left the New Tower of Babel unchallenged, through various doors and the city received him, the great Metropolis which swayed in the dance of light and which was a dancer.

He stood in the street, drinking in the drunken air. He felt white silk on his body. On his feet he felt shoes which were soft and supple. He breathed deeply and the fullness of his own breath filled him with the most high intoxicating intoxication.

He saw a city which he had never seen. He saw it as a man he had never been. He did not walk in a stream of others: a stream twelve files deep . . . He wore no blue linen, no hard shoes, no cap. He was not going to work. Work was put away, another man was doing his work for him.

A man had come to him and had said: "We shall now exchange lives, Georgi; you take mine and I your's . . ."

"When you reach the street, take a car."

"You will find more than enough money in my pockets . . ."

"You will find more than enough money in my pockets . . ."

"You will find more than enough money in my pockets . . ."

Georgi looked at the city which he had never seen . . .

Ah! The intoxication of the lights. Ecstasy of Brightness! —Ah! Thousand-limbed city, built up of blocks of light. Towers of brilliance! Steep mountains of splendour! From the velvety sky above you showers golden rain, inexhaustibly, as into the open lap of the Danae.

Ah—Metropolis! Metropolis!

A drunken man, he took his first steps, saw a flame which hissed up into the heavens. A rocket wrote in drops of light on the velvety sky the word: "Yoshiwara . . ."

George ran across the street, reached the steps, and, taking three steps at a time, reached the roadway. Soft, flexible, a black willing beast, a car approached, stopped at his feet.

Georgi sprang into the car, fell back upon the cushions, the engine of the powerful automobile vibrating soundlessly. A recollection stiffened the man's body.

Was there not, somewhere in the world—and not so very far away, under the sole of the New Tower of Babel, a room which was run through by incessant trembling? Did not a delicate little machine stand in the middle of this room, shining with oil and having strong, gleaming limbs? Under the crouching body and the head, which was sunken on the chest, crooked legs rested, gnome-like upon the platform. The trunk and legs were motionless. But the short arms pushed and pushed and pushed, alternately forwards, backwards, and forwards. The floor which was of stone and seamless, trembled under the pushing of the little machine which was smaller than a five-year-old child.

The voice of the driver asked: "Where to, sir?"

Straight on, motioned Georgi with his hand. Anywhere . . .

The man had said to him: Change the car after the third street.

But the rhythm of the motor-car embraced him too delightfully. Third street . . . sixth street . . . it was still very far to the ninetieth block.

He was filled with the wonder of being thus couched, the bewilderment of the lights, the shudder of entrancement at the motion.

The further that, with the soundless gliding of the wheels, he drew away from the New Tower of Babel, the further did he seem to draw away from the consciousness of his own self.

Who was he—? Had he not just stood in a greasy patched, blue linen uniform, in a seething hell, his brain mangled by eternal watchfulness, with bones, the marrow of which was being sucked out by eternally making the same turn of the lever to eternally the same rhythm, with face scorched by unbearable heat, and in the skin of which the salty sweat tore its devouring furrows?

Did he not live in a town which lay deeper under the earth than the underground stations of Metropolis, with their thousand shafts—in a town the houses of which storied just as high above squares and streets as, above in the night, did the houses of Metropolis, which towered so high, one above the other?

Had he ever known anything else than the horrible sobriety of these houses, in which there lived not men, but numbers, recognisable only by the enormous placards by the house-doors?

Had his life ever had any purpose other than to go out from these doors, framed with numbers, out to work, when the sirens of Metropolis howled for him—and ten hours later, crushed and tired to death, to stumble into the house by the door of which his number stood?

Was he, himself, anything but a number—number 11811—crammed into his linen, his clothes, his cap? Had not the number also become imprinted into his soul, into his brain, into his blood, that he must even stop and think of his own name?

And now—?

And now—?

His body refreshed by pure cold water which had washed the sweat of labour from him, felt, with wonderful sweetness, the yielding relaxation of all his muscles. With a quiver which rendered all his muscles weak he felt the caressing touch of white silk on the bare skin of his body, and, while giving himself up to the gentle, even rhythm of the motion, the consciousness of the first and complete deliverance from all that which had put so agonising a pressure on his existence overcame him with so overpowering a force that he burst out into the laughter of a madman, his tears falling uncontrollably,

Violently, aye, with a glorious violence, the great city whirled towards him, like a sea which roars around mountains.

The workman No. 11811, the man who lived in a prison-like house, under the underground railway of Metropolis, who knew no other way than that from the hole in which he slept to the machine and from the machine back to the hole—this man saw, for the first time in his life, the wonder of the world, which was Metropolis: the city, by night shining under millions and millions of lights.

He saw the ocean of light which filled the endless trails of streets with a silver, flashing lustre. He saw the will-o'-the-wisp sparkle of the electric advertisements, lavishing themselves inexhaustibly in an ecstasy of brightness. He saw towers projecting, built up of blocks of light, feeling himself seized, overpowered to a state of complete impotence by this intoxication of light, feeling this sparkling ocean with its hundreds and thousands of spraying waves, to reach out for him, to take the breath from his mouth, to pierce him, suffocate him . . .

And then he grasped that this city of machines, this city of sobriety, this fanatic for work, sought, at night, the mighty counterpoise to the frenzy of the day's work—that this city, at night, lost itself, as one insane, as one entirely witless, in the intoxication of a pleasure, which, flinging up to all heights, hurtling down to all depths, was boundlessly blissful and boundlessly destructive.

Georgi trembled from head to foot. And yet it was not really trembling which seized his resistless body. It was as though all his members were fastened to the soundless evenness of the engine which bore them forwards. No, not to the single engine which was the heart of the motor-car in which he sat—to all these hundreds and thousands of engines which were driving an endlessly gliding, double stream of gleaming illuminated automobiles, on through the streets of the city in its nocturnal fever. And, at the same time, his body was set in vibration by the fire-works of spark-streaming wheels, ten-coloured lettering snow-white fountains of overcharged lamps, rockets, hissing upwards, towers of flame, blazing ice-cold.

There was a word which always recurred. From an invisible source there shot up a sheaf of light, which bursting apart at the highest point, dropped down letters in all colours of the rainbow from the velvet-black sky of Metropolis.

The letters formed themselves into the word: Yoshiwara.

What did that mean: Yoshiwara—?

From the iron-work of the elevated railway-track a yellow-skinned fellow hung, head downwards, suspended by the crocks of his knees, who let a snow-storm of white sheets of paper shower down upon the double row of motor-cars.

The pages fluttered and fell. Georgi's glance caught one of them. Upon it stood, in large, distorted letters: Yoshiwara.

The car stopped at a crossing. Yellow-skinned fellows, in many-coloured embroidered silk jackets, wound themselves, supple as eels, through the twelve-fold strings of waiting cars. One of them swung himself onto the foot-board of the black motor-car in which Georgi sat. For one second the grinning hideousness stared into the young, white, helpless face.

A sheaf of hand-bills were hurled through the window, falling upon Georgi's knee and before his feet. He bent down mechanically and picked up that for which his fingers were groping.

On these slips, which gave out a penetrating, bitter-sweet, seductive perfume, there stood, in large, bewitched-looking letters, the word: Yoshiwara . . .

Georgi's throat was as dry as dust. He moistened his cracked lips with his tongue, which lay heavy and as though parched in his mouth.

A voice had said to him: "You will find more than enough money in my pockets . . ."

Enough money . . . what for? To clutch and drag near this city—this mighty, heavenly, hellish city; to embrace her with both arms, both legs, in the impotence of mastering her; to despair, to throw one-self into her—take me!—take me! —To feel the filled bowl at one's lips—gulping, gulping—not drawing breath, the brim of the bowl set fast between the teeth-eternal, eternal insatiability, competing with the eternal, eternal overflow, over-pouring of the bowl of intoxication . . .

Ah—Metropolis! . . . Metropolis! . . .

"More than enough money . . ."

A strange sound came from Georgi's throat, and there was something in it of the throat-rattle of a man who knows he is dreaming and wants to awake, and something of the guttural sound of the beast of prey when it scents blood. His hand did not let go of the wad of bank-notes for the second time. It screwed it up in burning convulsive fingers.

He turned his head this way and that, as though seeking a way out, which, nevertheless, he feared to find . . .

Another car slipped silently along beside his, a great, black-gleaming shadow, the couch of a woman, set on four wheels, decorated with flowers, lighted by dim lamps. Georgi saw the woman very clearly, and the woman looked at him. She cowered rather than sat, among the cushions of the car, having entirely wrapped herself in her gleaming cloak, from which one shoulder projected with the dull whiteness of a swan's feather.

She was bewilderingly made-up—as though she did not wish to be human, to be a woman, but rather a peculiar animal, disposed, perhaps to play, perhaps to murder.

Calmly holding the man's gaze, she gently slipped her right hand, sparkling with stones, and the slender arm, which was quite bare and dull white, even as the shoulder, from the wrappings of her cloak, and began to fan herself in a leisurely manner with one of the sheets of paper on which the word Yoshiwara stood . . .

"No!" said the man. He panted, wiping the perspiration from his forehead. Coolness welled out from the fine, strange stuff with which he dried the perspiration from his brow.

Eyes stared at him. Eyes which were fading away. The all-knowing smile of a painted mouth.

With a panting sound Georgi made to open the door of the taxi and to jump out into the road. However, the movement of the car threw him back on to the cushions. He clenched his fists, pressing them before both eyes. A vision shot through his head, quite misty and lacking in outline, a strong little machine, no larger than a five-year-old child. Its short arms pushed and pushed and pushed, alternately forwards, backwards, forwards . . . The head, sunken on the chest, rose, grinning . . .

"No!" shrieked the man, clapping his hands and laughing. He had been set free from the machine. He had exchanged lives.

Exchanged—with whom?

With a man who had said: "You will find more than enough money in my pockets . . ."

The man bent back his head into the nape of his neck and stared at the roof suspended above him.

On the roof there flamed the word:

Yoshiwara . . .

The word Yoshiwara became rockets of light which showered around him, paralysing his limbs. He sat motionless, covered in a cold sweat. He clawed his fingers into the leather of the cushions. His back was stiff, as though his spine were made of cold iron. His jaws chattered.

"No—!" said Georgi, tearing his fists down. But before his eyes which stared into space, the word flamed up:

"Yoshiwara . . ."

Music was in the air, hurled into the nocturnal streets by enormous loud-speakers. Wanton was the music, most heated of rhythm, of a shrieking, lashing gaiety . . .

"No—!" panted the man. Blood trickled in drops from his bitten lips.

But a hundred multi-coloured rockets wrote in the velvet-black sky of Metropolis, the word:

"Yoshiwara . . ."

Georgi pushed the window open. The glorious town of Metropolis, dancing in the drunkenness of light, threw itself impetuously towards him, as though he were the only-beloved, the only-awaited. He leant out of the window, crying:

"Yoshiwara—!"

He fell back upon the cushions. The car turned in a gentle curve, round in another direction.

A rocket shot up and wrote in the sky above Metropolis:

Yoshiwara . . .

Graphic by Russian-born artist and designer Boris Bilinsky (1900-1948). French UFA movie poster promoting METROPOLIS. (See also pages 146, 158, and 228 for more samples of promotional materials from France).

There was a house in the great Metropolis which was older than the town. Many said that it was older, even, than the cathedral, and, before the Archangel Michael raised his voice as advocate in the conflict for God, the house stood there in its evil gloom, defying the cathedral from out its dull eyes.

CHAPTER IV
ROTWANG'S ROBOTRIX

THERE WAS A house in the great Metropolis which was older than the town. Many said that it was older, even, than the cathedral, and, before the Archangel Michael raised his voice as advocate in the conflict for God, the house stood there in its evil gloom, defying the cathedral from out its dull eyes.

It had lived through the time of smoke and soot. Every year which passed over the city seemed to creep, when dying, into this house, so that, at last it was a cemetery—a coffin, filled with dead tens of years.

Set into the black wood of the door stood, copper-red, mysterious, the seal of Solomon, the pentagram.

It was said that a magician, who came from the East (and in the track of whom the plague wandered) had built the house in seven nights. But the masons and carpenters of the town did not know who had mortared the bricks, nor who had erected the roof. No foreman's speech and no ribboned nosegay had hallowed the Builder's Feast after the pious custom. The chronicles of the town held no record of when the magician died nor of how he died. One day it occurred to the citizens as odd that the red shoes of the magician had so long shunned the abominable plaster of the town. Entrance was forced into the house and not a living soul was found inside. But the rooms, which received, neither by day nor by night, a ray from the great lights of the sky, seemed to be waiting for their master, sunken in sleep. Parchments and folios lay about, open, under a covering of dust, like silver-grey velvet.

Set in all the doors stood, copper-red, mysterious, the seal of Solomon, the pentagram.

Then came a time which pulled down antiquities. Then the words were

43

spoken: The house must die. But the house was stronger than the words, as it was stronger than the centuries. With suddenly falling stones it slew those who laid hands on its walls. It opened the floor under their feet, dragging them down into a shaft, of which no man had previously had any knowledge. It was as though the plague, which had formerly wandered in the wake of the red shoes of the magician, still crouched in the corners of the narrow house, springing out at men from behind, to seize them by the neck. They died, and no doctor knew the illness. The house resisted its destruction with so great a force that word of its malignity went out over the borders of the city, spreading far over the land, that, at last, there was no honest man to be found who would have ventured to make war against it. Yes, even the thieves and the rogues, who were promised remission of their sentence provided that they declared themselves ready to pull down the magician's house, preferred to go to the pillory, or even to the scaffold, rather than to enter within these spiteful walls, these latchless doors, which were sealed with Solomon's seal.

The little town around the cathedral became a large town and grew into Metropolis, and into the centre of the world.

One day there came to the town a man from far away, who saw the house and said: "I want to have that."

He was initiated into the story of the house. He did not smile. He stood by his resolution. He bought the house at a very low price, moved in at once and kept it unaltered.

This man was called Rotwang. Few knew him. Only Joh Fredersen knew him very well. It would have been easier for him to have decided to fight out the quarrel about the cathedral with the sect of Gothics than the quarrel with Rotwang about the magician's house.

There were in Metropolis, in this city of reasoned, methodical hurry, very many who would rather have gone far out of their way than have passed by Rotwang's house. It hardly reached knee-high to the house-giants which stood near it. It stood at an angle to the street. To the cleanly town, which knew neither smoke nor soot, it was a blot and an annoyance. But it remained. When Rotwang left the house and crossed the street, which occurred but seldom, there were many who covertly looked at his feet, to see if, perhaps, he walked in red shoes.

Before the door of this house, on which the seal of Solomon glowed, stood Joh Fredersen.

He had sent the car away and had knocked.

He waited, then knocked again.

A voice asked, as if the house were speaking in its sleep:

"Who is there?"

"Joh Fredersen," said the man.

The door opened.

He entered. The door closed. He stood in darkness. But Joh Fredersen knew the house well. He walked straight on, and as he walked, the shimmering tracks of two stepping feet glistened before him, along the passage, and the edge of the stair began to glow. Like a dog showing the track, the glow ran on before him, up the steps, to die out behind him.

He reached the top of the stairs and looked about him. He knew that many doors opened out here. But on the one opposite him the copper seal glowed like a distorted eye, which looked at him.

He stepped up to it. The door opened before him.

Many doors as Rotwang's house possessed, this was the only one which opened itself to Joh Fredersen, although, and even, perhaps, because, the owner of this house knew full well that it always meant no mean effort for Joh Fredersen to cross this threshold.

He drew in the air of the room, lingeringly, but deeply, as though seeking in it the trace of another breath . . .

His nonchalant hand threw his hat on a chair. Slowly, in sudden and mournful weariness, he let his eyes wander through the room.

It was almost empty. A large, time-blackened chair, such as are to be found in old churches, stood before drawn curtains. These curtains covered a recess the width of the wall.

Joh Fredersen remained standing by the door for a long time, without moving. He had closed his eyes. With incomparable impotence he breathed in the odour of hyacinths, which seemed to fill the motionless air of this room.

Without opening his eyes, swaying a little, but aim-sure, he walked up to the heavy, black curtains and drew them apart.

Then he opened his eyes and stood quite still . . .

On a pedestal, the breadth of the wall, rested the head of a woman in stone . . .

It was not the work of an artist, it was the work of a man, who, in agonies for which the human tongue lacks words, had wrestled with the white stone throughout immeasurable days and nights until at last it seemed to realise and form the woman's head by itself. It was as if no tool had been at work here— no, it was as if a man, lying before this stone, had called on the name of the woman, unceasingly, with all the strength, with all the longing, with all the despair, of his brain, blood and heart, until the shapeless stone took pity on him letting itself turn into the image of the woman, who had meant to two men all heaven and all hell.

Joh Fredersen's eyes sank to the words which were hewn into the pedestal, roughly, as though chiselled with curses.

HEL
born
to be my happiness, a blessing to all men,
lost
to Joh Fredersen
dying
in giving life to his son, Freder

Yes, she died then. But Joh Fredersen knew only too well that she did not die from giving birth to her child. She died then because she had done what she had to do. She really died on the day upon which she went from Rotwang to Joh Fredersen, wondering that her feet left no bloody traces behind on the way. She had died because she was unable to withstand the great love of Joh Fredersen and because she had been forced by him to tear asunder the life of another.

Never was the expression of deliverance at last more strong upon a human face than upon Hel's face when she knew that she would die.

But in the same hour the mightiest man in Metropolis had lain on the floor, screaming like a wild beast, the bones of which are being broken in its living body.

And, on his meeting Rotwang, four weeks later, he found that the dense, disordered hair over the wonderful brow of the inventor was snow-white, and in the eyes under this brow the smouldering of a hatred which was very closely related to madness.

In this great love, in this great hatred, the poor, dead Hel had remained alive to both men . . .

"You must wait a little while," said the voice which sounded as though the house were talking in its sleep.

"Listen, Rotwang," said Joh Fredersen. "You know that I treat your little juggling tricks with patience, and that I come to you when I want anything of you, and that you are the only man who can say that of himself. But you will never get me to join in with you when you play the fool. You know, too, that I

It was as if no tool had been at work here—no, it was as if a man, lying before this stone, had called on the name of the woman, unceasingly, with all the strength, with all the longing, with all the despair, of his brain, blood and heart, until the shapeless stone took pity on him letting itself turn into the image of the woman, who had meant to two men all heaven and all hell. [Rudolf Klein-Rogge (Rotwang)]

have no time to waste. Don't make us both ridiculous, but come!"

"I told you that you would have to wait a little while," explained the voice, seeming to grow more distant.

"I shall not wait. I shall go."

"Do so, Joh Fredersen!"

He wanted to do so. But the door through which he had entered had no key, no latch. The seal of Solomon, glowing copper-red, blinked at him.

A soft, far-off voice laughed.

Joh Fredersen had stopped still, his back to the room. A quiver ran down his back, running along the hanging arms to the clenched fists.

"You should have your skull smashed in," said Joh Fredersen, very softly . . . "You should have your skull smashed in . . . that is, if it did not contain so valuable a brain . . ."

"You can do no more to me than you have done," said the far-off voice.

Joh Fredersen was silent.

"Which do you think," continued the voice, "to be more painful: to smash in the skull, or to tear the heart out of the body?"

Joh Fredersen was silent.

"Are your wits frozen, that you don't answer, Joh Fredersen?"

"A brain like yours should be able to forget," said the man standing at the door, staring at Solomon's seal.

The soft, far-off voice laughed.

"Forget? I have twice in my life forgotten something . . . Once that Aetro-oil and quick-silver have an idiosyncrasy as regards each other; that cost me my arm. Secondly that Hel was a woman and you a man; that cost me my heart. The third time, I am afraid, it will cost me my head. I shall never again forget anything, Joh Fredersen."

Joh Fredersen was silent.

The far-off voice was silent, too.

Joh Fredersen turned round and walked to the table. He piled books and parchments on top of each other, sat down and took a piece of paper from his pocket. He laid it before him and looked at it.

It was no larger than a man's hand, bearing neither print nor script, being covered over and over with the tracing of a strange symbol and an apparently half-destroyed plan. Ways seemed to be indicated, seeming to be false ways, but they all led one way; to a place that was filled with crosses.

Suddenly he felt, from the back, a certain coldness approaching him. Involuntarily he held his breath.

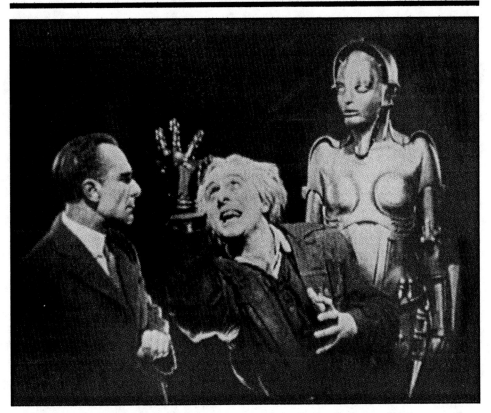

"A brain like yours should be able to forget," said the man standing at the door, staring at Solomon's seal. . . ."Forget? I have twice in my life forgotten something . . . Once that Aetro-oil and quick-silver have an idiosyncrasy as regards each other; that cost me my arm. Secondly that Hel was a woman and you a man; that cost me my heart. The third time, I am afraid, it will cost me my head. I shall never again forget anything, Joh Fredersen." [Left: Alfred Abel (Frederson); Right: Rudolf Klein-Rogge (Rotwang).]

No plaything, Joh Fredersen but a tool. Do you know what it means to have a woman as a tool? A woman like this, faultless and cool? And obedient— implicitly obedient . . . [Brigitte Helm as Futura (also above)]

A hand grasped along, by his head, a graceful, skeleton hand. Transparent skin was stretched over the slender joints, which gleamed beneath it like dull silver. Fingers, snow-white and fleshless, closed over the plan which lay on the table, and, lifting it up, took it away with it.

Joh Fredersen swung around. He stared at the being which stood before him with eyes which grew glassy.

The being was, indubitably, a woman. In the soft garment which it wore stood a body, like the body of a young birch tree, swaying on feet set fast together. But, although it was a woman, it was not human. The body seemed as though made of crystal, through which the bones shone silver. Cold streamed from the glazen skin which did not contain a drop of blood. The being held its beautiful hands pressed against its breast, which was motionless, with a gesture of determination, almost of defiance.

But the being had no face. The beautiful curve of the neck bore a lump of carelessly shaped mass. The skull was bald, nose, lips, temples merely traced. Eyes, as though painted on closed lids, stared unseeingly, with an expression of calm madness, at the man—who did not breathe.

"Be courteous, my parody," said the far-off voice, which sounded as though the house were talking in its sleep. "Greet Joh Fredersen, the Master over the great Metropolis."

The being bowed slowly to the man. The mad eyes neared him like two darting flames. The mass began to speak; it said in a voice full of a horrible tenderness:

"Good evening, Joh Fredersen . . ."

And these words were more alluring than a half-open mouth.

"Good, my Pearl! Good, my Crown-jewel!" said the far-off voice, full of praise and pride.

But at the same moment the being lost its balance. It fell, tipping forward, towards Joh Fredersen. He stretched out his hands to catch it, feeling them, in the moment of contact, to be burnt by an unbearable coldness, the brutality of which brought up in him a feeling of anger and disgust.

He pushed the being away from him and towards Rotwang, who was standing near him as though fallen from the air. Rotwang took the being by the arm.

He shook his head. "Too violent," he said. "Too violent. My beautiful parody, I fear your temperament will get you into much more trouble."

"What is that?" asked Joh Fredersen, leaning his hands against the edge of the table-top, which he felt behind him. Rotwang turned his face towards

But the being had no face. The beautiful curve of the neck bore a lump of carelessly shaped mass. The skull was bald, nose, lips, temples merely traced. Eyes, as though painted on closed lids, stared unseeingly, with an expression of calm madness, at the man—who did not breathe. [Brigitte Helm (Futura) and Rudolf Klein-Rogge (Rotwang)]

him, his glorious eyes glowing as watch fires glow when the wind lashes them with its cold lash.

"Who is it?" he replied. "Futura . . . Parody . . . whatever you like to call it. Also: delusion . . . In short: it is a woman . . . Every man-creator makes himself a woman. I do not believe that humbug about the first human being a man. If a male-god created the world (which is to be hoped, Joh Fredersen) then he certainly created woman first, lovingly and revelling in creative sport. You can test it, Joh Fredersen: it is faultless. A little cool—I admit, that comes of the material, which is my secret. But she is not yet completely finished. She is not yet discharged from the workshop of her creator. I cannot make up my mind to do it. You understand that? Completion means setting free. I do not want to set her free from me. That is why I have not yet given her a face. You must give her that, Joh Fredersen. For you were the one to order the new beings."

"I ordered machine men from you, Rotwang, which I can use at my machines. No woman . . . no plaything."

"No plaything, Joh Fredersen, no . . . you and I, we no longer play. Not for any stakes . . . We did it once. Once and never again. No plaything, Joh Fredersen but a *tool*. Do you know what it means to have a woman as a tool? A woman like this, faultless and cool? And obedient—implicitly obedient . . . Why do you fight with the Gothics and the monk Desertus about the cathedral? Send the woman to them Joh Fredersen! Send the woman to them when they are kneeling, scourging themselves. Let this faultless, cool woman walk through the rows of them, on her silver feet, fragrance from the garden of life in the folds of her garment . . . Who in the world knows how the blossoms of the tree smell, on which the apple of knowledge ripened. The woman is both: Fragrance of the blossom and the fruit . . .

"Shall I explain to you the newest creation of Rotwang, the genius, Joh Fredersen? It will be sacrilege. But I owe it to you. For you kindled the idea of creating within me, too . . . Shall I show you how obedient my creatures is? Give me what you have in your hand, Parody!"

"Stop . . . " said Joh Fredersen rather hoarsely. But the infallible obedience of the creature which stood before the two men brooked no delay in obeying. It opened its hands in which the delicate bones shimmered silver, and handed to its creator the piece of paper which it had taken from the table, before Joh Fredersen's eyes.

"That's trickery, Rotwang," said Joh Fredersen.

The great inventor looked at him. He laughed. The noiseless laughter drew back his mouth to his ears.

"No trickery, Joh Fredersen—the work of a genius! Shall Futura dance to you? Shall my beautiful Parody play the affectionate? Or the sulky? Cleopatra of Damayanti? Shall she have the gestures of the Gothic Madonnas? Or the gestures of love of an Asiatic dancer? What hair shall I plant upon the skull of your tool? Shall she be modest or impudent? Excuse me my many words, you man of few! I am drunk, d'you see, drunk with being a creator. I intoxicate myself, I inebriate myself, on your astonished face! I have surpassed your expectations, Joh Fredersen, haven't I? And you do not know everything yet: my beautiful Parody can sing, too! She can also read! The mechanism of her brain is as infallible as that of your own, Joh Fredersen!"

"If that is so," said the Master over the great Metropolis, with a certain dryness in his voice, which had become quite hoarse, "then command her to unriddle the plan which you have in your hand, Rotwang . . ."

Rotwang burst out into laughter which was like the laughter of a drunken man. He threw a glance at the piece of paper which he held spread out in his fingers, and was about to pass it, anticipatingly triumphant, to the being which stood beside him.

But he stopped in the middle of the movement. With open mouth, he stared at the piece of paper, raising it nearer and nearer to his eyes.

Joh Fredersen, who was watching him, bent forward. He wanted to say something, to ask a question. But before he could open his lips Rotwang threw up his head and met Joh Fredersen's glance with so green a fire in his eyes that the Master of the great Metropolis remained dumb.

Twice, three times did this green glow flash between the piece of paper and Joh Fredersen's face. And during the whole time not a sound was perceptible in the room but the breath that gushed in heaves from Rotwang's breast as though from a boiling, poisoned source.

"Where did you get the plan?" the great inventor asked at last. Though it was less a question than an expression of astonished anger.

"That is not the point," answered Joh Fredersen. "It is about this that I have come to you. There does not seem to be a soul in Metropolis who can make anything of it."

Rotwang's laughter interrupted him.

"Your poor scholars!" cried the laughter. "What a task you have set them, Joh Fredersen. How many hundredweights of printed paper have you forced them to heave over. I am sure there is no town on the globe, from the construction of the old Tower of Babel onward, which they have not snuffled through from North to South. Oh—if you could only smile, Parody! If only you already had eyes to wink at me. But laugh, at least, Parody! Laugh, rippingly, at the great scholars to whom the ground under their feet is foreign!"

The being obeyed. It laughed, ripplingly.

"Then you know the plan, or what it represents?" asked Joh Fredersen, through the laughter.

"Yes, by my poor soul, I know it," answered Rotwang. "But, by my poor soul, I am not going to tell you what it is until you tell me where you got the plan."

Joh Fredersen reflected. Rotwang did not take his gaze from him. "Do not try to lie to me, Joh Fredersen," he said softly, and with a whimsical melancholy.

"Somebody found the paper," began Joh Fredersen.

"Who—somebody?"

"One of my foremen."

"Grot?"

"Yes, Grot."

"Where did he find the plan?"

"In the pocket of a workman who was killed in the accident to the Geyser machine."

"Grot brought you the paper?"

"Yes."

"And the meaning of the plan seemed to be unknown to him?"

Joh Fredersen hesitated a moment with the answer.

"The meaning—yes; but not the plan. He told me he has often seen this paper in the workmen's hands, and that they anxiously keep it a secret, and that the men will crowd closely around him who holds it."

"So the meaning of the plan has been kept secret from your foreman."

"So it seems, for he could not explain it to me."

"H'm."

Rotwang turned to the being which was standing near him, with the appearance of listening intently.

"What do you say about it, my beautiful Parody?"

The being stood motionless.

"Well—?" said Joh Fredersen, with a sharp expression of impatience.

Rotwang looked at him, jerkily turning his great skull towards him. The glorious eyes crept behind their lids as though wishing to have nothing in common with the strong white teeth and the jaws of the beast of prey. But from beneath the almost closed lids they gazed at Joh Fredersen, as though they sought in his face the door to the great brain.

"How can one bind you, Joh Fredersen," he murmured, "what is a word to you—or an oath . . . Oh God . . . you with your own laws. What promise would you keep if the breaking of it seemed expedient to you?"

"Don't talk rubbish, Rotwang," said Joh Fredersen. "I shall hold my tongue because I still need you. I know quite well that the people whom we need are our solitary tyrants. So, if you know, speak."

Rotwang still hesitated; but gradually a smile took possession of his features—a good natured and mysterious smile, which was amusing itself at itself.

"You are standing on the entrance," he said.

"What does that mean?"

"To be taken literally, Joh Fredersen! You are standing on the entrance."

"What entrance, Rotwang? You are wasting time that does not belong to you . . ."

The smile on Rotwang's face deepened to serenity.

"Do you recollect, Joh Fredersen, how obstinately I refused, that time, to let the underground railway be run under my house?"

"Indeed I do! I still know the sum the detour cost me, also!"

"The secret was expensive, I admit, but it was worth it. Just take a look at the plan, Joh Fredersen, what is that?"

"Perhaps a flight of stairs . . ."

"Quite certainly a flight of stairs. It is a very slovenly execution in the drawing as in reality . . ."

"So you know them?"

"I have the honour, Joh Fredersen—yes. Now come two paces sideways. What is that?"

He had taken Joh Fredersen by the arm. He felt the fingers of the artificial hand pressing into his muscles like the claws of a bird of prey. With the right one Rotwang indicated the spot upon which Joh Fredersen had stood.

"What is that?" he asked, shaking the hand which he held in his grip.

Joh Fredersen bent down. He straightened himself up again.

"A door?"

"Right, Joh Fredersen! A door! A perfectly fitting and well shutting door. The man who built this house was an orderly and careful person. Only once did he omit to give heed, and then he had to pay for it. He went down the stairs which are under the door, followed the careless steps and passages which are connected with them, and never found his way back. It is not easy to find, for those who lodged there did not care to have strangers penetrate into their domain . . . I found my inquisitive predecessor, Joh Fredersen, and recognised him at once—by his pointed red shoes, which have preserved themselves wonderfully. As a corpse he looked peaceful and Christian-like, both of which he certainly was not in his life. The companions of his last hours probably contributed considerably to the conversion of the erst-while devil's disciple . . ."

He tapped with his right forefinger upon a maze of crosses in the centre of the plan.

"Here he lies. Just on this spot. His skull must have enclosed a brain which was worthy of your own, Joh Fredersen, and he had to perish because he once lost his way . . . What a pity for him . . ."

"Where did he lose his way?" asked Joh Fredersen.

Rotwang looked long at him before speaking.

"In the city of graves, over which Metropolis stands," he answered at last. "Deep below the moles' tunnels of your underground railway, Joh Fredersen, lies the thousand-year-old Metropolis of the thousand-year-old dead . . ."

Joh Fredersen was silent. His left eyebrow rose, while his eyes narrowed. He fixed his gaze upon Rotwang, who had not taken his eyes from him.

"What is the plan of this city of graves doing in the hands and pockets of my workmen?"

"That is yet to be discovered," answered Rotwang.

"Will you help me?"

"Yes."

"Tonight?"

"Very well."

"I shall come back after the changing of the shift."

"Do so, Joh Fredersen. And, if you take some good advice . . ."

"Well?"

"Come in the uniform of your workmen, when you come back!"

Joh Fredersen raised his head but the great inventor did not let him speak. He raised his hand as one calling for and admonishing to silence.

"The skull of the man in the red shoes also enclosed a powerful brain, Joh Fredersen, but nevertheless, he could not find his way homewards from those who dwell down there . . ."

Joh Fredersen reflected. He nodded and turned to go.

"Be courteous, my beautiful Parody," said Rotwang. "Open the doors for the Master over the great Metropolis."

The being glided past Joh Fredersen. He felt the breath of coldness which came forth from it. He saw the silent laughter between the half-open lips of Rotwang, the great inventor. He turned pale with rage, but he remained silent.

The being stretched out the transparent hand in which the bones shone silver, and, touching it with its finger-tips, moved the seal of Solomon, which glowed copperish.

The door yielded back. Joh Fredersen went out after the being, which stepped downstairs before him.

There was no light on the stairs, nor in the narrow passage. But a shimmer came from the being no stronger than that of a green-burning candle, yet strong enough to lighten up the stairs and the black walls.

At the house-door the being stopped still and waited for Joh Fredersen, who was walking slowly along behind it. The house-door opened before him, but not far enough for him to pass out through the opening.

The eyes stared at him from the mass-head of the being, eyes as though painted on closed lids, with the expression of calm madness.

"Be courteous, my beautiful Parody," said a soft, far-off voice, which sounded as though the house were talking in its sleep.

The being bowed. It stretched out a hand—a graceful skeleton hand. Transparent skin was stretched over the slender joints, which gleamed beneath it like dull silver. Fingers, snow-white and fleshless, opened like the petals of a crystal lily.

Joh Fredersen laid his hand in it, feeling it, in the moment of contact, to be burnt by an unbearable coldness. He wanted to push the being away from him but the silver-crystal fingers held him fast.

"Good-bye, Joh Fredersen," said the mass head, in a voice full of a horrible tenderness. "Give me a face soon, Joh Fredersen!"

A soft far-off voice laughed, as if the house were laughing in its sleep.

The hand let go, the door opened, Joh Fredersen reeled into the street.

The door closed behind him. In the gloomy wood of the door glowed, copper-red, the seal of Solomon, the pentagram.

When Joh Fredersen was about to enter the brain-pan of the New Tower of Babel Slim stood before him, seeming to be slimmer than ever.

"What is it?" asked Joh Fredersen.

Slim made to speak but at the sight of his master the words died on his lips.

"Well—?" said Joh Fredersen, between his teeth.

Slim breathed deeply.

"I must inform you, Mr. Fredersen," he said, "that, since your son left this room, he has disappeared!"

"What does that mean? . . . disappeared!"

"He has not gone home, and none of our men has seen him . . ."

Joh Fredersen screwed up his mouth.

"Look for him!" he said hoarsely. "What are you all here for? Look for him!"

He entered the brain-pan of the New Tower of Babel. His first glance fell upon the clock. He stepped to the table and stretched out his hand to the little blue metal plate.

"Who is it?" he replied. "Futura . . . Parody . . . whatever you like to call it. Also: delusion . . . In short: it is a woman . . . Every man-creator makes himself a woman . . . . A little cool—I admit, that comes of the material, which is my secret. But she is not yet completely finished . . . . That is why I have not yet given her a face. You must give her that, Joh Fredersen. For you were the one to order the new beings." [Brigitte Helm (Futura)]

CHAPTER V

MARIA!

THE MAN BEFORE the machine which was like Ganesha, the god with the elephant's head, was no longer a human being. Merely a dripping piece of exhaustion, from the pores of which the last powers of volition were oozing out in large drops of sweat. Running eyes no longer saw the manometer. The hand did not hold the lever—it clawed it fast in the last hold which saved the mangled man-creature before it from falling into the crushing arms of the machine.

The Pater-noster works of the New Tower of Babel turned their buckets with an easy smoothness. The eye of the little machine smiled softly and maliciously at the man who stood before it and who was now no more than a babel.

"Father!" babbled the son of Joh Fredersen, "to-day, for the first time, since Metropolis stood, you have forgotten to let your city and your great machines roar punctually for fresh food . . . Has Metropolis gone dumb, father? Look at us! Look at your machines! Your god-machines turn sick at the chewed-up ends in their mouths—at the mangled food that we are . . . Why do you strangle its voice to death? Will ten hours never, never come to an end? Our Father, which art in heaven—!"

But in this moment Joh Fredersen's fingers were pressing the little blue metal plate and the voice of the great Metropolis.

"Thank you, father!" said the mangled soul before the machine, which was like Ganesha. He smiled. He tasted a salty taste on his lips and did not know if it was from blood, sweat or tears. From out a red mist of long-flamed, drawn-out clouds, fresh men shuffled on towards him. His hand slipped from the lever and be collapsed. Arms pulled him up and led him away. He turned his head aside to hide his face.

The eye of the little machine, the soft, malicious eye, twinkled at him from behind.

"Good-bye, friend," said the little machine.

Freder's head fell upon his breast. He felt himself dragged further, heard the dull evenness of feet tramping onwards, felt himself tramping, a member of twelve members. The ground under his feet began to roll; it was drawn upwards, pulling him up with it.

Doors stood open, double doors. Towards him came a stream of men.

The great Metropolis was still roaring.

Suddenly she fell dumb and in the silence Freder became aware of the breath of a man at his ear, and of a voice—merely a breath—which asked:

"She has called . . . Are you coming?"

He did not know what the question meant, but he nodded. He wanted to get to know the ways of those who walked, as he, in blue linen, in the black cap, in the hard shoes.

With tightly closed eyelids he groped on, shoulder to shoulder with an unknown man.

She has called, he thought, half asleep. Who is that . . . she . . .?

He walked and walked in smouldering weariness. The way would never, never come to an end. He did not know where he was walking. He heard the tramp of those who were walking with him like the sound of perpetually falling water.

She has called! he thought. Who is that: she, whose voice is so powerful that these men, exhausted to death by utter weariness, voluntarily throw off sleep, which is the sweetest thing of all to the weary—to follow her when her voice calls? It can't be very much further to the centre of the earth . . .

Still deeper—still deeper down?

No longer any light round about, only, here and there, twinkling pocket torches, in men's hands.

At last, in the far distance, a dull shimmer.

Have we wandered so far to walk towards the sun, thought Freder, and does the sun dwell in the bowels of the earth?

The procession came to a standstill. Freder stopped too. He staggered against the dry, cool stones.

Where are we, he thought—in a cave? If the sun dwells here, then she

The man before the machine which was like Ganesha, the god with the elephant's head, was no longer a human being. Merely a dripping piece of exhaustion, from the pores of which the last powers of volition were oozing out in large drops of sweat. Running eyes no longer saw the manometer. The hand did not hold the lever—it clawed it fast in the last hold which saved the mangled man-creature before it from falling into the crushing arms of the machine. [Gustav Frˆöhlich (Freder)]

can't be at home now . . . I am afraid we have come in vain . . . Let us turn back, brother . . . Let us sleep . . .

He slid along the wall, fell on his knees, leant his head against the stone . . . how smooth it was.

The murmur of human voices was around him, like the rustling of trees, moved by the wind . . .

He smiled peacefully. It's wonderful to be tired . . .

Then a voice—a voice began to speak . . .

Oh—sweet voice, thought Freder dreamily. Tender beloved voice, your voice, Virgin-mother! I have fallen asleep . . . Yes, I am dreaming! I am dreaming of your voice, beloved!

But a slight pain at his temple made him think: I am leaning my head on stone . . . I am conscious of the coldness which comes out of the stone . . . I feel coldness under my knees . . . so I am not sleeping—I am only dreaming . . . suppose it is not a dream . . . ? Suppose it is reality . . . ?

With an exertion of will which brought a groan from him he forced open his eyes and looked about him.

A vault, like the vault of a sepulcher, human heads so closely crowded together as to produce the effect of clods on a freshly ploughed field. All heads turned towards one point: to the source of a light, as mild as God.

Candles burnt with sword-like flames. Slender, lustrous swords of light stood in a circle around the head of a girl, whose voice was as the Amen of God.

The voice spoke, but Freder did not hear the words. He heard nothing but a sound, the blessed melody of which was saturated with sweetness as is the air of a garden of blossoms with fragrance. And suddenly there sprang up above this melody the wild throb of a heart-beat. The air stormed with bells. The walls shook under the surf of an invisible organ. Weariness—exhaustion—faded out! He felt his body from head to foot to be one single instrument of blissfulness—all strings stretched to bursting point, yet tuned together into the purest, hottest, most radiant accord, in which his whole being hung, quivering.

He longed to stroke with his hands the stones on which he knelt. He longed to kiss with unbounded tenderness the stones on which he rested his head. God—God—God—beat the heart in his breast, and every throb was a thank-offering. He looked at the girl, and yet he did not see her. He saw only a shimmer; he knelt before it.

Gracious one, formed his mouth. Mine! Mine! My beloved! How could the world have existed before you were? How must God have smiled when he created you! You are speaking?—What are you saying?—My heart is shouting within me—I cannot catch your words . . . Be patient with me, gracious one, beloved!

Without his being aware of it, drawn by an invisible unbreakable cord, he pushed himself forward on his knees, nearer and nearer to the shimmer which the girl's face was to him. At last he was so near that he could have touched the hem of her dress with his outstretched hand.

"Look at me, Virgin!" implored his eyes. "Mother, look at me!"

But her gentle eyes looked out over him. Her lips said:

"My brothers . . ."

And stopped dumb, as though alarmed.

Freder raised his head. Nothing had happened—nothing to speak of, only that the air which passed through the room had suddenly become audible, like a raised breath, and that it was cool, as though coming in through open doors.

With a faint crackling sound the swords of flame bowed themselves. Then they stood still again.

"Speak, my beloved!" said Freder's heart.

Yes, now she spoke. This is what she said:

"Do you want to know how the building of the Tower of Babel began, and do you want to know how it ended? I see a man who comes from the Dawn of the World. He is as beautiful as the world, and has a burning heart. He loves to walk upon the mountains and to offer his breast unto the wind and to speak with the stars. He is strong and rules all creatures. He dreams of God and feels himself closely tied to him. His nights are filled with faces.

"One hallowed hour bursts his heart. The firmament is above him and his friends. 'Oh friends! Friends!' he cries, pointing to the stars. 'Great is the world and its Creator! Great is man! Come, let us build a tower, the top of which reaches the sky! And when we stand on its top, and hear the stars ringing above us, then let us write our creed in golden symbols on the top of the tower! Great is the world and its creator! And great is man!'

"And they set to, a handful of men, full of confidence, and they made bricks and dug up to the earth. Never have men worked more rapidly, for they all had one thought, one aim and one dream. When they rested from work in the evening each knew of what the other was thinking. They did not need speech to make themselves understood. But after some time they knew: The work was greater than their working hands. Then they enlisted new friends to their work. Then their work grew. It grew overwhelming. Then the builders

A vault, like the vault of a sepulcher, human heads so closely crowded together as to produce the effect of clods on a freshly ploughed field. All heads turned towards one point: to the source of a light, as mild as God. [Brigitte Helm (Maria)]

sent their messengers to all four winds of the world and enlisted Hands, working Hands for their mighty work.

"The Hands came. The Hands worked for wages. The Hands did not even know what they were making. None of those building Southwards knew one of those digging toward the North. The Brain which conceived the construction of the Tower of Babel was unknown to those who built it. Brain and Hands were far apart and strangers. Brain and Hands became enemies. The pleasure of one became the other's burden. The hymn of praise of one became the other's curse.

"'Babel!' shouted one, meaning: Divinity, Coronation, Eternal, Triumph!

"'Babel!' shouted the other, meaning: Hell, Slavery, Eternal, Damnation!

"The same word was prayer and blasphemy. Speaking the same words, the men did not understand each other.

"That men no longer understood each other, that Brain and Hands no longer understood each other, was to blame that the Tower of Babel was given up to destruction, that never were the words of those who had conceived it written on its top in golden symbols: Great is the world and its Creator! And great is man!

"That Brain and Hands no longer understand each other will one day destroy the New Tower of Babel.

"Brain and Hands need a mediator. The Mediator between Brain and Hands must be the Heart . . ."

She was silent. A breath like a sigh came up from the silent lips of the listeners.

Then one stood up slowly, resting his fists upon the shoulders of the man who crouched before him, and asked, raising his thin face with its fanatical eyes to the girl:

"And where is *our* mediator, Maria?"

The girl looked at him, and over her sweet face passed the gleam of a boundless confidence.

"Wait for him," she said. "He is sure to come."

A murmur ran through the rows of men. Freder bowed his head to the girl's feet, His whole soul said:

"It shall be I."

But she did not see him and she did not hear him.

"Be patient, my brothers!" she said. "The way which your mediator must take is long . . . There are many among you who cry, "Fight! Destroy!—Do not fight, my brothers, for that makes you to sin. Believe me: One will come, who will speak for you—who will be the mediator between you, the Hands, and the man whose Brain and Will are over you all. He will give you something which is more precious than anything which anybody could give you: To be free, without sinning."

She stood up from the stone upon which she had been sitting. A movement ran through the heads turned towards her. A voice was raised. The speaker was not to be seen. It was as if they all spoke:

"We shall wait, Maria. But not much longer—!"

The girl was silent. With her sad eyes she seemed to be seeking the speaker among the crowd.

A man who stood before her spoke up to her:

"And if we fight—where will you be then?"

"With you!" said the girl, opening her hands with the gesture of one sacrificing. "Have you ever found me faithless?"

"Never!" said the men. "You are like gold to us. We shall do what you expect of us."

"Thank you," said the girl, closing her eyes. With bowed head she stood there, listening to the sound of retiring feet—feet which walked in hard shoes.

Only when all about her had become silent and when the last footfall had died away she sighed and opened her eyes. Then she saw a man, wearing the blue linen and the black cap and the hard shoes, kneeling at her feet.

She bent down. He raised his head. She looked at him. And then she recognised him.

(Behind them, in a vault that was shaped like a pointed devil's-ear, one man's hand seized another man's arm.

"Hush! Keep quiet!" whispered the voice, which was soundless and yet which had the effect of laughter—like the laughter of spiteful mockery.)

The girl's face was as a crystal, filled with snow. She made a movement as if for flight. But her knees would not obey her. Reeds which stand in troubled water do not tremble more than her shoulders trembled.

"If you have come to betray us, son of Joh Fredersen, then you will have but little blessing from it," she said softly, but in a clear voice.

He stood up and remained standing before her.

"Is that all the faith you have in me?" he asked gravely. She said nothing, but looked at him. Her eyes filled with tears.

"You . . ." said the man. "What shall I call you? I do not know your name.

I have always called you just 'you.' In all the bad days and worse nights, for I did not know if I should find you again, I always called you only, 'you.' . . . Will you tell me, at last, what your name is?"

"Maria," answered the girl.

"Maria . . . That should be your name . . . you did not make it easy for me to find my way to you, Maria."

"And why did you seek your way to me? And why do you wear the blue linen uniform? Those condemned to wear it all their life long, live in an underground city, which is accounted a wonder of the world in all the five continents. It is an architectural wonder—that is true. It is light and shining bright and a model of tidiness. It lacks nothing but the sun and the rain—and the moon by night—nothing but the sky. That is why the children which are born there have their gnome-like faces . . . Do you want go down into this city under the earth in order the more to enjoy your dwelling which lies so high above the great Metropolis, in the light of the sky? Are you wearing the uniform, which you have on to-day, for fun?"

"No, Maria. I shall always wear it now."

"As Joh Fredersen's son?"

"He no longer has a son . . . unless—you, yourself, give him back his son."

(Behind them, in a vault that was shaped like a pointed devil's-ear, one man's hand was laid upon another man's mouth.

"It is written," whispered a laugh: "Therefore shall a man leave his father and his mother and cleave unto his wife . . . ")

"Won't you understand me?" asked Freder. "Why do you look at me with such stern eyes? You wish me to be a mediator between Joh Fredersen and those whom you call your brothers . . . There can be no mediator between heaven and hell who never was in heaven and hell . . . I never knew hell until yesterday. That is why I failed so deplorably, yesterday, when I spoke to my father for your brothers. Until you stood before me for the first time, Maria, I lived the life of a dearly loved son. I did not know what an unrealisable wish was. I knew no longing, for everything was mine . . . Young as I am, I have exhausted the pleasures of the earth, down to the very bottom. I had an aim—a gamble with Death: A flight to the stars . . . And then you came and showed me my brothers . . . From that day on I have sought you. I have so longed for you that I should gladly and unhesitatingly have died, had somebody told me that that was the way to you. But as it was, I had to live and seek another way . . ."

"To me, or to your brothers . . . ?"

"To you, Maria . . . I will not make myself out to you to be better than I am. I want to come to you, Maria—and I want you . . . I love mankind, not for its own sake, but for your sake—because you love it. I do not want to help mankind for its own sake, but for your sake—because you wish it. Yesterday I did good to two men; I helped one whom my father had dismissed. And I did the work of the man, whose uniform I have on . . . That was my way to you . . . God bless you . . ."

His voice failed him. The girl stepped up to him. She took his hands in both her hands. She gently turned the palms upward, and considered them, looked at them with her Madonna-eyes, and folded her hands tenderly around his, which she carefully laid together.

"Maria," he said, without a sound.

She let his hands fall and raised her's to his head. She laid her finger-tips on his cheeks. With her fingertips she stroked his eyebrows, his temples, twice, three times.

Then he snatched her to his heart and they kissed each other . . .

He no longer felt the stones under his feet. A wave carried him, him and the girl whom he held clasped to him as though he wished to die of it—and the wave came from the bottom of the ocean, roaring as though the whole sea were an organ; and the wave was of fire and flung right up to the heavens.

Then sinking . . . sinking . . . endlessly gliding down—right down to the womb of the world, the source of the beginning . . . Thirst and quenching drink . . . hunger and satiation . . . pain and deliverance from it . . . death and rebirth . . .

"You . . . " said the man to the girl's lips. "You are really the great mediatress . . . You are all that is most sacred on earth . . . You are all goodness . . . You are all grace . . . To doubt you is to doubt God . . . Maria—Maria—you called me—here I am!"

(Behind them, in a vault that was shaped like a pointed devil's-ear, one man leant towards another man's ear.

"You wanted to have the Futura's face from me . . . There you have your model . . ."

"Is that a commission?"

"Yes.")

"Now you must go, Freder," said the girl. Her Madonna eyes looked at him.

(Behind them, in a vault that was shaped like a pointed devil's-ear, one man leant towards another man's ear.
"You wanted to have the Futura's face from me . . . There you have your model . . . "
"Is that a commission?"
"Yes.")
[Rudolf Klein-Rogge (Rotwang)]

"Go—and leave you here?"

She turned grave and shook her head.

"Nothing will happen to me," she said. "There is not one, among those who know this place, whom I cannot trust as though he were my blood brother. But what is between us is nobody's affair; it would vex me to have to explain—" (and now she was smiling again)— "what is inexplicable . . . Do you see that?"

"Yes," he said. "Forgive me . . ."

(Behind them, in a vault that was shaped like a pointed devil's-ear, a man took himself away from the wall.

"You know what you have to do," he said in a low voice.

"Yes," came the voice of the other, idly, sleepily, out of the darkness, "But wait a bit, friend . . . I must ask you something . . ."

"Well?"

"Have you forgotten your own creed?"

For one second a lamp twinkled through the room, that was shaped like a pointed devil's ear, impaling the face of the man, who had already turned to go, on the pointed needle of its brilliance.

"That sin and suffering are twin-sisters . . . you will be sinning against two people, friend . . ."

"What has that to do with you?"

"Nothing . . . Or—little. Freder is Hel's son . . ."

"And mine . . ."

"Yes . . ."

"It is he whom I do not wish to lose."

"Better to sin once more?"

"Yes."

"And—"

"To suffer. Yes."

"Very well, friend," and in the voice was an inaudible laugh of mockery: "May it happen to you according to your creed . . .!")

The girl walked through the passages that were so familiar to her. The bright little lamp in her hand roved over the roof of stone and over the stone walls, where, in niches, the thousand-year-old dead slept.

The girl had never known fear of the dead; only reverence and gravity in face of their gravity. To-day she saw neither wall nor dead. She walked on, smiling and not knowing she did it. She felt like singing. With an expression of happiness, which was still incredulous and yet complete, she said the name of her beloved over to herself.

Quite softly: "Freder . . . " And once more: "Freder . . ."

Then she raised her head, listening attentively, standing quite still . . .

It came back as a whisper: An echo?—No.

Almost inaudibly a word was breathed:

"Maria . . ."

She turned around, blissfully startled. Was it possible that he had come back?

"Freder—!" she called. She listened.

No answer.

"Freder—!"

Nothing.

But suddenly there came a cool draught of air which made the hair at her neck quiver, and a hand of snow ran down her back.

There came an agonized sigh—a sigh which would not come to an end . . .

The girl stood still. The bright little lamp which she held in her hand let its gleam play tremblingly about her feet.

"Freder . . .?"

Now her voice, too, was only a whisper.

No answer. But, behind her, in the depths of the passage she would have to pass through, a gentle, gliding slink became perceptible: feet in soft shoes on rough stones . . .

That was . . . yes, that was strange. Nobody, apart from her, ever came this way. Nobody could be here. And, if somebody were here, then it was no friend . . .

Certainly nobody whom she wanted to meet.

Should she let him by?—yes.

A second passage opened to her left. She did not know it well. But she would not follow it up. She would only wait in it until the man outside—the man behind her—had gone by.

She pressed herself against the wall of the strange passage, keeping still and waiting quite silently. She did not breath. She had extinguished the lamp. She stood in utter darkness, immovable.

She listened: the gliding feet were approaching. They walked in darkness as she stood in darkness. Now they were here. Now they must . . . they must go past . . . But they did not go. They stood quite still. Before the opening to the passage in which she stood, the feet stopped still and seemed to wait.

For what . . .? For her . . .?

In the complete silence the girl suddenly heard her own heart . . . She heard her own heart, like pump-works, beating more and more quickly, throbbing more and more loudly. These loud throbbing heartbeats must also be heard by the man who kept the opening to the passage. And suppose he did not stay there any longer . . . suppose he came inside . . . she could not hear his coming, her heart throbbed so.

She groped, with fumbling hand, along the stone wall. Without breathing, she set her feet, one before the other . . . Only to get away from the entrance . . . Away from the place where the other was standing . . .

Was she wrong? Or were the feet really coming after her? Soft, slinking shoes on rough stones? Now the agonised, heavy breathing, heavier still, and nearer . . . cold breath on her neck . . . Then—

Nothing more. Silence. And waiting. And watching—keeping on the look-out . . .

Was it not as if a creature, such as the world had never seen: trunkless, nothing but arms, legs and head . . . but what a head! God—God in heaven! . . . was crouching on the floor before her, knees drawn up to chin, the damp arms supported right and left, against the walls, near her hips, so that she stood defenceless, caught? Did she not see the passage lighted by a pale shimmer— and did not the shimmer come from the being's jelly-fish head?

"Freder!" she thought. She bit the name tightly between her jaws, yet heard the scream with which her heart screamed it.

She threw herself forwards and felt—she was free—she was still free—and ran and stumbled, and pulled herself up again and staggered from wall to wall, knocking herself bloody, suddenly clutched into space, stumbled, fell to the ground, felt . . . Something lay there . . . what? No—No—No—!

The lamp had long since fallen from her hand. She raised herself to her knees and clapped her fists to her ears, in order not to hear the feet, the slinking feet coming nearer. She knew herself to be imprisoned in darkness and yet opened her eyes because she could no longer bear the circles of fire, the wheels of flame behind her closed lids—

And saw her own shadow thrown, gigantic, on the wall before her, and behind her was light, and before her lay a man—

A man?—That was not a man . . . That was the remains of a man, with his back half leaning against the wall, half slipped down, and on his skeleton feet, which almost touched the girl's knees, were the slender shoes, pointed and purple-red . . .

With a shriek which tore her throat, the girl threw herself up, backwards—

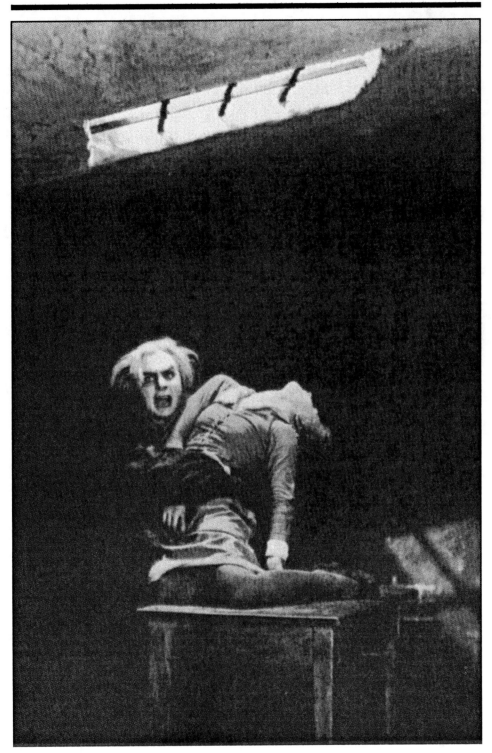

The girl turned around.
She saw a man sitting on the edge of the trap-door and saw his smile.
Then it was as though she were extinguished, and she plunged into nothing . . .
[Rudolf Klein-Rogge (Rotwang) and Brigitte Helm (Maria)]

and then on and on, without looking round, pursued by the light which lashed her own shadow in springs before her feet—pursued by long, soft, feathery feet-by feet which walked in red shoes, by the icy breath which blew at her back.

She ran, screamed and ran—

"Freder . . . ! Freder . . . !"

Her throat rattled, she fell.

There were some stairs . . . Crumbling stairs . . . She pressed her bleeding hands, right and left, against the stone wall, by the stone steps. She dragged herself up. She staggered up, step by step . . . There was the top.

The stairs ended in a stone trap-door.

The girl groaned: "Freder . . . !"

She stretched both fists above her. She pushed head and shoulders against the trap-door.

And one more groan: "Freder . . . "

The door rose and fell back with a crash.

Below—deep down—laughter . . .

The girl swung herself over the edge of the trapdoor. She ran hither and thither, with out-stretched hands. She ran along walls, finding no door. She saw the lustre which welled up from the depths. By this light she saw a door, which was latchless. It had neither bolt nor lock.

In the gloomy wood glowed, copper-red, the seal of Solomon, the pentagram.

The girl turned around.

She saw a man sitting on the edge of the trap-door and saw his smile.

Then it was as though she were extinguished, and she plunged into nothing . . .

CHAPTER VI
A MISTAKE

THE PROPRIETOR of Yoshiwara used to earn money in a variety of ways. One of them, and quite positively the most harmless, was to make bets that no man—be he never so widely travelled—was capable of guessing to what weird mixture of races he owed his face. So far he had won all such bets, and used to sweep in the money which they brought him with hands, the cruel beauty of which would not have shamed an ancestor of the Spanish Borgias, the nails of which, however, showed an inobliterable shimmer of blue; on the other hand, the politeness of his smile on such profitable occasions originated unmistakably in that graceful insular world, which, from the eastern border of Asia, smiles gently and watchfully across at mighty America.

There were prominent properties combined within him which made him appear to be a general representative of Great Britain and Ireland, for he was as red-haired, chaff-loving and with as good a head for drink as if his name had been McFosh, avaricious and superstitious as a Scotsman and—in certain circumstances, which made it requisite, of that highly bred obliviousness, which is a matter of will and a foundation stone of the British Empire. He spoke practically all living languages as though his mother had taught him to pray in them and his father to curse. His greed appeared to hail from the Levant, his contentment from China. And, above all this, two quiet, observant eyes watched with German patience and perseverance.

As to the rest, he was called, for reasons unknown, September.

The visitants to Yoshiwara had met September in a variety of emotions— from the block-headed dozing away of the well-contented bushman to the dance-ecstatic of the Ukrainer.

But to come upon his features in an expression of absolute bewilderment was reserved for Slim, when, on the morning after his having lost sight of his young master, he set throbbing the massive gong which demanded entrance to Yoshiwara.

It was most unusual that the generally very obliging door of Yoshiwara was not opened before the fourth gong-signal; and that this was performed by September himself and with this expression of countenance deepened the impression of an only tolerably overcome catastrophe. Slim bowed. September looked at him. A mask of brass seemed to fall over his face. But a chance glance at the driver of the taxi, in which Slim had come tore it off again.

"Would to God your tin-kettle had gone up in the air before you could have brought that lunatic here yesterday evening," he said. "He drove away my guests before they even thought of paying. The girls are huddling down in the corners like lumps of wet floor-cloth—that is, those who are not in hysterics. Unless I call in the police I might just as well close the house; for it doesn't look as though that chap will have recovered his five senses by this evening."

"Of whom are you speaking, September?" asked Slim.

September looked at him. At this moment the tiniest hamlet in North Siberia would have flatly refused to have been proclaimed the birth-place of so idiotic looking an individual.

"If it is the man for whom I have come here to look," continued Slim, "then I shall rid you of him in a more agreeable and swifter manner than the police."

"And for what man are you looking, sir?"

Slim hesitated. He cleared his throat slightly. "You know the white silk which is woven for comparatively few in Metropolis . . ."

In the long line of ancestors, the manifold sediment of whom had been crystalised into September, a fur-trader from Tarnopolis must also have been represented and he now smiled out from the corners of his great-grandson's wily eyes.

"Come in, sir!" the proprietor of Yoshiwara invited Slim, with true Singhalese gentleness.

Slim entered. September closed the door behind him.

In the moment when the matutinal roar of the great Metropolis no longer bellowed up from the streets, another roar from inside the building became perceptible—the roar of a human voice, hotter than the voice of a beast of prey, mad-drunk with triumph.

"Who is that?" asked Slim, involuntarily dropping his own voice.

"He—!" answered September, and how he could stow the smooth and pointed vengefulness of whole Corsica into the monosyllable remained his own secret.

Slim's glance became uncertain, but he said nothing. He followed September over soft and glossy straw mats, along walls of oiled paper, narrowly framed in bamboo.

Behind one of these walls the weeping of a woman was to be heard—monotonous, hopeless, heartbreaking, like a long spell of rainy days which envelope the summit of Fuji Yama.

"That's Yuki," murmured September, with a fierce glance at the paper prison of this pitiful weeping. "She's been crying since midnight, as if she wanted to be the source of a new salt sea . . . This evening she will have a swollen potato on her face instead of a nose . . . Who pays for it?—I do!"

"Why is the little snowflake crying?" asked Slim, half thoughtlessly, for the roaring of the human voice, coming from the depths of the house occupied all the ears and attention he possessed.

"Oh, she isn't the only one," answered September, with the tolerant mien of one who owns a prosperous harbour tavern in Shanghai. "But she is at least tame. Plum Blossom has been snapping about her like a young Puma, and Miss Rainbow has thrown the Saki bowl at the mirror and is trying to cut her artery with the chips—and all on account of this white silk youngster."

The agitated expression on Slim's face deepened. He shook his head.

"How did he manage to get such a hold over them . . . " he said, and it was not meant to be a question.

September shrugged his shoulders.

"Maohee . . . " he said in a sing-song tone, as though beginning one of those Greenland fairy tales, which, the quicker they sent one to sleep are the more highly appreciated.

"What is that: Maohee?" asked Slim, irritably.

September drew his head down between his shoulders. The Irish and the British blood-corpuscles in his veins seemed to be falling out, violently: but the impenetrable Japanese smile covered this up with its mantle before it could grow dangerous.

"You don't know what Maohee is . . . Not a soul in the great Metropolis knows . . . No . . . Nobody. But here in Yoshiwara they all know."

"I wish to know, too, September," said Slim.

Generations of Roman lackeys bowed within September as he said, "Certainly, sir!" But they did not get the better of the wink of the heavy-drinking lying grandfathers in Copenhagen. "Maohee, that is . . . Isn't it odd, that, of all the ten thousand who have been guests here in Yoshiwara and who had experienced in detail what Maohee stands for, outside they know nothing more about it? Don't walk so fast, sir. The yelling gentleman down there won't run away from us—and if I am to explain to you what Maohee means . . ."

"Drugs, I expect, September—?"

"My dear sir, the lion is also a cat. Maohee is a drug: but what is a cat beside a lion? Maohee is from the other side of the earth. It is the divine, the only thing—because it is the only thing which makes us feel the intoxication of the others."

"The intoxication—of the others . . . ?" repeated Slim, stopping still.

September smiled the smile of Hotei the god of Happiness, who likes little children. He laid the hand of the Borgia, with the suspiciously blue shimmering nails on Slim's arm. "The intoxication of the others—Sir, do you know what that means? Not of one other—no, of the multitude which rolls itself into a lump, the rolled up intoxication of the multitude gives Maohee its friends . . ."

"Has Maohee many friends, September?"

The proprietor of Yoshiwara grinned, apocalyptically.

"Sir, in this house there is a round room. You shall see it. It has not its like. It is built like a winding seashell, like a mammoth shell, in the windings of which thunders the surf of seven oceans; in these windings people crouch, so densely crowded that their faces appear as one face. No one knows the other, yet they are all friends. They all fever. They are all pale with expectation. They have all clasped hands. The trembling of those who sit right down at the bottom of the shell runs right through the windings of the mammoth shell, right up to those, who, from the gleaming top of the spiral, send out their own trembling towards it . . ."

September gulped for breath. Sweat stood like a fine chain of beads on his brow. An international smile of insanity parted his prating mouth.

"Go on, September!" said Slim.

"On?—On?—Suddenly the rim of the shell begins to turn . . . gently . . . ah how gently, to music such as would bring a tenfold murderer-bandit to sobs and his judges to pardon him on the scaffold—to music on hearing which deadly enemies kiss, beggars believe themselves to be kings, the hungry forget their hunger—to such music the shell revolves around its stationary heart, until it seems to free itself from the ground and, hovering, to revolve about itself. The people scream—not loudly, no, no!—they scream like the birds that bathe in the sea. The twisted hands are clenched to fists. The bodies rock in one rhythm.

Then comes the first stammer of: Maohee . . . The stammer swells, becomes waves of spray, becomes a spring tide. The revolving shell roars: Maohee . . . Maohee . . . ! It is as though a little flame must rest on everyone's hair parting, like St. Elmo's fire . . . Maohee . . . Maohee! They call on their god. They call on him whom the finger of the god touches today . . . No one knows from where he will come today . . . He is there . . . They know he is amongst them . . . He must break out from the rows of them . . . He must . . . He must, for they call him: Maohee . . . Maohee! And suddenly—!"

The hand of the Borgia flew up and hung in the air like a brown claw.

"And suddenly a man is standing in the middle of the shell, in the gleaming circle, on the milk-white disc. But it is no man. It is the embodied conception of the intoxication of them all. He is not conscious of himself . . . A slight froth stands on his mouth. His eyes are stark and bursting and are yet like rushing meteors which leave waving tracks of fire behind them on the route from heaven to earth . . . He stands and lives his intoxication. He is what his intoxication is. From the thousands of eyes which have cast anchor into his soul the power of intoxication streams into him. There is no delight in God's creation which does not reveal itself, surmounted by the medium of these intoxicated souls. What he says becomes visible, what he hears becomes audible to all. What he feels: Power, desire, madness, is felt by them all. On the shimmering area, around which the shell revolves, to music beyond all description, one in ecstasy lives the thousandfold ecstasy which embodies itself in him, for thousands of others . . ."

September stopped and smiled at Slim. "That, sir, is Maohee . . ."

"It must indeed be a powerful drug," said Slim with a feeling of dryness in his throat, "which inspires the proprietor of Yoshiwara to such a hymn. Do you think that that yelling individual down there would join in this song of praise?"

"Ask him yourself, sir," said September.

He opened the door and let Slim enter. Just over the threshold Slim stopped, because at first he saw nothing. A gloom, more melancholy than the deepest darkness, spread over a room, the dimensions of which he could not estimate. The floor under his feet inclined in a barely perceptible slope. Where it stopped there appeared to be gloomy emptiness. Right and left, spiral walls, billowing outwards, swept away to each side.

That was all Slim saw. But from the empty depths before him came a white shimmer, no stronger than if coming from a field of snow. On this shimmer there floated a voice, that of a murderer and of one being murdered.

"Light, September!" said Slim with a gulp. An unbearable feeling of thirst gnawed at his throat.

The room slowly grew brighter, as though the light were coming unwillingly. Slim saw, he was standing in one of the windings of the round room, which was shaped like a shell. He was standing between the heights and the depths, separated by a low banister from the emptiness from which came the snow-like light and the murderer's voice and the voice of his victim. He stepped to the banister, and leaned far over it. A milk-white disc, lighted from beneath and luminous. At the edge of the disc, like a dark, rambling pattern on a plate-rim, women, crouching, kneeling there, in their gorgeous attire, as though drunken. Some had dropped their foreheads to the ground, their hands clutched above their ebony hair. Some crouched, huddled together in clumps, head pressed to head, symbols of fear. Some were swaying rhythmically from side to side as if calling on gods. Some were weeping. Some were as if dead.

But they all seemed to be the hand-maids of the man on the snow-light illuminated disk.

The man wore the white silk woven for comparatively few in Metropolis. He wore the soft shoes in which the beloved sons of mighty fathers seemed to caress the earth. But the silk hung in tatters about the body of the man and the shoes looked as though the feet within them bled.

"Is that the man for whom you are looking, sir?" asked a Levantine cousin from out September, leaning confidently towards Slim's ear.

Slim did not answer. He was looking at the man.

"At least," continued September, "it is the youngster who came here yesterday by the same car as you to-day. And the devil take him for it! He has turned my revolving shell into the fore-court of hell! He has been roasting souls! I have known Maohee-drugged beings to have fancied themselves Kings, Gods, Fire, and Storm—and to have forced others to feel themselves Kings, Gods, Fire, and Storm. I have known those in the ecstasy of desire to have forced women down to them from the highest part of the shell's wall, that they, diving, like seagulls, with out-spread hands, have swooped to his feet, without injuring a limb, while others have fallen to their death. That man there was no God, no Storm, no Fire, and his drunkenness most certainly inspired him with no desire. It seems to me that he had come up from hell and is roaring in the intoxication of damnation. He did not know that the ecstasy for men who are damned is also damnation . . . The fool! The prayer he is praying will not redeem him. He believes himself to be a machine and is praying to himself. He has forced the others to pray to him. He has ground them down.

He has pounded them to a powder. There are many dragging themselves around Metropolis to-day who cannot comprehend why their limbs are as if broken . . ."

"Be quiet, September!" said Slim hoarsely. His hand flew to his throat which felt like a glowing cork, like smouldering charcoal.

September fell silent, shrugging his shoulders. Words seethed up from the depths like lava.

"I am the Three-in-one—Lucifer—Belial—Satan—! I am the everlasting Death! I am the everlasting Noway! Come unto me—! In my hell there are many mansions! I shall assign them to you! I am the great king of all the damned—! I am a machine! I am the tower above you all! I am a hammer, a fly-wheel, a fiery oven! I am a murderer and of what I murder I make no use. I want victims and victims do not appease me! Pray to me and know: I do not hear you! Shout at me: Pater-noster! Know: I am deaf!"

Slim turned around; he saw September's face as a chalky mask at his shoulder. Maybe that, among September's ancestresses there was one who hailed from an isle in the South sea, where gods mean little—spirits everything.

"That's no more a man," he whispered with ashen lips. "A man would have died of it long ago . . . Do you see his arms, sir? Do you think a man can imitate the pushing of a machine for hours and hours at a time without its killing him? He is as dead as stone. If you were to call to him he'd collapse and break to pieces like a plaster statue."

It did not seem as though September's words had penetrated into Slim's consciousness. His face wore an expression of loathing and suffering and he spoke as one who speaks with pain.

"I hope, September, that to-night you have had your last opportunity of watching the effects of Maohee on your guests . . ."

September smiled his Japanese smile. He did not answer.

Slim stepped up to the banister at the edge of the curve of the shell in which he stood. He bent down towards the milky disc. He cried a high sharp tone which had the effect of a whistle:

"Eleven thousand eight hundred and eleven—!"

The man on the shimmering disc swung around as though he had received a blow in the side. The hellish rhythm of his arms ceased, running itself out in vibration. The man fell to earth like a log and did not move again.

Slim ran down the passage, reached the end and pushed asunder the circle of women, who, stiffened with shock, seemed to be thrown into deeper horror more by the end of that which they had brought to pass than by the beginning. He knelt down beside the man, looked him in the face and pushed the tattered silk away from his heart. He did not give his hand time to test his pulse. He lifted the man up and carried him out in his arms. The sighing of the women soughed behind him like a dense, mist-coloured curtain.

September stepped across his path. He swept aside as he caught Slim's glance at him. He ran along by him, like an active dog, breathing rapidly; but he said nothing.

Slim reached the door of Yoshiwara. September, himself, opened it for him. Slim stepped into the street. The driver pulled open the door of the taxi; he looked in amazement at the man who hung in Slim's arms, in tatters of white silk with which the wind was playing, and who was more awful to look on than a corpse.

The proprietor of Yoshiwara bowed repeatedly while Slim was climbing into the car. But Slim did not give him another glance. September's face, which was as grey as steel, was reminiscent of the blades of those ancient swords, forged of Indian steel, in Shiras or Ispahan and on which, hidden by ornamentation, stand mocking and deadly words.

The car glided away: September looked after it. He smiled the peaceable smile of Eastern Asia.

For he knew perfectly well what Slim did not know, and what, apart from him, nobody in Metropolis knew, that with the first drop of water or wine which moistened the lips of a human being, there disappeared even the very faintest memory of all which appertained to the wonders of the drug, Maohee.

The car stopped before the next medical depot. Male nurses came and carried away the bundle of humanity, shivering in tatters of white silk, to the doctor on duty. Slim looked about him. He beckoned to a policeman who was stationed near the door.

"Take down a report," he said. His tongue would hardly obey him, so parched was it with thirst.

The policeman entered the house after him.

"Wait!" said Slim, more with the movement of his head than in words. He saw a glass jug of water standing on the table and the coolness of the water had studded the jug with a thousand pearls.

Slim drank like an animal which finds drink on coming from the desert. He put down the jug and shivered. A short shudder passed through him.

He turned around and saw the man he had brought with him lying on a bed over which a young doctor was bending.

The lips of the sick man were moistened with wine. His eyes stood wide open, staring up at the ceiling, tears upon tears running gently and incessantly from the corners of his eyes, down over his temples. It was as though they had nothing to do with the man—as though they were trickling from a broken vessel and could not stop trickling until the vessel had run quite empty.

Slim looked the doctor in the face; the latter shrugged his shoulders. Slim bent over the prostrate man.

"Georgi," he said in a low voice, "can you hear me?"

The sick man nodded; it was the shadow of a nod.

"Do you know who I am?"

A second nod.

"Are you in a condition to answer two or three questions?"

Another nod.

"How did you get the white silk clothes?"

For a long time he received no answer apart from the gentle falling of the tear drops. Then came the voice, softer than a whisper.

" . . . He changed with me . . . "

"Who did?"

"Freder . . . Joh Fredersen's son . . . "

"And then, Georgi?"

"He told me I was to wait for him . . . "

"Wait where, Georgi?"

A long silence. And then, barely audible:

"Ninetieth Street. House seven. Seventh floor . . . "

Slim did not question him further. He knew who lived there. He looked at the doctor; the latter's face wore a completely impenetrable expression.

Slim drew a breath as though he were sighing. He said, more deploringly than inquiringly:

"Why did you not rather go there, Georgi . . . "

He turned to go but stopped still as Georgi's voice came wavering after him;

" . . . The city . . . all the lights . . . more than enough money . . . It is written . . . Forgive us our trespasses . . . lead us not into temptation . . ."

His voice died away. His head fell to one side. He breathed as though his soul wept, for his eyes could do so no longer.

The doctor cleared his throat cautiously.

Slim raised his head as though somebody had called him, then dropped it again.

"I shall come back again," he said softly. "He is to remain under your care..."

Georgi was asleep.

Slim left the room, followed by the policeman.

"What do you want?" Slim asked with an absent-minded look at him.

"The report, sir."

"What report?"

"I was to take down a report, sir."

Slim looked at the policeman very attentively, almost meditatively. He raised his hand and rubbed it across his forehead.

"A mistake," he said. "That was a mistake..."

The policeman saluted and retired, a little puzzled, for he knew Slim.

He remained standing on the same spot. Again and again he rubbed his forehead with the same helpless gesture.

Then he shook his head, stepped into the car and said:

"Ninetieth block..."

CHAPTER VII

NO, NO, NO . . . !

"WHERE IS GEORGI?" asked Freder, his eyes wandering through Josaphat's three rooms, which stretched out before him—beautiful, with a rather bewildering super-abundance of armchairs, divans and silk cushions, with curtains which goldenly obscured the light.

"Who?" asked Josaphat, listlessly. He had waited, had not slept and his eyes stood excessively large in his thin, almost white face. His gaze, which he did not take from Freder, was like hands which are raised adoringly.

"Georgi," repeated Freder. He smiled happily with his tired mouth.

"Who is that?" asked Josaphat.

"I sent him to you."

"Nobody has come."

Freder looked at him without answering.

"I sat all night in this chair," continued Josaphat, misinterpreting Freder's silence. "I did not sleep a wink. I expected you to come at any second, or a messenger to come from you, or that you would ring me up. I also informed the watchman. Nobody has come, Mr. Freder."

Freder still remained silent. Slowly, almost stumblingly be stepped over the threshold, into the room raising his right hand to his head, as though to take off his hat, then noticing that he was wearing the cap, the black cap, which pressed the hair tightly down, he swept it from his head; it fell to the ground. His hand sank from his brow, over his eyes, resting there a little while. Then the other joined it, as though wishing to console its sister. His form was like that of a young birch tree pressed sideways by a strong wind.

Josaphat's eyes hung on the uniform which Freder wore.

"Mr. Freder," he began cautiously, "how comes it that you are wearing these clothes?"

Freder remained turned away from him. He took his hands from his eyes and pressed them to his face as though he felt some pain there.

"Georgi wore them . . . " He answered. "I gave him mine . . ."

"Then Georgi is a workman?"

"Yes . . . I found him before the Pater-noster machine. I took his place and sent him to you . . ."

"Perhaps he'll come yet," answered Josaphat.

Freder shook his head.

"He should have been here hours ago. If he had been caught when leaving the New Tower of Babel, then someone would have come to me when I was standing before the machine. It is strange, but there it is; he has not come."

"Was there much money in the suit which you exchanged with Georgi?" asked Josaphat tentatively, as one who bares a wounded spot.

Freder nodded.

"Then you must not be surprised that Georgi has not come," said Josaphat. But the expression of shame and pain on Freder's face prevented him from continuing.

"Won't you sit down, Mr. Freder," he begged. "Or lie down? You look so tired that it is painful to look at you."

"I have no time to sit down and no time to lie down, either," answered Freder. He walked through the rooms, aimlessly, senselessly, stopping wherever a chair, a table, offered him a hold. "The fact, is this, Josaphat: I told Georgi to come here and to wait here for me—or for a message from me . . . It is a thousand to one that Slim, in searching for me, is already on Georgi's track, and it's a thousand to one he gets out of him where I sent him . . ."

"And you do not want Slim to find you?"

"He must not find me, Josaphat—not for anything on earth . . ."

The other stood silent, rather helpless. Freder looked at him with a trembling smile.

"How shall we obtain money, now, Josaphat?"

"That should offer no difficulty to Joh Fredersen's son."

"More than you think, Josaphat, for I am no longer Joh Fredersen's son . . ."

Josaphat raised his head.

"I do not understand you," he said, after a pause.

"There is nothing to misunderstand, Josaphat. I have set myself free from my father, and am going my own way . . ."

The man who had been the first secretary to the Master over the great Metropolis held his breath back in his lungs, then released it in streams.

"Will you let me tell you something, Mr. Freder?"

"Well . . ."

"One does not set oneself free from your father. It is he who decides whether one remains with him or must leave him.

"There is nobody who is stronger than Joh Fredersen. He is like the earth. As regards the earth we have no will either. Her laws keep us eternally perpendicular to the centre of the earth, even if we stand on our head . . . When Joh Fredersen sets a man free it means just as much as if the earth were to shut off from a man her powers of attraction. It means falling into nothing . . . Joh Fredersen can set free whom he may; he will never set free his son . . ."

"But what," answered Freder, speaking feverishly, "if a man overcomes the laws of nature?"

"Utopia, Mr. Freder."

"For the inventive spirit of man there is no Utopia: there is only a Not-yet. I have made up my mind to venture the path. I must take it—yes, I must take it! I do not know the way yet, but I shall find it because I must find it . . ."

"Wherever you wish, Mr. Freder—I shall go with you . . ."

"Thank you," said Freder, reaching out his hand. He felt it seized and clasped in a vice-like grip.

"You know, Mr. Freder, don't you—" said the strangled voice of Josaphat, "that everything belongs to you—everything that I am and have . . . It is not much, for I have lived like a madman . . . But for to-day, and to-morrow and the day after to-morrow . . ."

Freder shook his head without losing hold of Josaphat's hand.

"No, no!" he said, a torrent of red flowing over his face. "One does not begin new ways like that . . . We must try to find other ways . . . It will not be easy. Slim knows his business."

"Perhaps Slim could be won over to you . . ." said Josaphat, hesitatingly. "For—strange though it may sound, he loves you . . ."

"Slim loves all his victims. Which does not prevent him, as the most considerate and kindly of executioners, from laying them before my father's feet. He is the born tool, but the tool of the strongest. He would never make himself the tool of the weaker one, for he would thus humiliate himself. And you have just told me, Josaphat, how much stronger my father is than I . . ."

"If you were to confide yourself to one of your friends . . ."

"I have no friends, Josaphat."

Josaphat wanted to contradict, but he stopped himself. Freder turned his eyes towards him. He straightened himself up and smiled—the other's hand still in his.

"I have no friends, Josaphat, and, what weighs still more, I have no friend. I had play-fellows—sport-fellows—but friends? A friend? No, Josaphat! Can one confide oneself to somebody of whom one knows nothing but how his laughter sounds?"

He saw the eyes of the other fixed upon him, discerned the ardour in them and the pain and the truth.

"Yes," he said with a worried smile. "I should like to confide myself to you . . . I must confide myself to you, Josaphat . . . I must call you 'Friend' and 'Brother' . . . for I need a man who will go with me in trust and confidence to the world's end. Will you be that man?"

"Yes."

"Yes—?" He came to him and laid his hands upon his shoulders. He looked closely into his face. He shook him. "You say: 'Yes—!' Do you know what that means—for you and for me? What a last plummet-drop that is—what a last anchorage? I hardly know you—I wanted to help you—I cannot even help you now, because I am poorer now than you are—but, perhaps, that is all to the good . . . Joh Fredersen's son can, perhaps, be betrayed—but I, Josaphat? A man who has nothing but a will and an object? It cannot be worth while to betray him—eh, Josaphat?"

"May God kill me as one kills a mangy dog . . ."

"That's all right, that's all right . . ." Freder's smile came back again and stood, clear and beautiful in his tired face. "I am going now, Josaphat. I want to go to my father's mother, to take her something which is very sacred to me . . . I shall be here again before evening. Shall I find you here then?"

"Yes, Mr. Freder, most certainly!"

They stretched out their hands towards each other. Hand held hand, gripped. They looked at each other. Glance held glance, gripped. Then they loosened their grip in silence and Freder went.

A little while later (Josaphat was still standing on the same spot on which Freder had left him) there came a knock at the door.

Though the knocking was as gentle, as modest, as the knocking of one who has come to beg, there was something in it which chased a shiver down Josaphat's spine. He stood still, gazing at the door, incapable of calling out "Come in," or of opening it himself.

The knocking was repeated, becoming not in the least louder. It came for the third time and was still as gentle. But just that deepened the impression that it was inescapable, that it would be quite pointless to play deaf permanently.

"Who is there?" asked Josaphat hoarsely. He knew very well who was standing outside. He only asked to gain time—to draw breath, which he badly needed. He expected no answer; neither did he receive one.

The door opened.

In the doorway stood Slim.

They did not greet each other; neither greeted the other. Josaphat: because his gullet was too dry: Slim: because his all-observing eye had darted through the room in the second in which he put his foot on the threshold, and had found something: a black cap, lying on the floor.

Josaphat followed Slim's gaze with his eyes. He did not stir. With silent step Slim went up to the cap, stooped and picked it up. He twisted it gently this way and that, he twisted it inside out.

In the sweat-sodden lining of the cap stood the number, 11811.

Slim weighed the cap in almost affectionate hands, He fixed his eyes, which were as though veiled with weariness on Josaphat and asked, speaking in a low voice:

"Where is Freder, Josaphat?"

"I do not know . . ."

Slim smiled sleepily. He fondled the black cap. Josaphat's hoarse voice continued:

" . . . But if I did know you would not get it out of me, anyway . . ."

Slim looked at Josaphat, still smiling, still fondling the black cap.

"You are quite right," said he courteously. "I beg your pardon. It was an idle question. Of course you will not tell me where Mr. Freder is. Neither is it at all necessary . . . It is quite another matter . . ."

He pocketed the cap, having carefully rolled it up, and looked around the room. He went up to an armchair, standing near a low, black, polished table.

"You permit me?" he asked courteously, seating himself.

Josaphat made a movement of the head, but the "Please do so," dried up in his throat. He did not stir from the one spot.

You live very well here," said Slim, leaning back and surveying the room with a sweeping movement of his head. "Everything of a soft, half-dark tone. The atmosphere about these cushions is a tepid perfume. I can well understand how difficult it will be for you to leave this flat."

"I have no such intention, however," said Josaphat. He swallowed.

Slim pressed his eye-lids together, as though he wished to sleep.

"No . . . Not yet . . . But very soon . . ."

"I should not think of it," answered Josaphat. His eyes grew red, and he looked at Slim, hatred smouldering in his gaze.

"No . . . Not yet . . . But very soon . . ."

Josaphat stood quite still: but suddenly he smote the air with his fist, as though beating against an invisible door.

"What do you want exactly?" he asked pantingly. "What is that supposed to imply? What do you want from me—?"

It appeared at first as though Slim had not heard the question. Sleepily, with closed eye-lids, he sat there, breathing inaudibly. But, as the leather of the chair-back squeaked under Josaphat's grasp, Slim said, very slowly, but very clearly:

"I want you to tell me for what sum you will give up this flat, Josaphat."

" . . . When?" . . ."

"Immediately."

" . . . What is that supposed to mean . . . Immediately? . . ."

Slim opened his eyes, and they were as cold and bright as a pebble in a brook.

"Immediately means within an hour . . . Immediately means long before this evening . . ."

A shiver ran down Josaphat's back. The hands on his hanging arms slowly clenched themselves into fists.

"Get out, sir . . ." he said quietly. "Get out of here—! Now—! At once—! *Immediately!*—"

"The flat is very pretty," said Slim. "You are unwilling to give it up. It is of value to one who knows how to appreciate such things. You will not have time to pack any large trunks, either. You can only take what you need for twenty-four hours. The journey—new outfit—a year's expenses—all this is to be added to the sum: what is the price of your flat, Josaphat?"

"I shall chuck you into the street," stammered Josaphat with feverish mouth. "I shall chuck you seven stories down into the street—through the window, my good sir!—through the closed window—if you don't get out this very second!"

"You love a woman. The woman does not love you. Women who are not in love are very expensive. You want to buy this woman. Very well. The threefold cost of the flat . . . Life on the Adriatic coast—in Rome—on Teneriffe—on a splendid steamer around the world with a woman who wants to be bought anew every day—comprehensible, Josaphat, that the flat will be expensive . . . but to tell you the truth, I must have it, so I must pay for it."

He plunged his hands into his pocket and drew out a wad of banknotes. He pushed it across to Josaphat over the black, polished mirror-like table. Josaphat clutched at it, leaving his nail marks behind on the table-top and threw it into Slim's face. He caught it with a nimble, thought-swift movement, and gently laid it back on the table. He laid a second one beside it.

"Is that enough?" he asked sleepily.

"No—!" shouted Josaphat's laughter.

"Sensible!" said Slim. "Very sensible. Why should you not make full use of your advantages. An opportunity like this, to raise your whole life by one hundred rungs, to become independent, happy, free, the fulfilment of every wish, the satisfaction of every whim—to have your own, and a beautiful woman before you, will come only once in your life and never again. Seize it, Josaphat, if you are not a fool! In strict confidence: The beautiful woman of whom we spoke just now has already been informed and is awaiting you near the aeroplane which is standing ready for the journey . . . Three times the price, Josaphat, if you do not keep the beautiful woman waiting!"

He laid the third bundle of banknotes on the table. He looked at Josaphat. Josaphat's reddened eyes devoured his. Josaphat's hands fumbled across blindly and seized the three brown wads. His teeth showed white under his lips; while his fingers tore the notes to shreds, they seemed to be biting them to death.

Slim shook his head. "That's of no account," he said undisturbedly. "I have a cheque-book here, some of the blank leaves of which bear the signature, Joh Fredersen. Let us write a sum on the first leaf—a sum the double of the amount agreed upon up to now . . . Well, Josaphat?"

"I will not—!" said the other, shaken from head to foot.

Slim smiled.

"No," he said. "Not yet . . . But very soon . . ."

Josaphat did not answer. He was staring at the piece of paper, white, printed and written on, which lay before him on the blue-black table. He did not see the figure upon it. He only saw the name upon it:

Joh Fredersen.

The signature, as though written with the blade of an axe:

Joh Fredersen.

Josaphat turned his head this way and that as though he felt the blade of the axe at his neck.

"No," he croaked. "No, no, no . . .!"

"Not enough yet?" asked Slim.

"Yes!" said he in a mutter. "Yes! It is enough."

Slim got up. Something which he had drawn from his pocket with the bundles of banknotes, without his having noticed it, slid down from his knees.

It was a black cap, such as the workmen in Joh Fredersen's works used to wear . . .

A howl escaped Josaphat's lips. He threw himself down on both knees. He seized the black cap in both hands. He snatched it to his mouth. He stared at Slim. He jerked himself up. He sprang, like a stag before the pack, to gain the door.

But Slim got there before him. With a mighty leap he sprang across table and divan, rebounded against the door and stood before Josaphat. For the fraction of a second they stared each other in the face. Then Josaphat's hands flew to Slim's throat. Slim lowered his head. He threw forward his arms, like the grabbing arms of the octopus. They held each other, tightly clasped, and wrestled together, burning and ice-cold, raving and reflecting, teeth-grinding and silent, breast to breast.

They tore themselves apart and dashed at each other. They fell, and, wrestling, rolled along the floor. Josaphat forced his opponent beneath him. Fighting, they pushed each other up. They stumbled and rolled over armchairs and divans. The beautiful room, turned into a wilderness, seemed to be too small for the two twisted bodies, which jerked like fishes, stamped like steers, struck at each other like fighting bears.

But against Slim's unshakeable, dreadful coldness the white-hot fury of his opponent could not stand its ground. Suddenly, as though his knee joints had been hacked through, Josaphat collapsed in Slim's hands, fell on his knees and remained there, his back resting against an over-turned armchair, staring up with glassy eyes.

Slim loosened his hold. He looked down at him.

"Had enough yet?" he asked, and smiled sleepily.

Josaphat did not answer. He moved his right hand. In all the fury of the fight he had not lost hold of the black cap which Freder had worn when he came to him.

He raised the cap painfully on to his knees, as though it weighed a hundredweight. He twisted it between his fingers. He fondled it . . .

"Come, Josaphat, get up!" said Slim. He spoke very gravely and gently and a little sadly. "May I help you? Give me your hands! No, no. I shall not take the cap away from you . . . I am afraid I was obliged to hurt you very much. It was no pleasure. But you forced me into it."

He left go of the man, who was now standing upright, and he looked around him with a gloomy smile.

"A good thing we settled the price beforehand," he said. "Now the flat would be considerably cheaper."

He sighed a little and looked at Josaphat.

"When will you be ready to go?"

"Now," said Josaphat.

"You will not take anything with you?"

"No. "

"You will go just as you are—with all the marks of the struggle, all tattered and torn?"

"Yes."

"Is that courteous to the lady who is waiting for you?"

Sight returned to Josaphat's eyes. He turned a reddened gaze towards Slim.

"If you do not want me to commit the murder on the woman which did not succeed on you—then send her away before I come . . .

Slim was silent. He turned to go. He took the cheque, folded it together and put it into Josaphat's pocket.

Josaphat offered no resistance.

He walked before Slim towards the door. Then he stopped again and looked around.

He waved the cap which Freder had worn, in farewell to the room, and burst out into ceaseless laughter. He struck his shoulder against the door post . . .

Then he went out. Slim followed him.

Architectural sketch of METROPOLIS and the New Tower of Babel.
Artist: Eric Kettelhut, City from above with Tower of Babel.

Still from the film, METROPOLIS, showing the City and the New Tower of Babel in the background. See page 96 for details of bottom half of this image.

During the filming, these workman move the cars on the miniature set between still shots. Note the New Tower of Babel, again, in the background.

Still from the film showing the City, bridges and traffic (see also pages 94-95).

CHAPTER VIII

I AM MAD

FREDER WALKED UP the steps of the cathedral hesitatingly; he was walking up them for the first time. Hel, his mother, used often to go to the cathedral. But her son had never yet done so. Now he longed to see it with his mother's eyes and to hear with the ears of Hel, his mother, the stony prayer of the pillars, each of which had its own particular voice.

He entered the cathedral as a child, not pious, yet not entirely free from shyness—prepared for reverence, but fearless. He heard, as Hel, his mother the Kyrie Eleison of the stones and the Te Deum Laudamus—the De Profundis and the Jubilate. And he heard, as his mother, how the powerfully ringing stone chair was crowned by the Amen of the cross vault . . .

He looked for Maria, who was to have waited for him on the belfry steps; but he could not find her. He wandered through the cathedral, which seemed to be quite empty of people. Once he stopped. He was standing opposite Death.

The ghostly minstrel stood in a side-niche, carved in wood, in hat and wide cloak, scythe on shoulder, the hour-glass dangling from his girdle; and the minstrel was playing on a bone as though on a flute. The Seven Deadly Sins were his following.

Freder looked Death in the face. Then he said:

"If you had come earlier you would not have frightened me . . . Now I pray you: Keep away from me and my beloved!"

But the awful flute-player seemed to be listening to nothing but the song he was playing upon a bone.

Freder walked on. He came to the central nave. Before the high altar, over which hovered God Incarnate, a dark form lay stretched out upon the stones, hands clutching out to each side, face pressed into the coldness of the stone, as though the blocks must burst asunder under the pressure of the brow. The form wore the garment of a monk, the head was shaven. An incessant trembling shook the lean body from shoulder to heel, and it seemed to be stiffened as though in a cramp.

But suddenly the body reared up. A white flame sprang up: a face; black flames within it: two blazing eyes. A hand rose up, clutching high in the air towards the crucifix which hovered above the altar.

A voice spoke, like the voice of fire:

"I will not let thee go, God, God, except thou bless me!"

The echo of the pillars yelled the words after him.

The son of Joh Fredersen had never seen the man before. He knew, however, as soon as the flame-white face unveiled the black flames of its eyes to him: it was Desertus the monk, his father's enemy . . .

Perhaps his breath had become too loud. Suddenly the black flame struck across at him. The monk arose slowly. He did not say a word. He stretched out his hand. The hand indicated the door.

"Why do you sent me away, Desertus?" asked Freder. "Is not the house of your God open to all?"

"Hast thou come here to seek God?" asked the rough, hoarse voice of the monk.

Freder hesitated. He dropped his head.

"No." He answered. But his heart knew better.

"If thou hast not come to seek God, then thou hast nothing to seek here," said the monk.

Then Joh Fredersen's son went.

He went out of the cathedral as one walking in his sleep. The daylight smote his eyes cruelly. Racked with weariness, worn out with grief, he walked down the steps, and aimlessly onwards.

The roar of the streets wrapped itself, as a diver's helmet, about his ears. He walked on in his stupefaction, as though between thick glass walls. He had no thought apart from the name of his beloved, no consciousness apart from his longing for her. Shivering with weariness, he thought of the girl's eyes and lips, with a feeling very like homesickness.

Ah!—brow to brow with her—then mouth to mouth—eyes closed—breathing . . .

Peace . . . Peace . . .

"Come," said his heart. "Why do you leave me alone?"

He walked along in a stream of people, fighting down the mad desire to stop amid this stream and to ask every single wave, which was a human being, if it knew of Maria's whereabouts, and why she had let him wait in vain.

He came to the magician's house. There he stopped.

He stared at a window.

Was he mad?

There was Maria, standing behind the dull panes. Those were her blessed hands, stretched out towards him . . . a dumb cry: "Help me—!"

Then the entire vision was drawn away, swallowed up by the blackness of the room behind it, vanishing, not leaving a trace, as though it had never been. Dumb, dead and evil stood the house of the magician there.

Freder stood motionless. He drew a deep, deep breath. Then he made a leap. He stood before the door of the house.

Copper-red, in the black wood of the door, glowed the seal of Solomon, the pentagram.

Freder knocked.

Nothing in the house stirred.

He knocked for the second time.

The house remained dull and obstinate.

He stepped back and looked up at the windows.

They looked out in their evil gloom, over and beyond him. He went to the door again. He beat against it with his fists. He heard the echo of his drumming blows shake the house, as in dull laughter.

But the copper Solomon's seal grinned at him from the unshaken door.

He stood still for a moment. His temples throbbed. He felt absolutely helpless and was as near crying as swearing.

Then he heard a voice—the voice of his beloved.

"Freder—!" and once more: "Freder—!"

He saw blood before his eyes. He made to throw himself with the full weight of his shoulders against the door . . .

But in that same moment the door opened noiselessly. It swung back in ghostly silence, leaving the way into the house absolutely free.

That was so unexpected and alarming that, in the midst of the swing which was to have thrown him against the door, Freder caught both his hands against the door-posts, and stood fixed there. He buried his teeth in his lips. The heart of the house was as black as midnight . . .

But the voice of Maria called to him from the heart of the house: "Freder—! Freder—!"

He ran into the house as though he had gone blind. The door fell to behind him. He stood in blackness. He called. He received no answer. He saw nothing. He groped. He felt walls—endless walls . . . Steps . . . He climbed up the steps . . .

A pale redness swam about him like the reflection of a distant gloomy fire.

Suddenly—he stopped still, clawing his hand into the stonework behind him—a sound was coming out of the nothingness: The weeping of a woman sorrowing, sorrowing unto death.

It was not very loud, but yet it was as if the source of all lamentation were streaming out of it. It was as though the house were weeping—as though every stone in the wall were a sobbing mouth, set free from eternal dumbness, once and once only, to mourn an everlasting agony.

Freder shouted—he was fully aware that he was only shouting in order not to hear the weeping any more.

"Maria—Maria—Maria—!"

His voice was clear and wild as an oath: "I am coming!"

He ran up the stairs. He reached the top of the stairs. A passage, scarcely lighted. Twelve doors opened out here.

In the wood of each of these doors glowed, copper-red, the seal of Solomon, the pentagram.

He sprang to the first one. Before he had touched it it swung noiselessly open before him. Emptiness lay behind it. The room was quite bare.

The second door. The same.

The third. The fourth. They swung open before him as though his breath had blown them off the latch.

Freder stood still. He screwed his head down between his shoulders. He raised his arm and wiped it across his forehead. He looked around him. The open doors stood agape. The mournful weeping ceased. All was quite silent.

But out of the silence there came a voice, soft and sweet, and more tender than a kiss . . .

"Come . . . ! Do come . . . ! I am here, dearest . . . !"

Freder did not stir. He knew the voice quite well. It was Maria's voice, which he so loved. And yet it was a strange voice. Nothing in the world could be sweeter than the tone of this soft allurement—and nothing in the world has ever been so filled to overflowing with a dark, deadly wickedness.

Freder felt the drops upon his forehead.

"Who are you?" he asked expressionlessly.

"Don't you know me?"

"Who are you?"

" . . . Maria . . . "

"You are not Maria . . . "

"Freder—!" mourned the voice—Maria's voice.

"Do you want me to lose my reason?" said Freder, between his teeth. "Why don't you come to me?"

"I can't come, beloved . . . "

"Where are you?"

"Look for me!" said the sweetly alluring, the deadly wicked voice, laughing softly.

But through the laughter there sounded another voice—being *also* Maria's voice, sick with fear and horror.

"Freder . . . help me, Freder . . . I do not know what is being done to me . . . But what is being done is worse than murder . . . My eyes are on . . . "

Suddenly, as though cut off, her voice choked. But the other voice—which was *also* Maria's voice, laughed, sweetly, alluringly, on:

"Look for me, beloved!"

Freder began to run. Senselessly and unreasoningly, he began to run. Along walls, by open doors, upstairs, downstairs, from twilight into darkness, drawn on by the cones of light, which would suddenly flame up before him, then dazzled and plunged again into a hellish darkness.

He ran like a blind animal, groaning aloud. He found that he was running in a circle, always upon his own tracks, but he could not get free of it, could not get out of the cursed circle. He ran in the purple mist of his own blood, which filled his eyes and ears, heard the breaker of his blood dash against his brain, heard high above, like the singing of birds, the sweetly, deadly wicked laugh of Maria . . .

"Look for me, beloved! . . . I am here! . . . I am here! . . . "

At last he fell. His knees collided against something which was in the way of their blindness; he stumbled and fell. He felt stones under his hands, cool, hard stones, cut in even squares. His whole body, beaten and racked, rested upon the cool hardness of these blocks. He rolled over on his back. He pushed himself up, collapsed again violently, and lay upon the floor. A suffocating blanket sank downwards. His consciousness yielded up, as though drowned . . .

Rotwang had seen him fall. He waited attentively and vigilantly to see if this young wildling, the son of Joh Fredersen and Hel, had had enough at last, or if he would pull himself together once more for the fight against nothing.

But it appeared that he had had enough. He lay remarkably still. He was not even breathing now. He was like a corpse.

The great inventor left his listening post. He passed through the dark house on soundless soles. He opened a door and entered a room. He closed the door and remained standing on the threshold. With an expectation that was fully aware of its pointlessness, he looked at the girl who was the occupant of the room.

He found her as he always found her. In the farthest corner of the room, on a high, narrow chair, hands laid, right and left, upon the arms of the chair, sitting stiffly upright, with eyes which appeared to be lidless. Nothing about her was living apart from these eyes. The glorious mouth, still glorious in its pallor, seemed to enclose within it the unpronounceable. She did not look at the man—she looked over and beyond him.

Rotwang stooped forward. He came nearer to her. Only his hands, his lonely hands groped through the air, as though they wanted to close around Maria's countenance. His eyes, his lonely eyes, enveloped Maria's countenance.

"Won't you smile just once?" he asked. "Won't you cry just once? I need them both—your smile and your tears . . . Your image, Maria, just as you are now, is burnt into my retina, never to be lost . . . I could take a diploma in your horror and in your rigidity. The bitter expression of contempt about your mouth is every bit as familiar to me as the haughtiness of your eyebrows and your temples. But I need your smile and your tears, Maria. Or you will make me bungle my work . . . "

He seemed to have spoken to the deaf air. The girl sat dumb, looking over and beyond him.

Rotwang took a chair; he sat down astride it, crossed his arms over the back and looked at the girl. He laughed gloomily.

"You two poor children!" he said, "to have dared to pit yourselves against Joh Fredersen! Nobody can reproach you for it; you do not know him and do not know what you are doing. But the son should know the father. I do not believe that there is one man who can boast ever having got the better of Joh Fredersen. You could more easily bend to your will the inscrutable God, who is said to rule the world, than Joh Fredersen . . . "

The girl sat like a statue, immovable.

"What will you do, Maria, if Joh Fredersen takes you and your love so seriously that he comes to you and says: "Give me back my son!"

The girl sat like a statue, immovable.

"He will ask you: 'Of what value is my son to you?' and if you are wise you will answer him: 'Of no more and of no less value than he is to you!...' He will pay the price, and it will be a high price, for Joh Fredersen has only one son..."

The girl sat like a statue, immovable.

"What do you know of Freder's heart?" continued the man. "He is as young as the morning at sunrise. This heart of the young morning is yours. Where will it be at midday? And where at evening? Far away from you, Maria— far, far, away. The world is very large and the earth is very fair... His father will send him around the world. Out over the beautiful earth he will forget you, Maria, before the clock of his heart is at midday."

The girl sat like a statue, immovable. But around her pale mouth, which was like the bud of a snowrose, a smile began to bloom—a smile of such sweetness, of such depths, that it seemed as though the air about the girl must begin to beam.

The man looked at the girl. His lonely eyes were starved and parched as the desert which does not know the dew. In a hoarse voice he went on:

"Where do you get your sainted confidence from? Do you believe that you are Freder's first love? Have you forgotten the 'Club of the Sons,' Maria? There are a hundred women there—and all are his! These loving little women could all tell you about Freder's love, for they know more about it than you do, and you have only one advantage over them: You can weep when he leaves you; for they are not allowed to weep... When Joh Fredersen's son celebrates his marriage it will be as though all Metropolis celebrated its marriage. When?—Joh Fredersen will decide that... With whom?—Joh Fredersen will decide that... But you will not be the bride, Maria! The son of Joh Fredersen will have forgotten you by the day of his wedding."

"Never!" said the girl. "Never—never!"

And the painless tears of a great, true love fell upon the beauty of her smile.

The man got up. He stood still before the girl. He looked at her. He turned away. As he was crossing the threshold of the next room his shoulder fell against the door-post.

He slammed the door to. He stared straight ahead. He looked on the being—his creature of glass and metal—which bore the almost completed head of Maria.

His hands moved towards the head, and, the nearer they came to it, the more did it appear as if these hands, these lonely hands, wished not to create but to destroy.

"We are bunglers, Futura!" he said. "Bunglers!—Bunglers! Can I give you the smile which you make angels fall gladly down to hell? Can I give you the tears which would redeem the chiefest Satan, and make him beatify?—Parody is your name! And Bungler is mine!"

Shining cool and lustrous, the being stood there and looked at its creator with its baffling eyes. And, as he laid his hands on its shoulders, its fine structure tinkled in mysterious laughter . . .

Freder, on recovering, found himself surrounded by a dull brightness. It came from a window, in the frame of which stood a pale, grey sky. The window was small and gave the impression that it had not been opened for centuries.

Freder's eyes wandered through the room. Nothing that he saw penetrated into his consciousness. He remembered nothing. He lay, his back resting on stones which were cold and smooth. All his limbs and joints were wracked by a dull pain.

He turned his head to one side. He looked at his hands which lay beside him as though not belonging to him, thrown away, bled white.

Knuckles knocked raw . . . shreds of skin . . . brownish crusts . . . were these his hands?

He stared at the ceiling. It was black, as if charred. He stared at the walls; grey, cold walls . . .

Where was he—? He was tortured by thirst and a ravenous hunger. But worse than the hunger and thirst was the weariness which longed for sleep and which could not find it.

Maria occurred to him . . .

Maria? . . . Maria—?

He jerked himself up and stood on sawn-through ankles. His eyes sought for doors: There was one door. He stumbled up to it. The door was closed, was latchless, would not open.

His brain commanded him: Don't be surprised at anything . . . Don't let anything startle you . . . Think . . .

Over there, there was a window. It had no frame. It was a pane of glass set into stone. The street lay before it—one of the great streets of the great Metropolis, seething with human beings.

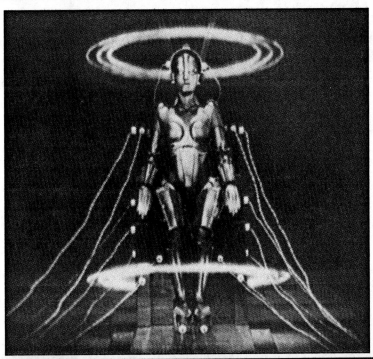

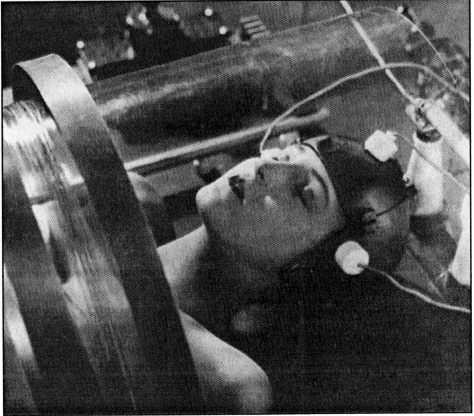

He slammed the door to. He stared straight ahead. He looked on the being—his creature of glass and metal—which bore the almost completed head of Maria. [Brigitte Helm]

The glass window-pane must be very thick. Not the least sound entered the room in which Freder was captive, though the street was so near.

Freder's hands fumbled across the pane. A penetrating coldness streamed out of the glass, the smoothness of which was reminiscent of the sucking sharpness of a steel blade. Freder's finger tips glided towards the setting of the pane . . . and remained, crooked, hanging in the air, as though bewitched. He saw: Down there, below, Maria was crossing the street . . .

Leaving the house which held him captive, she turned her back on him and walked with light, hurried step towards the Maelstrom, which the street was . . .

Freder's fists smote against the pane. He cried the girl's name. He yelled: "Maria . . .!" She must hear him. It was impossible that she did not hear him, Regardless of his raw knuckles he banged with his fists against the pane.

But Maria did not hear him. She did not turn her head around. With her gentle but hurried step she submerged herself in the surf of people as though into her very familiar element.

Freder leaped for the door. He heaved with his whole body, with his shoulders, his knees, against the door. He no longer shouted. His mouth was gaping open. His breath burnt his lips grey. He sprang back to the window. There, outside, hardly ten paces from the window, stood a policeman, his face turned towards Rotwang's house. The man's face registered absolute nonchalance. Nothing seemed to be farther from his mind than to watch the magician's house. But the man who was striving, with bleeding fists, to shatter a window pane in his house could not have escaped even his most casual glance.

Freder paused. He stared at the policeman's face with an unreasoning hatred, born of fear of losing time where there was no time to be lost. He turned around and snatched up the rude foot-stool, which stood near the table. He dashed the foot-stool with full force at the window pane. The rebound jerked him backwards. The pane was undamaged.

Sobbing fury welled up in Freder's throat. He swung the foot-stool and hurled it at the door. The foot-stool crashed to earth. Freder dashed to it, snatched it up and struck and struck, again and again, at the booming door, in a ruddy, blind desire to destroy.

Wood splintered, white. The door shrieked like a living thing. Freder did not pause. To the rhythm of his own boiling blood, he beat against the door until it broke, quivering.

Freder dragged himself through the hole. He ran through the house. His wild eyes sought an enemy and fresh obstacles in each corner. But he found neither one nor the other. Unchallenged, he reached the door, found it open and reeled out into the street.

He ran in the direction which Maria had taken. But the surf of the people had washed her away. She had vanished.

For some minutes Freder stood among the hurrying mob, as though paralysed. One senseless hope befogged his brain: Perhaps—perhaps she would come back again . . . if he were patient and waited long enough . . .

But he remembered the cathedral—waiting in vain—her voice in the magician's house—words of fear—her sweet, wicked laugh . . .

No—no waiting—! He wanted to know.

With clenched teeth he ran . . .

There was a house in the city where Maria lived. An interminably long way. What should he ask about? With bare head, with raw hands, with eyes which seemed insane with weariness, he ran towards his destination: Maria's abode.

He did not know by how many precious hours Slim had come before him . . .

He stood before the people with whom Maria was supposed to live: a man—a woman—the faces of whipped curs. The woman undertook the reply. Her eyes twitched. She held her hands clutched under her apron.

No—no girl called Maria lived here—never had lived here . . .

Freder stared at the woman. He did not believe her. She must know the girl. She must live here.

Half stunned with fear that this last hope of finding Maria could prove fallacious too, he described the girl, as memory came to the aid of this poor madman.

She had such fair hair . . . She had such gentle eyes . . . She had the voice of a loving mother . . . She wore a severe but lovely gown . . .

The man left his position, near the woman, and stooped down sideways, hunching his head down between his shoulders as though he could not bear to hear how that strange young man there, at the door, spoke of the girl, for whom he was seeking. Shaking her head in angry impatience for him to be finished, the woman repeated the same unvarnished words: The girl did not live here, once and for all . . . Hadn't he nearly finished with his catechism?

Freder went. He went without a word. He heard how the door was slammed to, with a bang. Voices were retiring, bickering. Interminable steps brought him to the street again.

Yes . . . what next?

He stood helpless. He did not know which way to turn.

Exhausted to death, drunken with weariness, he heard, with a sudden wince, that the air around him was becoming filled with an overpowering sound.

It was an immeasurably glorious and transporting sound, as deep and rumbling as and more powerful than any sound on earth. The voice of the sea when it is angry, the voice of falling torrents, the voice of very close thunderstorms would be miserably drowned in this Behemoth-din. Without being shrill it penetrated all walls and, as long as it lasted, all things seemed to swing in it. It was omnipresent, coming from the heights and from the depths, being beautiful and horrible, being an irresistible command.

It was high above the town. It was the voice of the town.

Metropolis raised her voice. The machines of Metropolis roared; they wanted to be fed.

"My father," thought Freder, half unconsciously, "has pressed his fingers upon the blue metal plate. The brain of Metropolis controls the town. Nothing happens in Metropolis which does not come to my father's ears. I shall go to my father and ask him if the inventor, Rotwang, has played with Maria and with me in the name of Joh Fredersen."

He turned around to wend his way to the New Tower of Babel. He set off with the obstinacy of one possessed, with screwed up lips, sharp lines between the eyebrows, clenched fists on his weak, dangling arms. He set off as though he wanted to pound the stone beneath his feet. It seemed as though every drop of blood in his face had collected in his eyes alone. He ran, and, on the interminable way, at every step, he had the feeling: I am not he who is running . . . I am running, a spirit, by the side of my own self . . . I, the spirit, am forcing my body to run onwards, although it is tired to death . . .

Those who stared at him when he arrived at the New Tower of Babel seemed to be seeing, not him, but a spirit . . .

He was about to enter the Pater-noster, which was pumping its way, a scoop-wheel for human beings, through the New Tower of Babel. But a sudden shudder pushed him away from it. Did there not crouch below, deep, deep, down, under the sole of the New Tower of Babel, a little, gleaming machine, which was like Ganesha, the god with the elephant's head? Under the crouching body, and the head, which was sunken on the chest, crooked legs rested, gnome-like, upon the platform. The trunk and legs were motionless. But the short arms pushed and pushed and pushed, alternately, forwards, backwards, forwards.

Who was standing before the machine now, cursing the Lord's Prayer—

the Lord's Prayer of the Pater-noster machine?

Shivering with horror, he ran up the stairs.

Stairs and stairs and stairs . . . They would never come to an end . . . The brow of the New Tower of Babel lifted itself very near to the sky. The tower roared like the sea. It howled as deep as the storm. The hurtling of a water-fall boomed in its veins.

"Where is my father?" Freder asked the servants.

They indicated a door. They wanted to announce him. He shook his head. He wondered: Why were these people looking so strangely at him?

He opened a door. The room was empty. On the other side, a second door, ajar. Voices behind it. The voice of his father and that of another . . .

Freder suddenly stood still. His feet seemed to be nailed to the floor. The upper part of his body was bent stiffly forwards. His fists dangled on helpless arms, seeming no longer capable of freeing themselves from their own clench. He listened; the eyes in his white face were filled with blood, the lips were open as though forming a cry.

Then he tore his deadened feet from the floor, stumbled to the door and pushed it open . . .

In the middle of the room, which was filled with a cutting brightness, stood Joh Fredersen, holding a woman in his arms. And the woman was Maria. She was not struggling. Leaning far back in the man's arms, she was offering him her mouth, her alluring mouth, that deadly laugh . . .

"You . . . !" shouted Freder.

He dashed to the girl. He did not see his father. He saw only the girl—no, neither did he see the girl, only her mouth and her sweet, wicked laugh.

Joh Fredersen turned around, broad and menacing. He let the girl go. He covered her with the might of his shoulders, with the great cranium, flamed with blood, and in which the strong teeth and the invincible eyes were very visible.

But Freder did not see his father. He only saw an obstacle between him and the girl.

He rushed at the obstacle. It pushed him back. Scarlet hatred for the obstacle choked him. His eyes flew around. They sought an implement—an implement which could be used as a battering ram. He found none. Then he threw himself toward as a battering ram. His fingers clutched into stuff. He bit into the stuff. He heard his own breath like a whistle, very high and shrill. Yet within him there was only one sound, only one cry: "Maria—!" Groaningly, beseechingly: "Maria—!!"

A man dreaming of hell shrieks out no more, in his torment, than did he.

And still, between him and the girl, the man, the lump of rock, the living wall . . .

He threw his hands forward. Ah . . . look! . . . there was a throat! He seized the throat. His fingers snapped fast like iron fangs.

"Why don't you defend yourself?" he yelled, staring at the man.

I'll kill you—! I'll take your life—! I'll murder you—!"

But the man before him held his ground while he throttled him. Thrown this way and that by Freder's fury, the body bent, now to the right, now to the left. And as often as this happened Freder saw, as through a transparent mist, the smiling countenance of Maria, who, leaning against the table, was looking on with her sea water eyes at the fight between father and son.

His father's voice said: "Freder . . ."

He looked the man in the face. He saw his father. He saw the hands which were clawing around his father's throat. They were his, were the hands of his son.

His hands fell loose, as though cut off . . . he stared at his hands, stammering something which sounded half like an oath, half like the weeping of a child that believes itself to be alone in the world.

The voice of his father said: "Freder . . ."

He fell on his knees. He stretched out his arms. His head fell forward into his father's hands. He burst into tears, into despairing sobs . . .

A door slid to.

He flung his head around. He sprang to his feet. His eyes swept the room.

"Where is she?" he asked.

"Who?"

"She . . ."

"Who—?"

"She . . . who was here . . ."

"Nobody was here, Freder . . ."

The boy's eyes glazed.

"What did you say—?" he stammered.

"There has not been a soul here, Freder, but you and I."

Freder twisted his head around stiffly. He tugged the shirt from his throat. He looked into his father's eyes as though looking into well-shafts.

"You say there was not a soul here . . . I did not see you . . . when you were holding Maria in your arms . . . I have been dreaming . . . I am mad, aren't I? . . ."

"I give you my word," said Joh Fredersen, "when you came to me there was neither a woman nor any other living soul here . . ."

Freder remained silent. His bewildered eyes were still searching along the walls.

And as often as this happened Freder saw, as through a transparent mist, the smiling countenance of Maria, who . . . was looking on with her sea water eyes at the fight between father and son. [Brigitte Helm (Futura/Maria)]

> "Now we shall see whether people believe the Robot is a creature of flesh and blood."

"You are ill, Freder," said his father's voice.

Freder smiled. Then he began to laugh. He threw himself into a chair and laughed and laughed. He bent down, resting both elbows upon his knees, burrowing his head between his hands and arms. He rocked himself to and fro, shrieking with laughter.

Joh Fredersen's eyes were upon him.

CHAPTER IX

TURN BACK!

THE AEROPLANE which had carried Josaphat away from Metropolis swam in the golden air of the setting sun, rushing towards it at a tearing speed, as though fastened to the westward sinking ball by metal cords.

Josaphat sat behind the pilot. From the moment when the aerodrome had sunk below them and the stone mosaic of the great Metropolis had paled away into the inscrutable depths, he had not given the least token that he was a human being with the faculty for breathing and moving. The pilot seemed to be taking a pale grey stone, which had the form of a man, with him as freight and, when he once turned around, he looked full into the wide open eyes of this petrified being without meeting a glance or the least sign of consciousness.

Nevertheless Josaphat had intercepted the movement of the pilot's head with his brain . . . Not immediately. Not soon. Yet the vision of this cautious, yet certain and vigilant movement remained in his memory until he at last comprehended it.

Then the petrified image seemed to become a human being again, whose breast rose in a long neglected breath, who raised his eyes upwards, looking into the empty greenish blue sky and down again to the earth which formed a flat, round carpet, deep down in infinity—and at the sun which was rolling westwards like a glowing ball.

Last of all, however, at the head of the pilot who sat before him, at the airman's cap which turned, neckless, into shoulders filled with a bull-like strength and a forceful calm.

The powerful engine of the aeroplane worked in perfect silence. But the air through which the aeroplane tore was filled with a mysterious thunder, as though the dome of heaven were catching up the roaring in the globe and throwing it angrily back again.

The aeroplane hovered homelessly above a strange earth, like a bird not able to find its nest.

Suddenly, amid the thunder of the air, the pilot heard a voice at his left ear saying, almost softly:

"Turn back . . ."

The head in the airman's cap was about to bend backwards. But at the first attempt to do so it came in contact with an object of resistance, which rested exactly on the top of his skull. This object of resistance was small, apparently angular and extraordinarily hard.

"Don't move!" said the voice at his left ear, which was so soft, yet making itself understood through the thunder of the air. "Don't look round, either! I have no revolver with me. Had I had one handy I should probably not be here. What I have in my hand is an implement the name and purpose of which are unknown to me. But it is made of solid steel and quite sufficient to smash in your skull with should you not obey me immediately . . . Turn back!"

The bull-like shoulders under the airman's cap raised themselves in a short, impatient shrug. The glowing ball of the sun touched the horizon with an inexpressibly light hovering movement. For a few seconds it seemed to dance along it in soft, blazing rhythm. The nose of the aeroplane was turned towards it and did not alter its course by a hand's breadth.

"You do not seem to have understood me," said the voice behind the pilot. "Turn back! I wish to return to Metropolis, do you hear? I must be there before nightfall . . . well?"

"Shut your mouth," said the pilot.

"For the last time, will you obey or will you not—?"

"Sit down and keep quiet, back there . . . damn it all, what do you mean by it—?"

"You won't obey—?"

"What the hell . . ."

A young girl, turning the bay in a wide, undulating field, by the last light of the setting sun, had sighted the rushing bird above her, in the evening sky and was watching it with eyes heated by work and tired by the summer.

How strangely the aeroplane was rising and falling! It was making jumps like a horse that wants to shake off its rider. Now it was racing towards the sun, now it was turning its back upon it. The young girl had never seen so wild and unruly a creature in the air before. Now it had swung westwards and was dashing in long, spurting bounds along the sky. Something freed itself from it; a broad, silver-grey cloth, which swelled itself out.

Drifted hither and thither by the wind, the silver-grey cloth fluttered down to earth—in the webs of which a gigantic, black spider seemed to be hanging.

Screaming, the young girl began to run. The great, black spider spun itself lower and lower on the thin cords. Now it was already like a human being. A white, death-like face bent earthwards. The earth curved itself gently towards the sinking creature. The man left go of the cord and leaped. And fell. Picked himself up again. And fell once more.

Like a snow-cloud, gentle and shimmering, the silver-grey cloth sank over him, quite covering him.

The young girl came running up.

She was still screaming, wordlessly, breathlessly, as though these primitive shrieks were her actual language. She bundled the silver silken cloth up before her young breast with both arms in order to bring the man who lay beneath it into the light again.

Yes, he lay there now, stretched out at his length on his back, and the silk which was so strong as to have borne him tore under the grip of his fingers. And where his fingers lost hold of the silk, to find another patch which they could tear, there remained moist, red marks upon the stuff, such as are left behind by an animal that had dipped its paws into the blood of its enemy.

The girl was silenced by the sight of these marks.

An expression of horror came into her face, but, at the same time, an expression such as mother-beasts have when they scent an enemy and do not want to betray themselves nor their offspring in any way.

She clenched her teeth together so forcibly that her young mouth became quite pale and thin. She knelt down beside the young man and lifted his head into her lap.

The eyes opened in the white face which she was holding. They stared into the eyes which were bending over them. They glanced sideways and searched across the sky.

A rushing black point in the scarlet of the westerly sky, from which the sun had sunk . . .

The aeroplane . . .

Now it had indeed carried out its will and was flying towards the sun, further and further westward. At its wheel sat the man who would not turn back, as dead as could be. The airman's cap hung down in shreds from the gaping skull, on to the bull-like shoulders. But the fists had not lost hold of the wheel. They still held it fast . . .

Farewell, pilot . . .

The face which lay in the young girl's lap began to smile, began to ask.

Where was the nearest town?

There was no town, far and wide.

Where was the nearest railway?

There was no railway, far and wide.

Josaphat pushed himself up. He looked about him.

Stretching out far and wide were fields and meadows, hemmed in by forests, standing there in their evening stillness. The scarlet of the sky had faded away. The crickets chirped. The mist about the distant, solitary willows brewed milky white. From the hallowed purity of the great sky the first star appeared with still glimmer.

"I must go," said the man with the white, deathlike face.

"You must rest, first," said the young girl.

The man's eyes looked up at her in astonishment. Her clear face, with its low, unintelligent brow and its beautiful, foolish mouth stood out, as if under a dome of sapphire, against the sky which curved above her.

"Aren't you afraid of me?" asked the man.

"No," said the young girl.

The head of the man fell into her lap. She bent forward and covered up the shivering body with the billowing, silver silk.

"Rest . . . " said the man with a sigh.

She made no reply. She sat quite motionless.

"Will you awaken me," asked the man—and his voice quavered with weariness—"as soon as the sun comes?"

"Yes," said the young girl. "Keep quiet . . ."

He sighed deeply. Then he lay still.

It grew darker and darker.

In the far distance a voice was to be heard, calling a name, long drawn out, again and again . . .

The stars stood glorious above the world. The distant voice was silent. The young girl looked down upon the man whose head lay in her lap. In her eyes was the never sleeping watchfulness which one sees in the eyes of animals and of mothers.

CHAPTER X

THE GHOSTLY MINSTREL AGAIN

WHENEVER JOSAPHAT tried, during the days which followed, to break through the barrier which was drawn around Freder, there was always a strange person there, and always a different one, who said, with expressionless mien:

"Mr. Freder cannot receive anybody. Mr. Freder is ill."

But Freder was not ill—at least not as illness generally manifests itself among mankind. From morning until evening, from evening until morning, Josaphat watched the house, the crown of the tower of which was Freder's flat. He never saw Freder leave the house. But for hours at a time he saw, during the night, behind the white-veiled windows, which ran the breadth of the wall, a shadow wandering up and down—and saw at the hour of twilight, when the rooves of Metropolis still shone, bathed in the sun, and the darkness of the ravines of its streets was flooded out by streams of cold light, the same shadow, a motionless form, standing on the narrow balcony which ran around this, almost the highest house in Metropolis.

Yet what was expressed by the shadow's wandering up and down, by the motionless standing still of the shadow form, was not illness. It was uttermost helplessness. Lying on the roof of the house which was opposite Freder's flat, Josaphat watched the man who had chosen him as friend and brother, whom he had betrayed and to whom he had returned. He could not discern his face but he read from the pale patch which this face was in the setting sun, in the shower-bath of the search-light, that the man over there, whose eyes were staring across Metropolis, did not see Metropolis.

Sometimes people would emerge beside him, would speak to him, expecting an answer. But the answer never came. Then the people would go, crushed.

Once Joh Fredersen came—came to his son, who stood on the narrow balcony, seeming not to know that his father was near. Joh Fredersen spoke to him for a long time. He laid his hand on his son's hand, which was resting on the railing. The mouth received no answer. The hand received no answer. Only once did Freder turn his head, then with difficulty, as though the joints of his neck were rusted. He looked at Joh Fredersen.

Joh Fredersen went.

And when his father had gone Freder turned his head back again on idle joints and stared out once more across Metropolis, which was dancing in a whirl of light, staring with blind eyes.

The railing of the narrow balcony on which he stood appeared as an insuperable wall of loneliness, of deep, inward consciousness of having been deserted. No calling, no signalling, not even the loudest of sounds penetrated this wall which was washed about by the strong, lustrous surf of the great Metropolis.

But Josaphat did not want to have ventured the leap from heaven to earth, to have sent a man, who was but performing his duty, into infinity, impotently to make a halt before this wall of loneliness.

There came a night which hung, glowing and vapourous over Metropolis. A thunder storm, which was still distant, burnt its warning fires in deep clouds. All the lights of the great Metropolis seemed more violently, seemed more wildly to lavish themselves on the darkness.

Freder stood by the railing of the narrow balcony, his hot hands laid on the railing. A sultry, uneasy puff of wind tugged at him, making the white silk which covered his now much emaciated body to flutter.

Around the ridge of the roof of the house right opposite him there ran, in a shining border, a shining word, running in an everlasting circuit around, behind itself . . .

Phantasus . . . Phantasus . . . Phantasus . . .

Freder did not see this row of words. The retina received it—not the brain.

Eternal hammering similarity of the wandering word . . .

Phantasus . . . Phantasus . . . Phantasus . . .

Suddenly the word picture was extinguished and in its place numbers sparkled out of the darkness, disappearing again, again emerging, and, this coming and disappearing, coming again and again disappearing, and coming anew had the effect in its unmistakability, of a penetrating, persistent call.

90................ 7................ 7................
90................ 7................ 7................

90............... 7............... 7...............

Freder's eyes caught the numbers

90............... 7............... 7...............

They turned around, they came back again

90............... 7............... 7...............

Thoughts stumbled through his brain.

90— — —? and 7— — —? a second 7—?

What did that mean? . . . How obtrusive these numbers were.

90............... 7............... 7...............

90............... 7............... 7...............

90............... 7............... 7...............

Freder closed his eyes. But now the numbers were within him. He saw them flame up, sparkle, go out . . . flame up, sparkle, go out.

Was that—no . . . or yes?

Did not these numbers, some time ago, what seemed to him an immeasurably long period ago, also convey something to him?

90 — — — 90 — — —

Suddenly a voice in his head said:

Ninetieth Block . . . Ninetieth Block . . . House seven . . . seventh floor . . .

Freder opened his eyes. Over there, on the house just opposite, the numbers jerked up, asked and called . . .

90............... 7............... 7...............

Freder bent forward over the railing so that it seemed he must hurtle into space. The numbers dazzled him. He made a movement with his arm as though he wanted to cover them up or put them out.

They went out. The shining border went out. The house stood in gloom, only half its height washed around by the shimmer from the white street. The stormy sky, becoming suddenly visible, lay above its roof and lightning seemed to be crackling.

In the faded light, over there, stood a man.

Freder stepped back from the railing. He raised both hands before his mouth. He looked to the right, to the left; he raised both arms. Then he turned away, as if removed by a natural power from the spot on which he stood, ran into the house, ran through the room, stopped still again . . .

Carefully . . . carefully now . . .

He reflected. He pressed his head between his fists. Was there among his servants, one single soul who could be trusted not to betray him to Slim?

What a miserable state—what a miserable state—!

But what alternative had he to the leap in the dark, the blind trust—the ultimate test of confidence?

He would have liked to extinguish the lights in his room, but he did not dare to, for up to this day he had not been able to bear darkness about him. He paced up and down. He felt the perspiration on his forehead and the trembling of his joints. He could not calculate the time which elapsed. The blood roared in his veins like a cataract. The first flash of lightning flickered over Metropolis, and, in the tardy responding rumble of thunder the rushing of the rain at last, mixed itself soothingly. It swallowed up the sound of the opening of the door. When Freder turned around Josaphat was standing in the middle of the room. He was dressed in workman's uniform.

They walked up to each other as though driven by an outward power. But, halfway, they both stopped and looked at each other, and each had for the other the same horrified question on his face. Where have you been since I saw you last? To what hell have you descended?

Freder with his feverish haste, was the first to collect himself. He seized his friend by the arm.

"Sit down!" he said in his toneless voice, which occasionally held the morbid dryness of things burnt. He sat down beside him, not taking his hand from the arm. "You waited for me—in vain and in vain . . . I could not send you a message, forgive me!"

I have nothing to forgive you, Mr. Freder," said Josaphat, quietly. "I did not wait for you . . . On the evening on which I was to have waited for you, I was far, far away from Metropolis and from you . . ."

Freder's waiting eyes looked at him.

"I betrayed you, Mr. Freder," said Josaphat.

Freder smiled, but Josaphat's eyes extinguished his smile. "I betrayed you, Mr. Freder," repeated the man. "Slim came to me . . . He offered me much money . . . But I only laughed . . . I threw it at his head. But then he laid on the table a slip with your father's signature . . . You must believe me, Mr. Freder; He would never have caught me with the money. There is no sum of money for which I would have sold you . . . But when I saw your father's hand-writing . . . I still put up a fight. I would gladly have throttled him. But I had no more strength . . . JOH FREDERSEN was written on the slip . . . I had no more strength then . . ."

"I can understand that," said Joh Fredersen's son.

"Thank you . . . I was to go away from Metropolis—right far away . . . I flew . . . The pilot was a strange man. We kept flying straight towards the sun. The sun was setting. Then it occurred to my empty brain that now the hour would come in which I was to wait for you. And I should not be there when you came . . . I wanted to turn back. I asked the pilot. He wouldn't. He wanted to carry me away by force, farther and farther from Metropolis. He was as obstinate as only a man can be when he knows Slim's will to be behind him. I begged and I threatened. But nothing was of any use. So then, with one of his own tools, I smashed in his skull."

Freder's fingers, which were still resting on Josaphat's arm, tightened their hold a little; but they lay still again immediately.

"Then I jumped out, and I was so far away from Metropolis that a young girl who picked me up in the field did not know the great Metropolis even by name . . . I came here and found no message from you, and all that I found out was that you were ill . . ."

He hesitated and was silent, looking at Freder.

"I am not ill," said Freder, looking straight ahead. He loosened his fingers from Josaphat's arm and bent forward, laying the palms of both hands flat on his head. He spoke into space . . . But do you believe, Josaphat, that I am mad?"

"No."

"But I must be," said Freder, and he shrank .together, so narrow that it seemed as if a little boy, filled with a mighty fear, were sitting in his place. His voice sounded suddenly quite high and thin and something in it brought the water to Josaphat's eyes.

Josaphat stretched out his hand, fumbled, and found Freder's shoulder. His hand closed around his neck and drew him gently towards him, holding him still and fast.

"Just tell me about it, Mr. Freder!" he said. "I do not think there are many things which seem insuperable to me since I sprang, as though from heaven to earth, from the aeroplane which was steered by a dead man. Also," he continued in a soft voice, "I learnt in one single night that one can bear very much when one has some one near one who keeps watch, asks nothing and is simply there."

"I am mad, Josaphat," said Freder. "But—I don't know if it is any consolation—I am not the only one . . ."

Josaphat was silent. His patient hand lay motionless on Freder's shoulder.

And suddenly, as though his soul were an over-filled vessel, which had lost its balance, toppled over and poured out in streams, Freder began to speak. He told his friend the story of Maria, from the moment of their first meeting in the "Club of Sons," to when they saw each other again right down under the

earth in the City of the Dead—his waiting for her in the cathedral, his experi-
ences in Rotwang's house, his vain search, the curt "no" at Maria's home, up
to the moment when, for her sake, he wanted to be the murderer of his own
father—no, not for her sake: for that of a being who was not there, whom he
only believed himself to see . . .

Was that not madness—?"

"Hallucination, Mr. Freder . . ."

"Hallucination—? I will tell you some more about hallucination, Josaphat,
and you mustn't believe that I am speaking in delirium or that I am not fully
master of my thoughts. I wanted to kill my father . . . It was not my fault that
the attempt at parricide was unsuccessful . . . But ever since that moment I
have not been human . . . I am a creature that has no feet, no hands and
hardly a head. And this head is only there eternally to think that I wanted to
kill my own father. Do you believe that I shall ever get free from this hell—
? Never, Josaphat. Never—never in all eternity. I lay during the night hearing
my father walking up and down in the next room. I lay in the depths of a
black pit; but my thoughts ran along behind my father's steps, as though
chained to his soles. What horror has come upon the world that this could
happen? Is there a comet in the heavens which drives mankind to madness? Is a fresh plague coming, or Anti-Christ? Or the end of the world? A
woman, who does not exist, forces herself between father and son and
incites the son to murder against the father . . . It may be that my thoughts
were running themselves a little hot at the time . . . Then my father came in
to me . . ."

He stopped and his wasted hands twisted themselves together upon his
damp hair.

"You know my father. There are many in the great Metropolis who do
not believe Joh Fredersen to be human, because he seems not to need to
eat and drink and he sleeps when he wishes to; and usually he does not
wish to . . . They call him The Brain of Metropolis, and if it is true that fear is
the source of all religion then the brain of Metropolis is not very far off
from becoming a deity . . . This man, who is my father came up to my bed
. . . He walked on tiptoe, Josaphat. He bent over me and held his breath . . .
My eyes were shut. I lay quite still and it seemed to me as though my father
must hear my soul crying within me. Then I loved him more than anything
on earth. But if my life had been dependent on it, I should still not have
been able to open my eyes. I felt my father's hand smoothing my pillow.
Then he went again as he had come, on tip-toe, closing the door quiet

soundlessly behind him. Do you know what he had done?"

"No . . ."

"No . . . I don't see how you could. I only realised it myself some hours later . . . For the first time since the great Metropolis had stood, Joh Fredersen had omitted to press on the little blue metal plate and to let the Behemoth-voice of Metropolis roar out, because he did not wish to disturb his son's sleep . . ."

Josaphat lowered his head; he said nothing. Freder let his intertwined hands sink.

"Then I realised," he continued, "that my father had quite forgiven me . . . And when I realised that, I really fell asleep . . ."

He stood up and remained standing, seeming to be listening to the rushing of the rain. The lightning was still flashing out over Metropolis, the angry thunder bounding after. But the rushing of the rain drowned it.

"I slept . . ." Freder went on—so softly that the other could scarcely follow his words—"then I began to dream . . . I saw this city—this great Metropolis—in the light of a ghostly unreality. A weird moon stood in the sky; as though along a broad street this ghostly, unreal light flowed down upon the city, which was deserted to the last soul. All the houses were distorted and had faces. They squinted evilly and spitefully down at me, for I was walking deep down between them, along the glimmering street.

"Quite narrow was this street, as though crushed between the houses; it was as though made of a greenish glass—like a solidified, glazen river. I glided along it and looked down through it into the cold bubbling of a subterranean fire.

"I did not know my destination, but I knew I had one, and went very fast in order to reach it the sooner. I quieted my step as well as I could, but its sound was excessively loud and awakened a rustling whisper over the crooked house-walls as though the houses were murmuring against me. I quickened my pace and ran, and, at last, raced along, and the more swiftly I raced the more hoarsely did the echo of the steps sound after me, as though there were an army at my heels. I was dripping with sweat . . .

"The town was alive. The houses were alive. Their open mouths snarled after me. The window-caverns, open eyes, winked blindly, horribly, maliciously.

"Graspingly, I reached the square before the cathedral . . .

"The cathedral was lighted up. The doors stood open—no, they did not stand open. They reeled to and fro like swing doors through which an invisible stream of guests was passing. The organ rolled, but not with music. Croaking,

123

bawling, screeching and whimpering sounded from the organ and intermingled were wanton dance tunes, wailing whore-songs.

"The swing-doors, the light, the organ's witches sabbath, everything appeared to be mysteriously excited, hurried, as though there were no time to be lost, and full of a deep evil satisfaction.

"I walked over to the cathedral and up the steps. A door laid hold of me, like an arm, and wafted me gustily in the cathedral.

"But that was as little the cathedral as the town was Metropolis. A pack of lunatics seemed to have taken possession of it, and not even human beings, at that. Dwarf-like creatures, resembling half monkey, half devil. In place of the saints, goat-like figures, petrified in the most ridiculous of leaps, reigned in the pillar niches. And around every pillar danced a ring, raving to the bawling of the music.

"Empty, ungodded, splintered, hung the crucifix above the high altar, from which the holy vessels had vanished.

"A fellow, dressed in black, the caricature of a monk, stood in the pulpit, howling out in a pulpit-voice:

" 'Repent! The kingdom of heaven is at hand!'

"A loud neigh answered him.

"The organ-player—I saw him, he was like a demon—stood with his hands and feet on the keys and his head beat time to the ring-dance of the spirits.

"The fellow in the pulpit pulled out a book, an enormous, black book with seven locks. Whenever his fingers touched a lock it sprang up in flame and shot open.

"Murmuring incantations, he opened the cover. He bent over the book. A ring of flames suddenly stood around his head.

"From the heights of the cathedral it struck midnight. But it was as though it was not enough for the clock to proclaim the hour of demons just once. Over and over again did it strike the ghastly twelve, in dreadful, baited haste.

"The light in the cathedral changed colour. Were it possible to speak of a blackish light this would be the expression best applied to the light. Only in one place did it shine, white, gleaming, cutting, a sharply whetted sword: there where death is figured as a minstrel.

"Suddenly the organ stopped, and suddenly the dance. The voice of the preacher-fellow in the pulpit stopped. And through the silence which did not dare to breathe, rang the sound of a flute. Death was playing. The minstrel was playing the song which nobody plays after him, on his flute which was a human bone.

"The ghostly minstrel stepped from out his side-niche, carved in wood, in hat

124

and wide cloak, scythe on shoulder, the hour-glass dangling from his girdle. Playing his flute, he stepped out of his niche and made his way through the cathedral. And behind him came the seven Deadly Sins as the following of Death.

"Death performed a circle around every pillar. Louder and ever louder rang the sound of his flute. The seven Deadly Sins seized hands. As a widely swung chain they paced behind Death; and gradually their paces became a light dance.

'The seven Deadly Sins danced along behind Death, who was playing the flute.

"Then the cathedral was filled with a light which seemed to be made from rose-leaves. An inexpressibly sweet, overpowering perfume hovered up, like incense, between the pillars. The light grew stronger and it seemed to ring. Pale red lightning flashed from the heights collecting itself in the central nave, to the magnificent radiance of a crown.

"The crown rested on the head of a woman. And the woman was sitting upon a scarlet-coloured beast, having seven heads and ten horns. And the woman was arrayed in purple and scarlet and decked with gold, precious stones and pearls. She had in her hand a golden cup. On the crowned brow of the woman there stood, mysteriously written: Babylon.

"Like a deity, she grew up and radiated. Death and the seven Deadly Sins bowed low before her.

"And the woman who bore the name Babylon had the features of Maria, whom I loved . . .

"The woman arose. She touched the cross-arched vault of the lofty cathedral with her crown. She seized the hem of her cloak and opened it. And spread out her cloak with both hands . . . Then one saw that the golden cloak was embroidered with the images of manifold demons. Beings with women's bodies and snakes' heads—beings half bull, half angel—devils adorned with crowns, human faced lions.

"The flute song of Death was silenced. But the fellow in the pulpit raised his yelling voice:

" 'Repent! The kingdom of heaven is at hand!'

"The church-clock was still hammering the wild twelve-time of midnight.

"The woman looked Death in the face. She opened her mouth. She said to Death: 'Go!'

"Then Death hung the flute on his girdle, by the hourglass, took the scythe down from his shoulder and went. He went through the cathedral and went out of the cathedral.

And from the cloak of the great Babylon, the demons freed themselves, come to life, and flew after Death.

"Death went down the steps of the cathedral, into the town; black birds with human faces rustling around him. He raised the scythe as if indicating the way. Then they divided themselves and swooped apart. The broad wings darkened the moon.

"Death flung back his wide cloak. He stretched himself up and grew. He grew much taller even than the houses of Metropolis. The highest hardly reached to his knee.

"Death swung his scythe and made a whistling cut. The earth and all the stars quivered. But the scythe did not seem to be sharp enough for him. He looked about him as though seeking a seat. The New Tower of Babel seemed to suit Death. He sat down on the New Tower of Babel, propped up the scythe, took the whet-stone from his girdle, spat on it and began to whet the scythe. Blue sparks flew out of the steel. Then Death arose and made a second blow. A rain of stars poured down from the sky.

"Death nodded with satisfaction, turned around and set off, on his way through the great Metropolis."

CHAPTER XI

DIN OF THE BEHEMOTH

"YES," SAID JOSAPHAT hoarsely, "but that was a dream . . ."

Of course it was a dream . . . And they say dreams are bubbles, don't they? But just listen to this, Josaphat . . . I emerged from this dream back into reality with a feeling of sadness, which seemed to hack me, as with a knife, from head to foot. I saw Maria's brow, that white temple of goodness and virginity, besmirched with the name of the great harlot of Babylon. I saw her send Death out over the city. I saw how abominations upon abominations loosened themselves from about her and fluttered away, swarming through the city—plague spirits, messengers of evil before the path of Death. I stood out there and looked over at the cathedral, which seemed to me to be desecrated and soiled. Its doors stood open. Dark, human snakes were creeping into the cathedral, and collecting themselves upon the steps. I thought: Perhaps, among all those pious people, is my Maria too . . . I said to my father: 'I wish to go to the cathedral . . . ' He let me go. I was no captive. As I reached the cathedral the organ was thundering like the Trump of Doom. Singing from a thousand throats. *Dies Irae* . . . The incense clouded above the head of the multitude, which was kneeling before the eternal God. The crucifix hovered above the high altar, and, in the light of the restless candles, the drops of blood on the thorn-crowned brow of the son of Mary seemed to come to life, to run. The saints in the pillar-niches looked at me sadly, as though they knew of my evil dream.

"I sought Maria. Oh, I knew quite well that all the thousands could not hide her from me. If she were here I should find her out, as a bird finds its way to its nest. But my heart lay as if dead in my breast. Yet I could not help looking

127

for her. I wandered about the place where I had already waited for her once before . . . Yes—so may a bird wander about the place where was its nest which it cannot find again, because the lightning or the storm has destroyed it.

"And, when I came to, the side-niche, in which Death stands, as a minstrel, playing upon a human bone, the niche was empty, Death had disappeared . . .

"It was as though the Death of my dream had not returned home to his following . . .

"Do not speak, Josaphat! It is really of no importance . . . a coincidence . . . The carving was, perhaps, damaged—I do not know! Believe me: it is of no importance.

"But now a voice yelled out:

" 'Repent! The kingdom of heaven is at hand!'

"It was the voice of Desertus, the monk. His voice was like a knife. The voice peeled bare my spine. Deathly stillness reigned in the church. Among all the thousands round about, not one seemed to breathe. They were kneeling and their faces, pale masks of horror, were turned towards the preacher.

"His voice flew through the air like a spear.

" 'Repent! The kingdom of heaven is at hand!'

"Before me, by a pillar, stood a young man, once a fellow member of mine, of the 'Club of the Sons.' If I had not personally experienced how vastly human faces can change, in a short time, I should not have recognised him.

"He was older than I, and was, it is true, not the happiest of us all, but the gayest. And the women loved him and feared him equally, for he was in no way to be captivated, either by laughter or by tears. Now he had the thousand-year-old face of men, who, yet living, are dead. It was as if a cruel executioner had removed his eyelids, that he was condemned never to sleep, so that he was perishing of weariness.

"But it surprised me more than all to find him here, in the cathedral, for he had been, all his life long, the greatest of scoffers.

"I laid my hand on his shoulder. He did not start. He only just turned his eyes—those parched eyes.

"I wanted to ask him: 'What are you doing here, Jan?' But the voice of the monk, that awful, spear-hurling voice, threw its sharpness between him and me . . . The monk Desertus began to preach . . ."

Freder turned around and came to Josaphat with violent haste, as though a sudden fear had taken him. He sat down by his friend, speaking very rapidly, with words which tumbled over each other in streaming out.

At first he had hardly listened to the monk. He had watched his friend, and the congregation which was still kneeling, head pressed to head. And, as he looked at them, it seemed to him as though the monk were harpooning the congregation with his words, as though he were throwing spears, with deadly, barbed hooks, right down into the most secret soul of the listeners, as though he were tugging groaning souls out of bodies, quivering with fear.

"Who is she, who has laid fire to this city? She is herself a flame—an impure flame. You were given of a brand, might. She is a fiery blaze over man. She is Lilith, Astarte, Rose of Hell. She is Gomorrah, Babylon—*Metropolis!* Your own city—this fruitful, sinful *City!*—has born this woman from out the womb of its hell. Behold her! I say unto you: Behold her! She is the woman who is to appear before the judgment of the world.

"He who has ears to hear, let him hear.

"Seven angels shall stand before God, and there shall be given unto them seven trumpets. And the seven angels, which have the seven trumpets, shall prepare themselves to sound. A star shall fall from heaven to earth and there shall be given up the key to the pit of the abyss. And it shall open the pit of the abyss and there shall go up a smoke out of the pit as the smoke of a great furnace; and the sun and the air shall be darkened by reason of the smoke of the pit. And an angel shall fly in mid heaven, saying with a great voice: 'Woe, woe, woe, for them that dwell on the earth!' And another angel shall follow after him and shall say: Fallen, fallen, is Babylon the great!'

"Seven angels come out from the heavens, and they bear in their hands the bowls of the wrath of God. And Babylon the great will be remembered in the sight of God, to give unto her the cup of the wine of the fierceness of His wrath—she who is sitting there upon a scarlet-coloured beast full of the names of blasphemy, having seven heads and ten horns. And the woman is arrayed in purple and scarlet, decked with gold and precious stones and pearls, having in her hand a golden cup, full of abominations and unclean things. And upon her forehead a name is written: Mystery . . . Babylon the Great . . . The Mother of Harlots and of the Abominations of the Earth.

"He who has ears to hear, let him hear! For the woman whom ye see is the great city, which reignest over the kings of the earth. Come forth, my people, out of her, that he have no fellowship with her sins! For her sins have reached even unto heaven, and God has remembered her iniquities!

"Woe, woe, the great city, Babylon, the strong city! For in one hour is thy judgment come! In one hour shalt thou be made desolate. Rejoice over her, thou heaven, and ye saints, and ye apostles; for God will judge your judgment on her. And a strong angel takes up a stone and casts it into the sea, saying: 'Thus with a mighty fall, shall Babylon the great city be cast down, and shall be found no more at all!"

"He who has ears to hear, let him hear!

"The woman who is called Babylon, the Mother of the Abominations of the Earth, wanders as a blazing brand through Metropolis. No wall and no gate bids her halt. No tie is sacred. An oath turns to mockery before her. Her smile is the last seduction. Blasphemy is her dance. She is the flame which says: 'God is very wrath! Woe unto the city in which she shall appear!' "

Freder bent across to Jan.

"Of whom is he speaking?" he asked, with strangely cold lips. "Is he speaking of a person? . . . of a woman? . . ."

He saw that the brow of his friend was covered with sweat.

"He is speaking of *her,*" said Jan, as though he were speaking with paralysed tongue.

"Of whom?"

"Of *her* . . . don't you know her?"

"I don't know," said Freder, "whom you mean . . ."

And his tongue, too, was heavy, and as though made of clay.

Jan gave no answer. He had hunched up his shoulders as though he were bitterly cold. Bewildered and undecided, he listened to the intermediate rolling of the organ.

"Let us go!" he said tonelessly, turning around. Freder followed him. They left the cathedral. They walked along together in silence for a long time. Jan seemed to have a destination of which Freder did not know. He did not ask. He waited. He was thinking of his dream and of the monk's words.

At last Jan opened his mouth; but he did not look at Freder, he spoke into space:

"You do not know who she is . . . But nobody knows . . . She was suddenly there . . . As a fire breaks out . . . No one can say who fanned the flame . . . But there it is, and now everything is ablaze . . ."

"A woman . . .?"

"Yes. A woman. Perhaps a maid, too. I don't know. It is inconceivable that this being would give herself to a man . . . (Can you imagine the marriage of ice?) . . . Or, if she were to do so, then she would raise herself up from the man's arms, bright and cool, in the awful, eternal virginity of the soulless . . ."

He raised his hand and seized his throat. He tugged something away from him which was not there. He was looking at a house which lay opposite him, on the other side of the street, with a gaze of superstitious hostility, which made his hands run cold.

"What is the matter with you?" asked Freder. There was nothing remarkable about this house, except that it lay next to Rotwang's house.

"Hush!" answered Jan, clasping his fingers around Freder's wrist.

"Are you mad?" Freder stared at his friend. "Do you think that the house can hear us across this infernal street?"

"It hears us!" said Jan, with an obstinate expression. "It hears us! You think it is a house just like any other? You're wrong . . . It began in this house . . ."

"What began?"

"The spirit . . ."

Freder felt that his throat was very dry. He cleared it vigorously. He wanted to draw his friend along with him. But he resisted him. He stood at the parapet of the street, which sheered down, steep as a gorge, and he was staring at the house opposite.

"One day," he said, "this house sent out invitations to all its neighbours. It was the craziest invitation on earth. There was nothing on the card but: 'Come this evening at ten o'clock! House 12, 113th Street!' One took the whole thing to be a joke. But one went. One did not wish to miss the fun. Strangely enough no one knew the house. Nobody could remember ever having entered it, or having known anything of its occupants. One turned up at ten. One was well dressed. One entered the house and found a big party. One was received by an old man, who was exceedingly polite, but who shook hands with nobody. It was an odd thing that all the people collected here seemed to be waiting for something, of which they did not know. One was well waited upon by servants, who seemed to be born mutes, and who never raised their eyes. Although the room in which we were all gathered was as large as the nave of a church, an unbearable heat prevailed, as though the floor were glowing hot, as though the walls were glowing hot, and all this in spite of the fact that, as one could see, the wide door leading to the street stood open.

"Suddenly one of the servants came up from the door to our host, with soundless step, and seemed wordlessly, with his silent presence, to give him some information. Our host inquired: 'Are we all met?' The servant inclined his head. 'Then close the door.' It was done. The servants swept aside and lined themselves up. Our host stepped into the middle of the great room. At the same moment so perfect a silence prevailed that one heard the noise of the street roaring like breakers against the walls of the house.

131

" 'Ladies and gentlemen,' said the old man courteously, 'may I have the honour of presenting my daughter to you!'" He bowed to all sides, and then he turned his back. Everyone waited. No one moved.

" 'Well, my daughter,' said the old man, with a gentle, but somehow horrible voice, softly clapping his hands.

"Then she appeared on the stairs and came slowly down the room . . ."

Jan gulped. His fingers, which still held Freder's wrist in their clutch, gripped tighter, as though they wished to crush the bones.

"Why am I telling you this?" he stammered. "Can one describe lightning? Or music? Or the fragrance of a flower? All the women in the hall suddenly blushed violently and feverishly and all the men turned pale. Nobody seemed capable of making the least movement or of saying a single word . . . You know Rainer? You know his young wife? You know how they loved each other? He was standing behind her. She was sitting, and he had laid his hands on her shoulders with a gesture of passionate and protective affection. As the girl walked by them—she walked, led by the hand of the old man, with gentle ringing step, slowly through the hall—Rainer's hands slipped from his wife's shoulders. She looked up at him, he down at her; and in the faces of those two were burnt, like a torch, a sudden, deadly hatred . . .

"It was as though the air was burning. We breathed fire. At the same time there radiated from the girl a coldness—an unbearable, cutting coldness. The smile which hovered between her half-open lips seemed to be the unspoken closing verse of a shameless song.

"Is there some substance through the power of which emotions are destroyed, as colours are by acids? The presence of this girl was enough to annul everything which spells fidelity in the human heart, even to a point of absurdity. I had accepted the invitation of this house because Tora had told me she would go too. Now I no longer saw Tora, and I have not seen her since. And the strange thing was that, among all these motionless beings who were standing there as though benumbed, there was not one who could have hidden his feelings. Each knew how it was with the other. Each felt that he was naked and saw the nakedness of the others. Hatred, born of shame, smouldered among us. Tora was crying. I could have struck her . . . Then the girl danced. No, it was no dance . . . She stood, freed from the hand of the old man, on the lowest step, facing us, and she raised her arms about the width of her garment with a gentle, a seemingly never-ending movement. The slender hands touched above her hair-parting. Over her shoulders, her breasts, her hips, her knees, there ran an incessant, a barely perceptible trembling. It was no frightened trembling. It

"Can one describe lightning? Or music? Or the fragrance of a flower? . . . It was as though the air was burning. We breathed fire. At the same time there radiated from the girl a coldness—an unbearable, cutting coldness. The smile which hovered between her half-open lips seemed to be the unspoken closing verse of a shameless song.
[Brigitte Helm (Futura/Maria)]

was like the trembling of the final spinal fins of a luminous, deep sea fish. It was as though the girl were carried higher and higher by this trembling, though she did not move her feet. No dance, no scream, no cry of an animal in heat, could have so lashing an effect as the trembling of this shimmering body, which seemed, in its calm, in its solitude, to impart the waves of its incitement to every single soul in the room.

"Then she went up the steps, stepping backwards, with tentative feet, without lowering her hands, and she disappeared into a velvet-deep darkness. The servants opened the door to the street. They lined up with backs bent.

"The people still sat motionless.

" 'Good night, ladies and gentlemen!' said the old man . . ."

Jan was silent. He took his hat from his head. He wiped his forehead.

"A dancer," said Freder, with cold lips, "but a spirit . . .?"

"Not a spirit! I will tell you another story . . . A man and a woman, of fifty and forty, rich and very happy, have a son. You know him, but I will not mention any names . . .

"The son sees the girl. He is as though mad. He storms the house. He storms the girl's father: 'Let me have her! I am dying for her!' The old man smiles, shrugs his shoulders, is silent, is exceedingly sorry, the girl is not to be attained.

"The young man wants to lay hands on the old man, but he is whirled out of the house and thrown into the street, by he does not know whom. He is taken home. He falls ill and is at Death's door. The doctors shrug their shoulders.

"The father, who is a proud but kindly man, and who loves his son above anything on earth, makes up his mind to visit the old man, himself. He gains entrance to the house without difficulty. He finds the old man, and with him, the girl. He says to the girl: 'Save my son!'

"The girl looks at him and says, with the most graciously inhuman of smiles: 'You have no son . . .'

"He does not understand the meaning of these words. He wants to know more. He urges the girl. She always gives the same answer. He urges the old man—he lifts his shoulders. There is a perfidious smile about his mouth . . .

"Suddenly the man comprehends . . . He goes home. He repeats the girl's words to his wife. She breaks down and confesses her sin—a sin which, after twenty years, has not yet died down. But she is not concerned with her own fate. She has no thought apart from her son. Shame, desertion, loneliness—all are nothing; but the son is everything.

"No dance, no scream, no cry of an animal in heat, could have so lashing an effect as the trembling of this shimmering body, which seemed, in its calm, in its solitude, to impart the waves of its incitement to every single soul in the room.

"Then she went up the steps, stepping backwards, with tentative feet, without lowering her hands, and she disappeared into a velvet-deep darkness.
[Brigitte Helm (Futura/ Maria)]

"She goes to the girl and falls on her knees before her: 'I beg you, in the name of God's mercy, save my son . . . !' The girl looks at her, smiles and says: 'You have no son . . . ' The woman believes that she has a lunatic before her. But the girl was right. The son, who had been a secret witness to the conversation between the husband and the mother, had ended his life . . ."

"Marinus?"

"Yes."

" . . . A terrible coincidence, Jan, but still, not a spirit."

"Coincidence?—Not a spirit?—And what do you call it, Freder," continued Jan, speaking quite close to Freder's ear, "when this girl can appear in two places at once?"

"That's absolute rubbish . . ."

"Rubbish—? It's the truth, Freder! The girl was seen standing at the window in Rotwang's house—and, at the same time, she was dancing her sinful dance in Yoshiwara . . ."

"That is not true—!" said Freder.

"It is true!"

"You have seen the girl . . . in Yoshiwara—?"

"You can see her yourself, if you like . . ."

"What's the girl's name?"

"Maria . . ."

Freder laid his forehead in his hands. He bent double, as in the throes of an agony, which otherwise God does not permit to visit mankind.

"You know the girl?" asked Jan, bending forward.

"No!"

"But you love her," said Jan, and behind these words lurked hatred, crouched to spring.

Freder took his hand and said: "Come!"

"But," continued Freder, fixing his eyes upon Josaphat, who was sitting there quite sunken together, while the rain was growing gentler, like hushed weeping, "Slim was suddenly standing there, beside me, and he said: 'Will you not return home, Mr. Freder?' "

Josaphat was silent for a long time: Freder, too, was silent. In the frame of the open door, which led out to the balcony, stood, hovering, the picture of the monster clock, on the New Tower of Babel, bathed in a white light. The large hand jerked to twelve.

Then a sound arose throughout Metropolis.

It was an immeasurably glorious and transporting sound, as deep and rumbling as, and more powerful than any sound on earth. The voice of the ocean when it is angry, the voice of falling torrents, the voice of very close thunder storms, would be miserably drowned in this Behemoth din. Without being shrill, it penetrated all walls, and, as long as it lasted, all things seemed to swing in it. It was omnipresent, coming from the heights and from the depths, being beautiful and horrible, being an irresistible command.

It was high above the town. It was the voice of the town.

Metropolis raised her voice. The machines of Metropolis roared: They wanted to be fed.

The eyes of Josaphat and Freder met.

"Now," said Josaphat, "many are going down into a city of the dead, and are waiting for one who is called Maria, and whom they have found as true as gold..."

"Yes!" said Freder, "you are a friend, and you are quite right... I shall go with them..."

And, for the first time this night, there was something like hope in the ring of his voice.

"The girl was seen standing at the window in Rotwang's house—and, at the same time, she was dancing her sinful dance in Yoshiwara . . .

"That is not true—!" said Freder.

"It is true!"

"You have seen the girl . . . in Yoshiwara—?"

"You can see her yourself, if you like . . . "

"What's the girl's name?"

"Maria . . . "

[Brigitte Helm (Futura/Maria)]

Freder laid his forehead in
his hands. He bent double,
as in the throes of an
agony, which otherwise
God does not permit to
visit mankind.
"You know the girl?" asked
Jan, bending forward.
"No!"
"But you love her," said Jan,
and behind these words
lurked hatred,
crouched to spring.
Freder took his hand
and said: "Come!"
[Brigitte Helm
(Futura/Maria)]

139

"Is there some substance through the power of which emotions are destroyed, as colours are by acids? The presence of this girl was enough to annul everything which spells fidelity in the human heart, even to a point of absurdity. . . ."
[Brigitte Helm (Futura/Maria)]

CHAPTER XII

JOH FREDERSEN GOES TO HEL

IT WAS ONE hour after midnight.

Joh Fredersen came to his mother's house.

It was a farmhouse, one-storied, thatch-roofed, overshadowed by a walnut tree and it stood upon the flat back of one of the stone giants, not far from
the cathedral. A garden full of lilies and hollyhocks, full of sweet peas and
poppies and nasturtiums, wound itself about the house.

Joh Fredersen's mother had only one son and him she had very dearly
loved. But the Master over the great Metropolis, the Master of the machine-
city, the Brain of the New Tower of Babel had become a stranger to her and
she hostile to him. She had had to look on once and see how one of Joh
Fredersen's machine-Titans crushed men as though they were dried up wood.
She had screamed to God. He had not heard her. She fell to the ground and
never got up again. Only head and hands retained their vitality in the paralysed
body. But the strength of a legion blazed in her eyes.

She opposed her son and the work of her son. But he did not let her
alone; he forced her to him. When she angrily vowed she wished to live in her
house—under the thatched roof, with its vault, the walnut tree—until her dying
day, he transplanted house and tree and gaily blossoming garden to the flat
roof of the stone house-giant which lay between the cathedral and the New
Tower of Babel. The walnut tree ailed one year long; and then it became green
again. The garden blossomed, a wonder of beauty, about the house.

When Joh Fredersen entered this house he came from sleepless nights
and evil days.

He found his mother as he always found her: sitting in the wide, soft chair

141

by the open window, the dark rug over the now paralysed knees, the great Bible on the sloping table before her, in the beautiful old hands the delicate figured lace at which she was sewing; and, as ever, when he came to her, she silently laid aside the fine work and folded her hands firmly in her lap as though she must collect all her will and every thought for the few minutes which the great son spent with his mother.

They did not shake hands; they did not do that any more.

"How are you, mother?" asked Joh Fredersen.

She looked at him with eyes in which gleamed the strength of a heavenly legion. She asked:

"What is it you want, Joh?"

He sat down opposite her and laid his forehead in his hands.

There was nobody in the great Metropolis, not anywhere else on earth who could have boasted ever having seen Joh Fredersen with sunken brow.

"I need your advice, mother," he said, looking at the floor.

The mother's eyes rested on his hair.

"How shall I advise you, Joh? You have taken a path along which I cannot follow you—not with my head, and certainly not with my heart. Now you are so far away from me that my voice can no longer reach you. And if it were able to reach you, Joh, would you listen to me were I to say to you: Turn back—? You did not do it then and would not do it to-day. Besides, all too much has been done which cannot be undone, you have done all too much wrong, Joh, and do not repent, but believe yourself to be in the right. How can I advise you then . . .?"

"It is about Freder, mother . . .?"

" . . . about Freder?"

"Yes."

"What about Freder . . ."

Joh Fredersen did not answer immediately.

His mother's hands trembled greatly, and, if Joh Fredersen had looked up, the fact could not have remained hidden from him. But Joh Fredersen's forehead remained sunken upon his hands.

"I had to come to you, mother, because Hel is no longer alive . . ."

"And of what did she die?"

"I know: of me . . . You have made it clear to me, mother, often and cruelly, and you have said I had poured boiling wine into a crystal. Then the most beautiful of glass must crack. But I do not repent it, mother. No, I do not repent it . . . For Hel was mine . . ."

"And died of it . . ."

"Yes. Had she never been mine perhaps she would still be alive. Better that she should be dead."

"She is, Joh. And Freder is her son."

"What do you mean by that, mother?"

"If you did not know just as well as I, Joh, you would not have come to me to-day."

Joh Fredersen was silent. Through the open window, the rustling of the walnut tree was to be heard, a dreamy, touching sound.

"Freder often comes to you, mother, doesn't he?" asked Joh Fredersen.

"Yes."

"He comes to you for aid against me . . ."

"He is in great need of it, Joh . . ."

Silence. Then Joh Fredersen raised his head. His eyes looked as though sprinkled with purple.

"I have lost Hel, mother," he said. "I can't lose Freder too . . ."

"Have you reason to fear that you will lose him?"

"Yes."

"Then I am surprised," said the old lady, "that Freder has not yet come to me . . ."

"He is very ill, mother . . ."

The old lady made a movement as though wishing to rise, and into her archangel eyes there came an angry glitter. "When he came here recently," she said, "he was as healthy as a tree in bloom. What ails him?"

Joh Fredersen got up and began to walk up and down the room. He smelt the perfume of flowers streaming up from the garden through the open window as something inflicting pain which ripped his forehead into lines.

"I do not know," he said suddenly, quite disjointedly, "how this girl could have stepped into his life. I do not know how she won this monstrous hold over him. But I heard from his own lips how he said to her: My father no longer has a son, Maria . . ."

"Freder does not lie, Joh. So you have lost him already."

Joh Fredersen did not answer. He thought of Rotwang. He had said the same words to him.

"Is it about this that you have come to me, Joh?" asked his mother. "Then you could have spared yourself the trouble. Freder is Hel's son. Yes . . . That means he has a soft heart. But he is your's too, Joh. That means he has a skull of steel. You know best, Joh, how much obstinacy a man can summon up to attain to the woman he wants."

"You cannot make that comparison, mother. Freder is almost a boy, still. When I took Hel to me I was a man, and knew what I was doing. Hel was more needful to me than the air to breathe. I could not do without Hel, Mother. I would have stolen her from the arms of God himself."

"From God, Joh, you can steal nothing, but something can be stolen from man. You have done that. You have sinned, Joh. You have sinned towards your friend. For Hel loved Rotwang and it was you who compelled her."

"When she was dying, mother, she loved me . . ."

"Yes. When she saw that you, too, were a man, when your head was beating against the floor and you were crying out. But do you believe, Joh, that this one smile in her dying hour outweighs all that which brought about her death?"

"Leave me my belief, Mother . . ."

"Delusion . . ."

Joh Fredersen looked at his mother.

"I should very much like to know," he said with darkened voice, "on what you feed your cruelty towards, me, mother."

"On my fears for you, Joh—on my fears!"

"You need have no fears for me, mother . . ."

"Oh yes, Joh—oh yes! Your sin walks behind you like a good dog on the trail. It does not lose your scent, Joh—it remains always and always at your back. A friend is unarmed against his friend. He has no shield before his breast, nor armour before his heart. A friend who believes in his friend is a defenceless man. A defenceless man was it whom you betrayed, Joh."

"I have paid for my sin, mother . . . Hel is dead. Now I have only Freder left. That is her legacy. I will not give up Hel's legacy. I have come to you to beg of you, mother: help me to win Freder back."

The old lady's eyes were fixed on him, sparklingly.

"What did you answer me, Joh, when I wanted to stop you on your way to Hel?"

"I don't remember."

"But I do, Joh! I still remember every syllable. You said: 'I don't hear a word you say—I only hear "Hel"! If I were to be blinded—I should still see Hel! If I were to be paralysed—with paralysed feet, I should still find my way to Hel!— ' Freder is your son. What do you think, Joh, he would answer me were I to say to him: give up the girl you love . . .?"

Joh Fredersen was silent.

"Take care, Joh," said the old mother. "I know what it means when your eyes grow cold, as now, and when you grow as pale as one of the stones of the wall. You have forgotten that lovers are sacred. Even if they are mistaken, Joh, their mistake itself is sacred. Even if they are fools, Joh, their folly itself is sacred. For where lovers are, there is God's garden, and no one has the right to drive them out. Not even God. Only their own sin."

"I must have my son back," said Joh Fredersen. "I had hoped you would help me, and you would certainly have been the gentlest means I could have chosen. But you will not, and now I must seek another means . . ."

"Freder is ill, you say . . ."

"He will get well again . . ."

"So you will continue in your way?"

"Yes."

"I believe, Joh, that Hel would weep were she to hear you!"

"Perhaps. But Hel is dead."

"Well, come here to me, Joh! I will give you a word to take with you on your way, which you cannot forget. It is easy to retain."

Joh Fredersen hesitated. Then he walked up to his mother. She laid her hand on the bible which lay before her. Joh Fredersen read: . . . *Whatsoever a man soweth, that shall he reap* . . .

Joh Fredersen turned around. He walked through the room. His mother's eyes followed him. As be turned toward her, suddenly, violently, with a violent word on his lips he found the gaze of her eyes set upon him. They could hide themselves no longer, and neither did they wish to—such an almighty love— such an almighty love, in their tear-washed depths that Joh Fredersen believed himself to see his mother to-day for the first time.

They looked at each other for a long time, in silence. Then the man stepped up to his mother.

"I am going, now, mother," he said, "and I don't believe I shall ever come to you again . . ."

She did not answer.

It seemed as though he wanted to stretch out his hand to her, but, half-way he let it drop again.

"For whom are you crying, mother," he asked, "for Freder or for me?"

"For you both," said the mother, "for you both, Joh . . ."

He stood in silence and the struggle of his heart was in his face. Then, without giving his mother another look, he turned around and went out of the house, over which the walnut tree rustled.

Artist Boris Bilinsky's rendition of the famous city of METROPOLIS (from French promotional material.).

CHAPTER XIII

THE STOLEN EGO

IT WAS MIDNIGHT and no light was burning. Only through the window there fell the radiance of the city, lying like a pale gleam upon the face of the girl who sat, leaning back against the wall, without moving, with closed eye-lids, her hands in her lap.

"Will you never answer me?" asked the great inventor.

Stillness. Silence. Immobility.

"You are colder than stone, harder than any stone. The tip of your finger must cut through the diamond as though it were water . . . I do not implore your love. What does a girl know of love? Her unstormed fortresses—her unopened Paradises—her sealed-up books, whom no one knows but the god who wrote them—what do you know of love? Women know nothing of love either. What does light know of light? Flame of burning? What do the stars know of the laws by which they wander? You must ask chaos—coldness, darkness, the eternal unredeemed which wrestles for the redemption of itself. You must ask the man what love is. The hymn of Heaven is only composed in Hell . . . I do not implore your love, Maria. But your pity, you motherly one, with the virgin face . . ."

Stillness. Silence. Immobility.

"I hold you captive . . . Is that my fault? I do not hold you captive for myself, Maria. Above you and me there is a Will which forces me into being evil. Have pity on him who must be evil, Maria! All the springs of good within me are choked up. I thought them to be dead; but they are only buried alive. My being is a rock of darkness. But deep within the sad stone I hear the springs rushing . . . If I defy the Will which is above you and me . . . If I destroy the work

147

I created after your image . . . It would only be what Joh Fredersen deserves and it would be better for me! . . . He has ruined me, Maria—he has ruined me! He stole the woman from me, who was mine, and whom I loved. I do not know if her soul was ever with me. But her pity was with me and made me good. Joh Fredersen took the woman from me. He made me evil. He, who grudged the stone the imprint of her shoe, made me evil to take her pity from me. Hel is dead. But she loved him. What a fearful law it is by which the beings of Light turn themselves to those of Darkness, but pass by those in the shade. Be more merciful than Hel was, Maria! I will defy the Will which is above you and me. I will open the doors for you. You will be able to go where you wish and nobody shall stop you. But would you remain with me of your own free will, Maria? I long to be good . . . will you help me?"

Stillness. Silence. Immobility.

"Neither do I implore your pity, Maria. There is nothing on earth more uncompassionate than a woman who only loves one single being . . . You cool murderesses in the name of Love . . . You goddesses of Death, with your smile! . . . The hands of your Beloved are cold. You ask: 'Shall I warm your hands for you, Beloved?' You do not wait for his 'Yes.' You set fire to a city. You burn down a kingdom, so that you can warm the hands of your Beloved at its blaze . . . You rise up and pluck from the heaven of the world its most radiant stars, without caring that you destroy the Universe and put the dance of the Eternal out of balance. 'Do you want the stars—Beloved?' And if he says 'No' then you let the stars fall . . . Oh! you blessed harmdoers! You may step, fearfully inviolable, before the throne of God and say: 'Get up, Creator of the World! I need the throne of the World for my beloved! . . . ' You do not see who dies by your side if only the one is living. A drop of blood on the finger of your Beloved frightens you more than the destruction of a continent . . . All this I know, and have never possessed it! . . . No, I do not call upon your pity, Maria. But I call upon your fidelity . . .!"

Still. Silence. Immobility.

"Do you know the subterranean City of the Dead? There used a girl called Maria, nightly to call her brothers together. Her brothers wear the blue linen uniform, the black caps, the hard shoes. Maria spoke to her brothers of a mediator, who would come to deliver them. 'The Mediator between Brain and Hands must be the Heart . . .' Wasn't it so?—The brothers of the girl believed in the girl. They waited. They waited long. But the mediator did not come. And the girl did not come. She sent no message. She was not to be found. But the brothers believed in the girl, for they had found her as true as gold. 'She will come!' they said. 'She will come again! She is faithful. She will not leave us alone! She said: "The mediator will come!" . . . Now he must come . . . Let us be patient and let us wait' . . .! But the mediator did not come. And—the girl did not come. The misery of the brothers has grown from day to day. Where once a thousand murmured—now murmur ten thousand. They will no more be fed with hope. They languish for fight, for destruction, for ruin, for downfall. And even the believers, even the patient ones ask: 'Where is Maria? Can it be that gold is faithless?' Will you leave them without an answer, Maria?"

Stillness. Silence. Immobility.

"You are silent . . . You are very obstinate . . . But now I shall tell you something which will surely break your obstinacy . . . Do you think I am holding you captive here for fun? Do you think Joh Fredersen knew no other way of getting you out of his son's sight than shutting you up behind the Solomon's seal on my doors? On no, Maria—oh no, my beautiful Maria! We have not been idle all these days. We have stolen your beautiful soul from you—your sweet soul, that tender smile of God. I have listened to you as the air has listened to you. I have seen you angry and in the depths of despair. I have seen you burning and dull as the earth. I have listened to you praying to God, and have cursed God because he did not hear you. I have intoxicated myself with your helplessness. Your pitiful weeping has made me drunken. When you sobbed the name of your Beloved, I thought I must die, and reeled . . . And thus, as one intoxicated, as one drunken, as one reeling, I became a thief of you, Maria, I created you anew—I became your second God! I have stolen you absolutely! In the name of Joh Fredersen, the Master over the great Metropolis, have I stolen your ego from you, Maria. And this stolen ego—your other self—sent a message to your brothers, calling them by night into the City of the Dead—and they all came. When you spoke to them before, you spoke for Peace . . . but Joh Fredersen does not want Peace any more—do you see?— He wants the decision! The hour has come! Your stolen ego may not speak for Peace any more. The mouth of Joh Fredersen speaks from out it . . . And among your brothers there will be one who loves you and who will not realize—who will not doubt you, Maria . . . Only just give me your hands, Maria— only your hands, no more . . . I do not ask for more . . . your hands must be wondrous. Pardon is the name of the right, Redemption of the left . . . If you give me your hands I will go with you into the City of the Dead, so that you can warn your brothers, so that you can unmask your stolen ego—so that the one who loves you finds you again and does not have to doubt you . . . .Did you say anything, Maria?"

He heard the soft, soft weeping of the girl. He fell, where he stood, upon his knees. He wanted to drag himself along on his knees to the girl. And suddenly stopped still. He listened. He stared. He said in a voice which was almost like a shriek, in its wide-awake attention:

"Maria . . .? Maria—don't you hear . . .? There's a strange man in the room . . ."

"Yes," said the quiet voice of Joh Fredersen.

And then the hands of Joh Fredersen seized the throat of Rotwang, the great inventor . . .

CHAPTER XIV

DESTROY THE MACHINES!

A VAULT, LIKE the vault of a sepulcher—human heads so closely crowded as to produce the effect of clods of a freshly ploughed field. All faces turned to one point: to the source of a light, as mild as God. Candles burnt with sword-like flames. Slender, lustrous swords of light stood in a circle around the head of a girl.

Freder stood pressed into the background of the arch—so far from the girl that he perceived of her face nothing but the shimmer of its pallor, the wonder of the eyes and the blood-red mouth. His eyes hung upon this blood-red mouth as though it were the middle point of the earth, to which, by eternal law, his blood must pour down. Tantalising was this mouth . . . All the seven Deadly Sins had such a mouth . . . The woman on the scarlet-coloured beast, who bore the name Babylon on her forehead, had such a mouth . . .

He pressed both hands to his eyes in order no longer to see this mouth of deadly sin.

Now he heard more clearly . . . Yes, that was her voice, the voice which sounded as though God could refuse it nothing . . . Was that really it? The voice came from out the blood-red mouth. It was like a flame, hot and pointed. It was full of a wicked sweetness . . .

The voice said: "My brothers . . ."

But no peace proceeded from out these words. Little red snakes hissed through the air. The air was hot—an agony to breathe . . .

Groaning heavily, Freder opened his eyes.

Dark, angry waves were the heads before him. These waves frothed, raged and roared. Here and there a hand shot up into the air. Words sprang

151

up, foam flecks of the surf. But the voice of the girl was like a tongue of fire, drawing, enticing, burning above the heads.

"Which is more pleasant: water or wine?"

" . . . Wine is more pleasant!"

"Who drinks the water?"

" . . . We!"

"Who drinks the wine?"

" . . . The masters! The masters of the machines!"

"Which is more pleasant: meat or dry bread?"

" . . . Meat is more pleasant!"

"Who eats the dry bread?"

" . . . We!"

"Who eats the meat?"

" . . . The masters! The masters of the machines!"

"Which is more pleasant to wear: blue linen or white silk?"

" . . . White silk is more pleasant to wear!"

"Who wears the blue linen?"

" . . . We!"

"Who wears the white silk?"

" . . . The masters! The sons of the masters!"

"Where is it more pleasant to live: upon or under the earth?"

" . . . It is more pleasant to live upon the earth!"

"Who lives under the earth?"

" . . . We!"

"Who lives upon the earth?"

" . . . The masters! The masters of the machines!"

"Where are your wives?"

" . . . In misery!"

"Where are your children?"

" . . . In misery!"

"What do your wives do?"

" . . . They starve!"

"What do your children do?"

" . . . They cry!"

"What do the wives of the masters of the machines do?"

" . . . They feast!"

"What do the children of the masters of the machines do?"

" . . . They play!"

Dark, angry waves were the heads before him. These waves frothed, raged and roared. . . . Words sprang up, foam flecks of the surf. But the voice of the girl was like a tongue of fire, drawing, enticing, burning above the heads. . . .

She said: "Come . . . ! Come . . . ! I will lead you . . . ! I will dance the dance of Death before you . . . ! I will dance the dance of the Murderers before you . . . !"
The multitude moaned. The multitude gasped. The multitude stretched out its hands.
[Brigitte Helm (Futura/Maria)]

153

"Who are the providers?"

" . . . We!"

"Who are the squanderers?"

" . . . The masters! The masters of the machines!"

"What are you?"

" . . . Slaves!"

"No!—what are you?"

" . . . Dogs!"

"No!—what are you?"

" . . . Tell us!—tell us!"

"You are fools! Blockheads! Blockheads! Throughout your morning, your midday, your evening, your night, the machine howls for food, for food, for food—! You are the food! You are the living food!—The machine devours you like fodder and then spews you up again! Why do you batten the machines with your bodies?—Why do you oil the joints of the machines with your brains?— Why do you not let the machines starve, you fools?—Why do you not let them perish, blockheads—? Why do you feed them—! The more you feed them the more they greed for your flesh, for your bones, for your brains. You are ten thousand! You are a hundred thousand! Why do you not throw yourselves—a hundred thousand murdering fists—upon the machines and strike them dead—? *You* are the masters of the machines—*you!* Not the others who walk in their white silk—! Turn the world about—! Stand the world on its head—! Murder the living and the dead—! Take the inheritance from living and dead—! You have waited long enough—! The hour has come!"

A voice shouted from among the multitude:

"Lead us on, Maria—!"

A mighty wave—all the heads broke forward. The blood-red mouth of the girl laughed and flamed. The eyes above it flamed, huge and greenish black. She raised her arms with an unspeakably difficult, burden-raising, sweet, mad gesture. The slim body grew and stretched itself up. The girl's hands touched above her hair—parting. Over her shoulders, her breasts, her hips, her knees, there ran an incessant, a barely perceptible trembling. It was as though the girl were carried higher and higher by this trembling, though she did not move her feet.

She said: "Come . . .! Come . . .! I will lead you . . .! I will dance the dance of Death before you . . .! I will dance the dance of the Murderers before you . . .!"

The multitude moaned. The multitude gasped. The multitude stretched out its hands. The multitude bowed head and neck low, as though its shoulders, its backs, should be a carpet for the girl. The multitude fell on its knees with a groan, one single beast felled with the hatchet. The girl raised her foot and stepped upon the neck of the outstretched beast . . .

A voice shouted out, sobbing with rage and pain: "You are not Maria—!"

The multitude turned around. The multitude saw a man standing in the background of the arch, a man, from whose shoulders the coat had fallen. Under the coat he wore the white silk. The man was more ghastly to see than one who has bled to death. He stretched out his hand and pointed to the girl. He yelled out:

"You are not Maria!! No—!! You are not Maria—!!"

The heads of the multitude stared at the man who was a stranger among them, who wore the white silk . . .

"You are not Maria—!" he yelled. "Maria preaches peace—and not murder—!"

The eyes of the multitude began to glare dangerously.

The girl stood bolt upright in the neck of the multitude. She began to totter. It seemed as though she would fall—fall over on to her white face in which the blood-red mouth—the mouth of deadly sin, flamed like hell-fire.

But she did not fall. She held herself upright. She swayed slightly, but she held herself upright. She stretched out her arm and pointed at Freder, calling in a voice which sounded like glass:

"Look—! Look—! The son of Joh Fredersen—! The son of Joh Fredersen is among you—!"

The multitude shouted. The multitude hurled itself around. The multitude made to lay hold of the son of Joh Fredersen. He did not resist. He stood pressed against the wall. He stared at the girl with a gaze in which belief in eternal damnation was to be read. It seemed as if he were already dead, and as though his lifeless body were falling, ghostlike upon the fists of those who wished to murder him.

A voice roared:

"Dog in white silken skin—!!"

An arm shot up, a knife flashed out . . .

Upon the billowing neck of the multitude stood the girl. It was as if the knife came flying from out her eyes . . .

But, before the knife could plunge into the white silk which covered the heart of the son of Joh Fredersen, a man threw himself as a shield before his breast, and the knife ripped open blue linen. Blue linen was dyed purple-red . . .

"Brothers . . .!" said the man. Dying, yet standing upright, he was covering the son of Joh Fredersen with his whole body. He turned his head a little to catch Freder's glance. He said with a smile which was transfigured in pain;

"Brothers . . ."

Freder recognised him. It was Georgi. It was number eleven thousand eight hundred and eleven which was now going out, and which, going out, was protecting him.

He wanted to push past Georgi. But the dying man stood like one crucified, with out-stretched arms and hands clawing into the edge of the niches which were behind him. He held his eyes, which were like jewels, fixedly set on the multitude which was storming towards him.

"Brothers . . ." he said.

"He said: 'Murderers . . . Brother murderers . . .' " said the dying mouth.

The multitude left him alone and raced on. On the shoulders of the multitude the girl was dancing and singing. She sang with her blood-red mouth of deadly sin!

"We've passed sentence upon the machines!
We have condemned the machines to death!
The machines must die—to hell with them!
Death!—Death!—Death to the machines—!"

Like the rush of a thousand wings the step of the multitude thundered through the narrow passages of the City of the Dead. The girl's voice died away. The steps died away. Georgi loosened his hands and pitched forward.

Freder caught him. He sank upon his knee. Georgi's head fell upon his breast.

"Warn . . . warn . . . the town . . ." said Georgi.

"And are you dying—?" gave Freder as answer. His bewildered eyes ran along the walls in the niches of which slept the thousand-year-old dead. "There is no justice in this world!"

"Uttermost justice . . ." said eleven thousand eight hundred and eleven. "From weakness—sin . . . From sin—atonement . . . Warn . . . the town!—Warn . . .!"

"I'm going to leave you alone—!"

"I beg you to . . . beg you—!"

Freder got up, despair in his eyes. He ran to the passage, in which the multitude had died away.

"Not that way—!" said Georgi. "You won't get through that way any more—!"

"I know no other way . . ."

"I'll take you . . ."

"You are dying, Georgi! The first step is your death—!"

"Won't you warn the town? Do you want to be an accessory?"

"Come!" said Freder.

He raised Georgi up. With his hand pressed to his wound, the man began to run.

"Pick up your lamp and come!" said Georgi. He ran so that Freder could hardly follow him. Into the ten-thousand-year-old dust dripped the blood which welled up from the freshly inflicted wound. He held Freder's arm clasped, pulling him forwards.

"Hurry!" he murmured. "Hurry—there's not time to lose!"

Passages—crossings—passages—steps—passages—a flight of stairs which led steeply upward . . . Georgi fell at the first step. Freder wanted to hold him. He pushed him away.

"Hurry!" he said. He indicated the stairs with his head. "Up—! You can't go wrong now . . . hurry up—!"

"And you, Georgi?—and you—?"

"I—" said Georgi, turning his head to the wall "I am not going to answer any more questions . . ."

Freder let go of Georgi's hand. He began to run up the stairs. Night embraced him—the night of Metropolis—this light-mad, drunken night . . .

Everything was still the same as usual. Nothing indicated the storm which was to break out from inside the earth, under Metropolis, to murder the machine-city.

But it seemed to Joh Fredersen's son as if the stones were giving way under his feet—as though he heard in the air the rushing of wings—the rushing of the wings of strange monsters: beings with women's bodies and snakes' heads—beings, half bull, half angel—devils adorned with crowns—human faced lions . . .

It seemed to him as if he saw death sitting on the New Tower of Babel, in hat and wide cloak, whetting his propped up scythe . . .

He reached the New Tower of Babel. Everything was as usual. The Dawn was fighting the first fight with the Early Morning. He looked for his father. He did not find him. Nobody could say where Joh Fredersen had gone at midnight.

The Brain-pan of the New Tower of Babel was empty.

Freder wiped from his brow the sweat which was running in drops over his temples.

"I must find my father—!" be said. "I must call him—cost what it may!"

Men, with servants eyes looked at him. Men who knew nothing apart from blind obedience—who could not advise, still less help . . .

Joh Fredersen's son stepped into his father's place, at the table where his great father used to sit. He was as white as the silk which he wore as he stretched out his hand and pressed his fingers on the little blue metal place, which no man ever touched apart from Joh Fredersen.

. . . Then the great Metropolis began to roar. Then she raised her voice—her Behemoth-voice. But she was not screaming for food—no, she was roaring:

Danger . . .!

Above the gigantic city, above the slumbering city, the monster-voice roared: *Danger—! Danger—!*

A barely perceptible trembling ran through the New Tower of Babel, as if the earth which bore it were shuddering, frightened by a dream, betwixt sleeping and waking . . .

French movie poster promoting the film METROPOLIS.

CHAPTER XV
METROPOLIS HEART ATTACK

MARIA DID NOT dare to stir. She did not even dare to breathe. She did not close her eyes for quaking fear that, between the lowering and raising of her eyelids, a fresh horror could come upon her and seize her.

She did not know how much time had elapsed since the hands of Joh Fredersen had closed around the throat of Rotwang, the great inventor. The two men had been standing in the shadow; and yet it seemed to the girl as if the outline of both of their forms had remained behind in the darkness, in fiery lines: The bulk of Joh Fredersen, standing there, his hands thrown forward, like two claws;—Rotwang's body, which hung in these claws, and which was dragged away—pulled forth—through the frame of the door, which closed behind them both.

What was happening behind this door? . . .

She heard nothing. She listened with all her senses—but she heard nothing, not the least sound . . .

Minutes passed—endless minutes . . . There was nothing to be heard, neither step nor cry . . .

Was she breathing, wall to wall, with murder?

Ah—that clutch at Rotwang's neck . . . That form, being dragged away, pulled from darkness into deeper darkness . . .

Was he dead? . . . Was he lying behind that door, in a corner, face twisted around to his back, with broken neck and glazed eyes? Was the murderer still standing behind that door?

The room in which she was seemed suddenly to become filled with the sound of a dull thumping. It grew louder and louder, more and more violent. It deafened the ears and yet remained dull . . . Gradually she realised: It was her own heart-beat . . . If somebody had come into the room, she would not have heard him, her heart was beating so.

Stammered words of a childish prayer passed through her brain, confusedly and senselessly . . . "Dear God, I pray Thee, bide with me, take care of me, Amen." . . . She thought of Freder . . . No—don't cry, don't cry—!

"Dear God, I pray Thee . . ."

This silence was no longer bearable! She must see—must be certain.

But she did not dare to take a step. She had got up and could not find courage to return to her old seat. She was as though sewn into a black sack. She held her arms pressed close to her body. Horrors stood at her neck and blew at her.

Now she heard—yes, she heard something. Yet the sound did not come from inside the house; it came from far away. This sound even penetrated the walls of Rotwang's house, which were otherwise penetrated by no sound, wherever it came from.

It was the voice of Metropolis. But she was screaming what she had never screamed before.

She was not screaming for food. She was screaming: *Danger—! Danger—! ! The screaming did not stop. It howled on, incessantly. Who had dared to unchain the voice of the great Metropolis, which otherwise obeyed no one but Joh Fredersen? Was Joh Fredersen no longer in this house? Or was this voice to call him?—this wild roar of: *Danger—! Danger—!* What danger was threatening Metropolis? Fire could not be alarming the city, to make her roar so, as though she had gone mad. No high tide was threatening Metropolis. The elements were subdued and quiet.

Danger—of man? . . . Revolt—?

Was that it—?

Rotwang's words fluttered through her brain . . . In the City of the Dead— what was going on in the City of the Dead? Did the uproar come from the City of the Dead? Was destruction welling up from the depths?

Danger—! Danger—! screamed the voice of the great city.

As though by power of a thrust within, Maria ran, all at once, to the door and tore it open. The room which lay before her, just as that which she had left, received its solitary light—and sparely enough—through the window. At the first glance round, the room seemed to be empty. A strong current of air, coming from an invisible source, streamed, hot and even, through the room, bringing in the roaring of the town with renewed force.

Maria stooped forward. She recognised the room. She had run along these walls in her despairing search for a door. There was a door, which had neither bolt nor lock. Copper-red, in the gloomy wood of the door, glowed the seal of Solomon, the pentagram. There, in the middle, was a square, the trap-door, through which, some time ago, a period which she could not measure, she had entered the house of the great inventor. The bright square of the window fell upon the square of the door.

A trap, thought the girl. She turned her head around . . .

Would the great Metropolis never stop roaring—?

Danger—! Danger—! Danger—! roared the town.

Maria took a step, then stopped again.

There was something lying over there. There was something lying there on the floor. Between her and the trap-door, something was lying on the floor. It was an unrecognisable heap. It was something dark and motionless. It might be human, and was, perhaps, only a sack. But it lay there and must be passed around if one wanted to reach the trap-door.

With a greater display of courage than had ever before in her life been necessary, Maria silently set one foot before the other. The heap on the floor did not move. She stood, bending far forward, making her eyes reconnoiter, deafened by her own heart-beat and the roar of the uproar-proclaiming city.

Now she saw clearly; What was lying there was a man. The man lay on his face, legs drawn tightly to his body, as though he had gathered them to him to push himself up and had then not found any more strength to do it. One hand lay thrown over his neck, and its crooked fingers spoke more eloquently than the most eloquent of mouths of a wild self-defence.

But the other hand of the heap of humanity lay stretched far away from it, on the square of the trapdoor, as though wishing, in itself, to be a bolt to the door. The hand was not of flesh and bone. The hand was of metal, the hand was the master-piece of Rotwang, the great inventor.

Maria threw a glance at the door, on which the seal of Solomon glowed. She ran up to it, although she knew it to be pointless to implore this inexorable door for liberty. She felt, under her feet, distant, quite dull, strong and impelling, a shake, as of distant thunder.

The voice of the great Metropolis roared: *Danger—!*

Maria clasped her hands and raised them to her mouth. She ran up to the trap-door. She knelt down. She looked at the heap of humanity which lay at the edge of the trapdoor. She knelt down. She looked at the heap of humanity which lay at the edge of the trap-door, the metal hand of which seemed obstinately to be defending the trap-door. The fingers of the other hand, thrown over the man's neck, were turned towards her, poised high, like a beast before the spring.

And the trembling shake again—and now much mightier—

Maria seized the iron ring of the trap-door. She pushed it up. She wanted to pull up the door. But the hand—the hand which lay upon it—held the door clutched fast.

Maria heard the chattering of her teeth. She pushed herself across on her knees towards the motionless heap of humanity. With infinite care, she grasped the hand which lay, as a steel bolt, across the trap-door. She felt the coldness of death proceeding from this hand. She pressed her teeth into her white lips. As she pushed back the hand with all her strength, the heap of humanity rolled over on its side, and the grey face appeared, staring upwards . . .

Maria tore open the trap-door. She swung herself down, into the black square. She did not leave herself time to close the door. Perhaps it was that she had not the courage, once more to emerge from the depths she had gained, to see what lay up there, at the edge of the trap-door. She felt the steps under her feet, and felt, right and left, the damp walls. She ran through the darkness, thinking only half-consciously: If you lose your way in the City of the Dead . . .

The red shoes of the magician occurred to her . . .

She forced herself to stand still, forced herself to listen . . .

What was that strange sound which seemed to be coming from the passages round about? . . . It sounded like yawning—it sounded as though the stone were yawning. There was a trickling . . . above her head a light grating sound grew audible, as though joint upon joint were loosening itself. Then all was still for a while. But not for long. Then the grating sound began again . . .

The stone was living. Yes—the stone was living . . . The stones of the City of the Dead were coming to life.

The shock of extreme violence shook the earth on which Maria was standing. Rumbling of falling stones, trickling, silence.

Maria was pitched against the stone wall. But the wall moved behind her. Maria shrieked. She threw up her arms and raced onwards. She stumbled over stones which lay across her way, but she did not fall. She did not know what was happening but the rustle of mystery which the storm drives along before it—the proclamation of a great evil, hung in the air above her, driving her forward.

There—a light in front of her! She ran towards it. An arched vault . . . Great burning candles . . . Yes, she knew the place. She had often stood here and spoken to those whom she called "brothers." . . . Who, but she, had the right to light these candles? For whom had they burnt today? The flames blew sideways in a violent draught of air; the wax dropped.

Maria seized a candle and ran on with it. She came to the background of the arched vault. A coat lay on the floor. None of her brothers wore such a coat over his blue linen uniform. She bent down. She saw, in the thousand-year-old dust of the arched vault, a trail of dark drops. She stretched out her hand and touched one of the drops. The tip of her finger was dyed red. She straightened herself up and closed her eyes. She staggered a little and a smile passed over her face as though she hoped she were dreaming.

"Dear God, I pray Thee, bide with me, take care of me . . . Amen . . ."

She leant her head against the stone wall. The wall quaked. Maria looked right up. In the dark, black vaulting of the stone roof above her, there gaped a winding cleft.

What did that mean . . .?

What was there—above her?

Up there were the mole-tunnels of the underground railway. What was happening up there—? It sounded as though three thousand giants were playing nine-pins with iron mountains, throwing them, one against the other, amid yells . . .

The cleft gaped wider. The air was filled with dust. But it was not dust. It was ground stone.

The structure of the City of the Dead quaked right down to the centre of the earth. It was as if a mighty fist had suddenly opened a sluice—but, instead of water, a maelstrom of stones hurtled from the dammed-up bed—blocks, mortar, crumbles, stone-splinters, ruins poured down from the arch—a curtain of stones—a hail of stones. And above the falling and the smashing was the power of a thunder which was roaring, and roaring long and resonantly, through the destruction.

A current of air, an irresistible whirl, swept the girl aside like a blade of straw. The skeletons rose up from the niches: bones rose up erect and skulls rolled! Doomsday seemed to be breaking over the thousand-year-old City of the Dead.

But above the great Metropolis the monster-voice was still howling and howling.

Red lay the morning above the stone ocean of the city. The red morning saw, amidst the stone ocean of the city, rolling along, a broad, an endless stream.

The stream was twelve files deep. They walked in even step. Men, men,

men, all in the same uniform; from throat to ankle in the dark blue linen, bare feet in the same hard shoes, hair tightly pressed down by the same black caps. And they all had the same faces. Wild faces, with eyes like fire-brands. And they all sang the same song—song without melody, but an oath—a storm vow:

"We've passed sentence upon the machines!
We have condemned the machines to death.
The machines must die, to hell with them!
Death!—Death!—Death to the machines—!"

The girl danced along before the streaming, bawling multitude.

She led the multitude on. She led the tramping multitude forward against the heart of the Machine city of Metropolis.

She said: "Come . . .! Come . . .! Come . . .! I will lead you . . .! I will dance the dance of Death before you . . .I will dance the dance of the murderers before you . . .!"

"Destroy—destroy—destroy—!" yelled the crowd.

They acted without plan, and yet following a law. Destruction was the name of the law; they obeyed it.

The multitude divided. A broad stream poured itself, frothing, down into the tunnel of the underground railway. The trains were standing ready on all the tracks. Searchlights wedged themselves into the darkness which crouched in the shafts, above the rails.

The multitude yelled. Here was a plaything for giants! Were they not as strong as three thousand giants? They dragged the drivers from the drivers' places. They released the trains and let them run—one after the other—for-ward—forwards!

The rails rumbled. The thundering carriage snakes, glitteringly lighted, hurled along by their emptiness, dashed into the brownish darkness. Two, three, four of the drivers fought like men possessed. But the mob sucked them up. "Will you shut your mouths, you dogs—? We are the masters! We want to play! We want to play like giants!"

They howled the song—the song of their deadly hatred:

"We've passed sentence upon the machines!
We have condemned the machines to death!"

They counted the seconds:

"Fifty-nine—sixty—sixty-one—sixty-two——now—!——

Somewhere in the depths of the tunnel, a crash, as if the globe were splitting . . .

"Once—and once again . . .

The mob howled:

"The machines must die—to hell with them!
    Death!—Death!—Death to the machines!"

Then—! What happened then?—Then!!—From one of the tunnels there broke forth a train, like a steed of fire, with sparkling lights, driverless, at a tearing speed—galloping death.

From whence did this hell-horse come?—Where were the giants, who were thus giving answer to the giants' game of the mob? The train vanished, amid shrieks— and, some seconds later, came the tearing crash from the depths of the pit. And the second train was crashing onwards, sent off by unknown hands.

The stones shook loose under the feet of the mob. Smoke gushed up from the pit. Suddenly the lights went out. Only the clocks, the whitish-shimmering clocks, hung, as patches of light, in a darkness which was filled with long, dim, drifting clouds.

The mob pressed towards the stairs and up them. Behind them, unchained demons, pulling their reeling carriages along behind them, the engines, now released, hurled themselves on, to fall upon each other and break into flames . . .

Metropolis had a brain.

Metropolis had a heart.

The heart of the machine city of Metropolis dwelt in a white, cathedral-like building. The heart of the machine city of Metropolis was guarded by one single man.

The man's name was Grot, and he loved his machine.

The machine was a universe to itself. Above the deep mysteries of its delicate joints, like the sun's disc, like the halo of a divine being, stood the silver spinning wheel, the spokes of which appeared, in the whirl of revolution, as a single gleaming disc. This disc filled out the back wall of the building, with its entire breadth and height.

No machine in all Metropolis which did not receive its power from this heart.

METROPOLIS

One single lever controlled this marvel of steel. All the treasures of the world heaped up before him would not, for Grot, have outweighed this, his machine.

When, at the grey hour of dawn, Grot heard the voice of the great Metropolis roaring, he glanced at the clock on the brow of the wall where was the door, and thought: "That's against all nature and regularity . . ."

When, at the red hour of sunrise, Grot saw the stream of the multitude rolling along, twelve files deep, led by a girl—dancing to the rhythm of the yelling mob, Grot set the lever of the machine to "Safety," carefully closed the door of the building and waited.

The mob thundered against his door.

"Oh—knock away!" thought Grot. "That door can stand a good bit . . ."

He looked at the machine. The wheel was spinning slowly. The beautiful spokes were playing, plainly to be seen. Grot nodded to his beautiful machine.

"They will not trouble us long," thought he. He waited for a signal from the New Tower of Babel. For a word from Joh Fredersen. The word did not come.

"He knows," thought Grot, "that he can rely on me . . ."

The door quaked like a giant drum. The mob hurled itself, a living battering ram, against it.

"There are rather a lot of them, it seems to me," thought Grot. He looked at the door, it trembled, but it held. And it looked as though it would still hold for a long time.

Grot nodded to himself in deep contentment. He would have loved to light his pipe, if only smoking had not been forbidden here. He heard the yelling of the mob, and rebound upon rebound against the singing door with a feeling of smog fierceness. He loved the door. It was his ally. He turned around and looked at his machine. He nodded at it affectionately: "We two—eh? . . . What do you say to that boozy lot of fatheads, machine?"

The storm before the door wound itself up into a typhoon. It was the hackling fury born of long resistance.

"Open the door,—!!" hackled the fury. "Open the door, you damned scoundrel—!!"

"Wouldn't that just suit you!" thought Grot. How well the door was holding! His gallant door!

What were those drunken apes out there singing about?

"We've passed sentence upon the machines!

166

We have condemned the machines to death!"

Ho ho ho—! He could sing too—could Grot! He could sing drunken songs, just fine! He kicked with both heels against the pedestal of the machine, upon which he was sitting. He pushed the black cap down lower in his neck. With his red fists resting upon his knees, opening wide his mouth, he sang with his whole throat, while his little, wild eyes were fixed on the door:

"Come on, you boozy lot, if you dare!
Come if you want a good hiding, you lousy apes!
Your mother forgot
To pull your pants tight
When you were little, you guttersnipes!
You're not even fit for pigs' swill!
You fell from the rubbish cart,
When it took the big curve!
And now you stand before the door,
Before my gallant door, and bawl: Open the door!
Open the door!
Let the devil open it for you,
You hen's bugs."

The pedestal of the machine boomed under the drumming rhythm of his boot-heels . . .

But suddenly they both stopped: drumming and singing. An exceedingly powerful, exceedingly white light flared up three times, under the dome of the building. A sound-signal, as gentle and as penetrating as the gong-beat of a temple bell, became audible, overpowering every sound.

"Yes!" said Grot, the guard of the Heart-machine.

He sprang to his feet. He raised his broad face, which shone with the joyful eagerness of obedience. "Yes, here I am!"

A voice said, slowly and clearly:

"Open the door, and give up the machine!"

Grot stood motionless. Fists like hammers hung down from his arms. He gulped. But he said nothing.

"Repeat instructions," said the quiet voice.

The guard of the heart machine swung his head violently this way and that, like a weighty bundle.

"I . . . I didn't understand," he said, gaspingly. The quiet voice spoke in a

167

A voice said, slowly and clearly:
"Open the door, and give up the machine!"
Grot stood motionless. Fists like hammers hung down from his arms. He gulped. But he said nothing.
"Repeat instructions," said the quiet voice.
[Alfred Abel (Joh Fredersen) and Heinrich George (Grot)]

more forceful tone: "Open the door and give up the machine!"

The man still said nothing, gazing stupidly upward.

"Repeat instructions," said the quiet voice.

The guard of the Heart-machine drew in a great draught of air.

"Who is speaking there—?" he asked. "What lousy swine is speaking there—?"

"Open the door, Grot . . ."

"The devil I will—!"

" . . . and give up the machine!"

The machine—?" said Grot, *"the—my machine?"*

"Yes," said the quiet voice.

The guard of the Heart-machine began to shake. His was a quite blue face, in which the eyes stood like whitish balls. The mob, which was throwing itself, as a buffer, against the ringing door yelled, hoarse with yelling:

"The machines must die—to Hell with them!
 Death! Death! Death to the machines!"

"Who is speaking there?" asked the man, so loudly that his words were a scream.

"Joh Fredersen is speaking."

"I want the pass-word."

"The pass-word is one thousand and three. The machine is running on half power. You have set the lever to 'Safety . . .' "

The guard of the Heart-machine stood like a log. Then the log turned itself clumsily around, staggered to the door, and tore at the bolts.

The mob heard it. It yelled triumph. The door flew open. The mob swept aside the man who was standing on its threshold. The mob hurled itself towards the machine. The mob made to lay hands upon the machine. A dancing girl was leading the mob on.

"Look—!" she shouted. "Look—! The beating heart of Metropolis! What shall be done to the heart of Metropolis—?

We've passed sentence upon the machines!

We have condemned the machines to death!

The machines must die—to hell with them!"

But the mob did not catch up the girl's song. The mob stared over, at the machine—at the beating heart of the great machine city, which was called Metropolis, and which they had fed. They pressed up slowly, as a single body, before the machine, which gleamed like silver. In the face of the mob stood hatred. In the face of the mob stood superstitious fear. Desire for the last destruction stood in the face of the mob.

But before it could take expression Grot, the guard, threw himself before his machine. There was no filthy word which he did not raise to chuck into the face of the mob. The dirtiest term of revilement was not dirty enough for him to apply to the mob. The mob turned red eyes upon him. The mob glared at him. The mob saw: The man there, in front of them, was abusing them in the name of the machine. For them, the man and the machine melted into one. Man and machine deserved the same hatred. They pushed forward against man and machine. They seized the man and meant the machine. They roared him down. They stamped him underfoot. They dragged him hither and thither and out of the door. They forgot the machine, for they had the man—had the guard of the heart-beat of all the machines—thinking that, in tearing the man away from the Heart-machine, they were tearing the heart from the breast of the great machine city.

What should be done to the heart of Metropolis?

It should be trodden underfoot by the mob.

"Death!" yelled the victorious mob. "Death to the machines!" yelled the victorious mob.

They did not see that they no longer had a leader. They did not see that the girl was missing from the procession. The girl was standing before the Heart-machine of the city. Her smile was cool and silver. She stretched out her hand, which was more delicate than glass, she seized the weighty lever, which was set to "Safety." She pressed the lever round, still smiling, then walked out, with light, mad, step.

Behind her the machine began to race. Above the deep mysteries of its delicate joints, like the sun's disc—like the halo of a divine being—stood the silver racing wheel, the spokes of which appeared, in the whirl of revolution, as a single circling disc.

The heart of Metropolis, Joh Fredersen's city, began to run up a temperature, seized by a deadly illness . . .

Wild faces, with eyes like fire-brands. And they all sang the same song—song without melody, but an oath—a storm vow:

"We've passed sentence upon the machines!
We have condemned the machines to death.
The machines must die, to hell with them!
Death!—Death!—Death to the machines—!"

171

UFA promotional movie poster for METROPOLIS, color lithograph, Anonymous.

CHAPTER XVI

THE DAY OF JUDGMENT

"FATHER—!!"

Joh Fredersen's son knew quite well that his father could not hear him, for he, the son, was standing in the lowest part of the pedestal of the New Tower of Babel, whither the twitching pulse of the street had thrown him, and his father was high, high, above the boiling of the city, the untouched brain, in the cool brain-pan. But yet he shouted for him and had to shout, and his shout, itself, was a cry for help and an accusation.

The round structure of the New Tower of Babel was throwing up people who pushed out into the street, laughing as if insane. They were sucked up by the pulp of those in the street. The New Tower of Babel was deserted. Those who had occupied its rooms and passages—those who had been poured by the buckets of the Pater-noster works down to the depths, up to the heights—who had taken up their positions on the stairs—who had received instructions and passed them on—who had suffocated amidst figures—who had listened in to the whispers of the world—all, all streamed out from the New Tower of Babel as blood streams out from a cut vein, until it stood there, horribly empty—bled white.

But the machines went on living.

Yes, they seemed to be coming to life for the first time.

Freder, who stood—a crumb of humanity—alone, in the hugeness of the round structure, heard the soft, deep, rushing howl, like the breath of the New Tower of Babel, growing louder and louder, clearer and clearer, and he saw, on turning round, that the empty cells of the Pater-noster were speeding more and more rapidly, more and more hurriedly, upwards and downwards. Yes,

173

now it was as if these cells, these empty cells, were dancing upwards and downwards and the howling which trans-sected the New Tower of Babel seemed to proceed from out their empty jaws.

"Father—!!" shouted Freder. And the whole round structure roared with him, with all its lungs.

Freder ran, but not to the heights of the Tower. He ran to the depths, driven by horror and curiosity—down into the hell—guided by luminous pillars—to the abode of the Pater-noster machine, which was like Ganesha, the god with the elephant's head.

The luminous pillars by which he ran did not shine as usual with their white, icy light. They blinked, they flashed lightning, they flickered. They burnt with an evil, green light. The stones, over which he ran, swayed like water. The nearer he came to the machine-room, the more bellowing did the voice of the tower become. The walls were baking. The air was colourless fire. If the door had not burst open by itself—no human hand could have opened it, for it was like a glowing curtain of liquid steel.

Freder held his arm flung before his forehead, as if wishing to protect his brain from bursting. His eyes sought the machine—the machine in front of which he had once stood. It was crouching in the centre of the howling room. It shone with oil. It had gleaming limbs. Under the crouching body and the head which was sunken on its chest, crooked legs rested, gnome-like, upon the platform. The trunk and legs were motionless. But the short arms pushed and pushed and pushed, alternately forwards, backwards, forwards.

And the machine was quite abandoned. Nobody was watching it. Nobody's hand held the lever. Nobody's gaze was fixed on the clock, the hands of which chased through the grades as though gone mad.

"Father—!!" shouted Freder, about to hurl himself forward. But at the same moment it was as if the hunched up body of the wild machine, which was like Ganesha, raised itself up to a furious height, as though its legs stretched themselves upon stumpy feet, to make a murderous leap, as though its arms no longer stretched themselves to push—no, to seize, to seize to crush—as though the howling voice of the New Tower of Babel broke from the lungs of the Pater-noster machine alone, howling:

"Murder—!"

And howling unceasingly:

"Murder—!"

The flame curtain of the door flew sideways, whistling. The monster-machine rolled itself down from the platform with pushing arms. The whole structure of the New Tower of Babel quivered. The walls shook. The ceiling groaned.

Freder turned around. He threw his arms about his neck and ran. He saw the luminous pillars stabbing at him. He heard a rattling gasp at his back and felt the marrow dry up, and ran and ran. He ran towards doors, pushed them open, slammed them to behind him and raced onwards.

"Father—!!" he shouted—and with a feeling as if his brain were overturning: "Our Father, Which art in heaven—"

Upstairs. Where did these stairs lead to—? Doors thundered open, rebounding against walls.

Aaah—! The temples of the machine-rooms? Deities, the machines—the shining Lords—the god-machines of Metropolis! All the great gods were living in white temples! Baal and Moloch and Huitzilopochtli and Durgha! Some frightfully companionable, some terribly solitary. There—Juggernaut's divine car! There—the Towers of Silence! There—Mahomet's curved sword! There—the crosses of Golgotha!

And not a soul, not a soul in the white rooms. The machines, these god-machines, left terribly alone. And they were all living—yes they were really living—an enhanced, an enflamed life.

For Metropolis had a brain.

Metropolis had a heart.

The heart of the machine-city of Metropolis dwelt in a white, cathedral-like building. The heart of the machine-city of Metropolis was, until this day and this hour, guarded by one single man. The heart of the machine-city of Metropolis was a machine and a universe to itself. Above the deep mysteries of its delicate joints, like the sun's disc—like the halo of a divine being—stood the silver-spinning wheel, the spokes of which appeared in the whirl of revolution, as a single, gleaming, disc.

No machine in all Metropolis which did not receive its power from this heart.

One single lever controlled this marvel of steel.

With the lever set to "Safety" all the machines would play with their curbed power, like tame animals. The shimmering spokes of the sun-wheel would circle, clearly to be distinguished, above the Heart-machine.

With the lever set to "6"—and it was generally set there—then work would spell slavery. The machines would roar. The powerful wheel of the Heart-machine would hang, an apparently motionless mirror of brightest silver, above it. And the mighty thunder of the machines, produced by the heart-beat of this one, would arch itself, a second heaven, above Metropolis, Joh Fredersen's city.

But never, as yet, since the construction of Metropolis, had the lever been set to "12."

Now it was set to "12." Now the lever was set to "12." A girl's hand, more delicate than glass, had pressed around the weighty lever, which was set to "Safety," until it touched "12." The heart of Metropolis, Joh Fredersen's great city had begun to run up a temperature, seized by a deadly illness, chasing the red waves of its fever along to all the machines which were fed by its pulse.

No machine in all Metropolis which did not receive its power from this heart.

Then all the god-machines were taken with the fever . . .

From the Towers of Silence there broke forth the vapour of decomposition. Blue flames hovered in the space above them. And the towers, the huge towers, which used otherwise to turn about but once in the course of the day, tottered around on their pedestals in a. drunken, spinning dance, full to bursting point.

Mahomet's curved sword was as circular lightning in the air. It met with no resistance, it cut and cut. It grew angry because it had nothing to cut. The power which, squandered too uselessly, was still increasing, now gathered itself together and, hissing, sent out snakes, green, hissing snakes, in all directions.

From the projecting arms of the crosses of Golgotha there swept long, white, crackling springs of sparks.

Swaying under impacts which had shaken the earth itself, the unslain, the man-crushing car of juggernaut began to glide, began to roll—checked itself, hanging crookedly on the platform—trembled like a ship, perishing on the rocks, lashed by the breakers—and shook itself free, amidst groans.

Then, from their glittering thrones, Baal and Moloch, Huitzilopochtli and Durgha arose. All the god-machines got up, stretching their limbs in a fearful liberty. Huitzilopochtli shrieked for the jewel-sacrifice. Durgha moved eight murderous arms, crackling the while. Hungry fires smouldered up from the bellies of Baal and Moloch, licking out of their jaws. And, roaring like a herd of a thousand buffaloes, at being cheated of a purpose, Asa Thor swung the infallible hammer.

A lost grain of dust among the soles of the gods, Freder reeled his way through the white rooms, the roaring temples.

"Father—!!" he shouted.

And he heard the voice of his father:

"Yes!—Here I am!—What do you want?—Come here to me!"

"Where are you?"

"Here—!"

"But I can't see you—!"

"You must look higher!"

Freder's gaze flitted through the room. He saw his father standing on a platform, between the out-stretched arms of the crosses of Golgotha from the ends of which long, white, crackling sprigs of sparks blazed. In the hellish fires his father's face was as a mask of unmistakable coldness. His eyes were blue-gleaming steel. Amidst the great, raving machine-gods, he was a greater god, and lord of all.

Freder ran over to him, but he could not get up to him. He clung to the foot of the flaming cross. Wild impacts crashed through the New Tower of Babel.

"Father—!" shrieked Freder. "Your city is going to ruin—!"

Joh Fredersen did not answer. The sweeping sprigs of flame seemed to be breaking from his temples.

"Father—! Don't you understand—? Your city is going to ruin!—Your machines have come to life!—They are dashing the town to pieces.—They are tearing Metropolis to tatters!—Do you hear—? Explosion after explosion—! I have seen a street in which the houses were dancing upon their shattered foundations—just like little children dancing upon the stomach of a laughing giant . . . A lava-stream of glowing copper poured itself out from the split-open tower of your boiler-factory, and a naked man was running before it, a man whose hair was charred and who was roaring: 'The end of the world has come—!' But then he stumbled and the copper stream overtook him . . . Where the Jethro works stood, there is a hole in the earth which is filling up with water. Iron bridges are hanging in shreds between towers which have lost their entrails, cranes are dangling on gallows like men hanged. And the people, incapable of flight as of resistance, are wandering about among houses and streets, both of which seemed doomed . . .

He clasped his hands about the stem of the cross and threw his head back into his neck, to see his father quite clearly, quite openly in the face.

"I cannot believe, father, that there is anything mightier than you! I have cursed your overwhelming might—your overwhelming might which has filled me with horror, from the bottom of my heart. Now I run to you and ask you on my knees: Why do you allow Death to lay hands on the city which is yours—?"

"Because Death has come upon the city by my will."

"By your will—?"

"Yes."

"The city is to perish—?"

"Don't you know why, Freder?"

There was no answer.

"The city is to go to ruin that you may built it up again . . ."

"—I—?"

"You."

"Then you are laying the murder of the city on my shoulders?"

"The murder of the city reposes on the shoulders of those alone who trampled Grot, the guard of the heart-machine, to death."

"Did that also take place by your will, father?"

"Yes!"

"Then you forced them to commit the crime—?"

"For your sake, Freder; that you could redeem them . . ."

"And what about those, father, who must die with your dying city, before I can redeem them!"

"Concern yourself about the living, Freder—not about the dead."

"And if the living come to kill you—?"

"That will not happen, Freder. That will not happen. The way to me, among the raving god-machines, as you called them, could only be found by one. And he found it. That was my son."

Freder dropped his head into his hands. He rocked it to and from as if in pain. He moaned softly. He was about to speak; but before he could speak a sound ripped the air, which sounded as though the earth were bursting to pieces. For a moment, everything in the white room seemed to hover in space, a foot above the ground—even Moloch and Baal and Huitzilopochtli and Durgha, even the hammer of Asa Thor and the Towers of Silence. The crosses of Golgotha, from the ends of the beams of which long, white crackling sprigs of sparks were blazing, fell together and then straightened up again. Then everything crashed back into its place with furious emphasis. Then all the lights went out. And from the depths and distance the city howled.

"Father—!" shouted Freder.

"Yes.—Here I am.—What do you want?"

" . . . I want you to put an end to this nightmare—!"

"Now?" Now—!"

"But I don't want any more people to suffer—! You must help them—you must save them, father—!"

"You must save them. Now—immediately!"

"Now? No!"

"Then," said Freder, pushing his fists out far before him, as if pushing something away from him, "then I must seek out the man who can help me—even if he is your enemy and mine."

"Do you mean Rotwang?"

No answer. Joh Fredersen continued:

"Rotwang cannot help you."

"Why not—"

"He is dead."

Silence. Then, tentatively, a strangled voice which asked: "Dead . . .?"

"Yes."

"How did he come . . . so suddenly . . . to die?"

"He died, chiefly, Freder, because he dared to stretch out his hands toward the girl whom you love."

Trembling fingers fumbled up the stem of the cross.

"Maria, father—Maria . . .?"

"So he called her."

"Maria—was with him?—In his house—?"

"Yes, Freder."

"Ah—I see.—I see—! . . . And now—!"

"I do not know."

Silence.

"Freder?"

No answer came.

"Freder—?"

But a shadow ran past the windows of the white machine-cathedral. It ran, ducked down, hands thrown behind its neck, as if it feared that Durgha's arms could snatch at it, or that Asa Thor could hurl his hammer, which never failed, at it from behind, in order, at Joh Fredersen's command, to prevent its flight.

It did not penetrate into the consciousness of the fugitive that all the machines were standing still because the heart, the unguarded heart of Metropolis, under the fiery lash of the "12," had raced itself to Death.

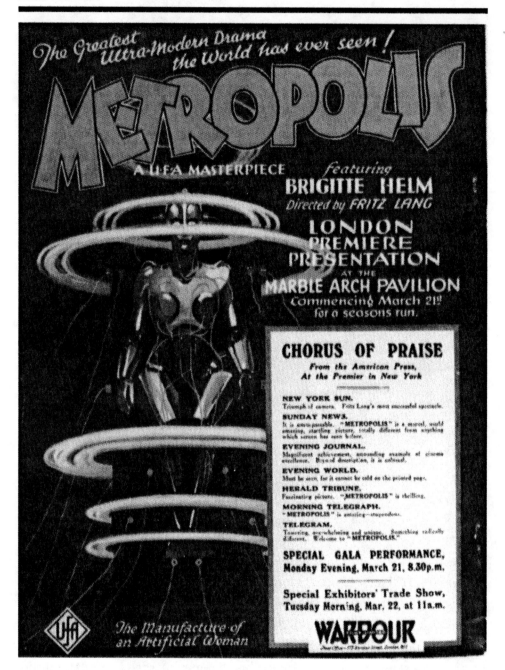

CHAPTER XVII
DOOMSDAY HAS COME!

MARIA FELT SOMETHING licking at her feet, like the tongue of a great, gentle dog. She bent down to fumble for the animal's head, and felt that it was water into which she was groping.

From where did the water come? It came silently. It did not splash. Neither did it throw up waves. It just rose—unhurriedly, yet persistently. It was not colder than the air round about. It lapped about Maria's ankles.

She snatched her feet back. She sat, crouched down, trembling, listening for the water which could not be heard. From where did it come?

It was said that a river wound its way deep under the city. Joh Fredersen had walled up its course when he built the subterranean city, the wonder of the world, for the workmen of Metropolis. It was also said that the stream fed a mighty water-basin and that there were pump-works there, which were powerful enough, inside of less than ten hours either completely to empty or to fill the water basin—in which there was room for a medium-sized city. One thing was certain—that, in the subterranean, workmen's city, the throbbing of these pumps was constantly to be heard, as a soft, incessant pulse-beat, if one laid one's head against a wall—and that, if this pulse-beat should ever become silent, no other interpretation would be conceivable than that the pumps had stopped, and that then the river was rising.

But they had never—never stopped.

And now—? From where was the silent water coming?—Was it still rising—?

She bent forward. She did not have to stretch her hand down very low to touch the cool brow of the water.

Now she felt, too, that it was flowing. It was making its way with great certainty of aim in one direction. It was making its way towards the subterranean city—

Old books tell of saintly women, whose smile at the moment of preparing themselves to gain the martyr's crown, was of such sweetness that the torturers fell at their feet and hardened heathens praised the name of God.

But Maria's smile was, perhaps, of a still sweeter kind. For, when setting about her race with the silent water, she thought, not of the crown of eternal bliss, but only of death and of the man she loved—

Yes, now the water seemed horribly cool, as her slender feet dipped down into it, and it murmured as she ran along through it. It soaked itself into the hem of her dress, clinging tight and making progress more and more difficult. But that was not the worst. The worst was that the water also began to have a voice.

The water quoth: "Do you know, beautiful Maria, that I am fleeter than the fleetest foot? I am stroking your sweet ankles. I shall soon clutch at your knees. No one has ever embraced your tender hips. But I shall do so, and before your steps number a thousand more. And I do not know, beautiful Maria, if you will reach your destination before you can refuse me your breast . . .

"Beautiful Maria, Doomsday has come! It is bringing the thousand-year-old dead to life. Know, that I have flooded them out of their niches and that the dead are floating along behind you! Do not look round, Maria, do not look round! For two skeletons are quarrelling about the skull which floats between them—swirling around and grinning. And a third, to whom the skull really belongs, is rearing up within me and falling upon them both . . .

"Beautiful Maria, how sweet are your hips . . . Is the man whom you love never to find that out? Beautiful Maria, listen to what I say to you: only a little to one side of this way, a flight of stairs leads steeply upward, leading to freedom . . . Your knees are trembling . . . how sweet that is! Do you think to overcome your weakness by clasping your hands? You call upon God, but believe me: God does not hear you! Since I came upon the earth as the great flood, to destroy all in existence but Noah's ark, God has been deaf to the scream of His creatures. Or did you think I had forgotten how the mothers screamed then? Have you more responsibility on your conscience than God on His? Turn back, beautiful Maria, turn back!

"Now you are making me angry, Maria—now I shall kill you! Why are you letting those hot, salty drops fall down into me? I am clasping you around your breast, but it no longer stirs me. I want your throat and your gasping mouth! I want your hair and your weeping eyes!

"Do you believe you have escaped me? No, beautiful Maria! No—now I shall fetch you with a thousand others—with all the thousand which you wanted to save . . ."

She dragged her dripping body up from the water. She crawled upwards, over stone slabs; she found the door. She pushed it open and slammed it behind her, peering to see if the water were already lapping over the threshold.

Not yet . . . not yet. But how much longer?

She could not see a soul as far as her eye could reach. The streets, the squares, lay as if dead—bathed in the whiteness of the moon-light. But she was mistaken—or was the light growing weaker and yellower from second to second?

An impact, which threw her against the nearest wall, ran through the earth. The iron door through which she had come flew from its bolts and gaped open. Black and silent, the water slipped over the threshold.

Maria collected herself. She screamed with her whole lungs:

"The water's coming in—!"

She ran across the square. She called for the guard, which, being on constant duty, had to give the alarm signal in danger of any kind.

The guard was not there.

A wild upheaval of the earth dragged the girl's feet from under her body and hurled her to the ground. She raised herself to her knees and stretched up her hands in order, herself, to set the siren howling. But the sound which broke from the metal throat was only a whimper, like the whimpering of a dog, and the light grew more and more pale and yellow.

Like a dark, crawling beast, in no hurry, the water wound its way across the smooth street.

But the water did not stand alone in the street. Suddenly, in the midst of a puzzling and very frightening solitude, a little half-naked child was standing there: her eyes, which were still being protected, by some dream, from the all too real, were staring at the beast, at the dark, crawling beast, which was licking at its bare little feet.

With a scream, in which distress and deliverance were equally mingled, Maria flew to the child and picked it up in her arms.

"Is there nobody here but you, child?" she asked, with a sudden sob. "Where is your father?"

"Gone . . ."

"Where is your mother?"

"Gone . . ."

Maria could understand nothing. Since her flight from Rotwang's house, she had been hurled from horror to horror, without grasping a single thing. She still took the grating of the earth, the jerking impacts, the roar of the awful, tearing thunder the water which gushed up from the shattered depths, to be the effects of the unchained elements. Yet she could not believe that there existed mothers who would not throw themselves as a barrier before their children when the earth opened her womb to bring forth horror into the world.

Only—the water which crawled up nearer and nearer, the impacts which racked the earth, the light which became paler and paler, gave her no time to think. With the child in her arms, she ran from house to house, calling to the others, which had hidden themselves.

Then they came, stumbling and crying, coming in troops, ghastly spectres, like children of stone, passionlessly begotten and grudgingly born. They were like little corpses in mean little shrouds, aroused to wakefulness on Doomsday by the voice of the angel, rising from out rent-open graves. They clustered themselves around Maria, screaming because the water, the cool water, was licking at their feet.

Maria shouted—hardly able to shout any more. There was in her voice the sharp cry of the mother-bird which sees winged Death above its brood. She waded about among the child-bodies, ten at her hands, at her dress, the others following closely, pushed along, torn along, with the stream. Soon the street was a wave of children's heads above which the pale, raised-up hands flitted like sea-gulls. And Maria's cry was drowned by the wailing of the children and by the laughter of the pursuing water.

The light in the Neon-lamps became reddish, flickering rhythmically and throwing ghostly shadows. The street sloped. There was the mustering-ground. But the huge elevators hung dead on their cables. Ropes, twisted from ropes—metal ropes, thick as a man's thigh, hung in the air, torn asunder. Blackish oil was welling in a leisurely channel from an exploded pipe. And over everything lay a dry vapour as if from heated iron and glowing stones.

Deep in the darkness of distant alleys the gloom took on a brownish hue. A fire was smouldering there . . .

"Go up—!" whispered Maria's dry lips. But she was not able to say the words. Winding stairs led upwards. The staircase was narrow—nobody used the stair-case which ran by the certain, infallible elevators. Maria crowded the children up the steps. But, up there, there reigned a darkness of impenetrable gloom and density. None of the children ventured to ascend alone.

Maria scrambled up. She counted the steps. Like the rushing of a thousand wings came the sound of the children's feet behind her, in the narrow spiral. She did not know how long she had been climbing up. Innumerable hands were clutching her damp dress. She dragged her burdens upward, praying, moaning the while—praying only for strength for another hour.

"Don't cry, little brothers!" she stammered. "My little sisters, please don't cry."

Children were screaming, down in the depths—and the hundred windings of the stair-way gave echo's trumpet to each cry:

"Mother—! Mother—!"

And once more:

"The water's coming—!"

Stop and lie down, halfway up the stairs—? No!

"Little sisters! Little brothers—do come along!"

Higher—winding ever and always higher upward; then, at last, a wide landing. Greyish light from above. A walled-in room; not yet the upper world, but its forecourt. A short, straight flight of stairs upon which lay a shaft of light. The opening, a trap-door, which seemed to be pressed inwards. Between the door and the square of the wall, a cleft, as narrow as a cat's body.

Maria saw that. She did not know what it meant. She had the uncertain feeling of something not being as it ought to be. But she did not want to think about it. With an almost violent movement she tore her hands, her gown, free from the children's tugging fingers, and dashed, hurled forward far more by her desperate will than by her benumbed feet, through the empty room and up the steep stairway,

She stretched out her hands and tried to raise the pressed-in door. It did not budge. Once more. No result. Head, arms, shoulders pushing, hips and knees pressing, as if to burst their sinews. No result. The door did not yield by a hair's breadth. If a child had tried to push the cathedral from its place it could not have acted more foolishly nor ineffectually.

For, upon the door, which alone led the way out of the depths, there towered, as high as houses, the corpses of the dead engines, which, when madness first broke out over Metropolis, had been the terrible playthings of the mob.

Train upon train, with carriages thundering along, all lights burning and on full power, had rushed along the rails, lashed by the bawling of the mob, had fallen upon each other, had become mixed and piled up together, had burnt down and were now lying, half-melted, still smouldering, a mass of ruins. And

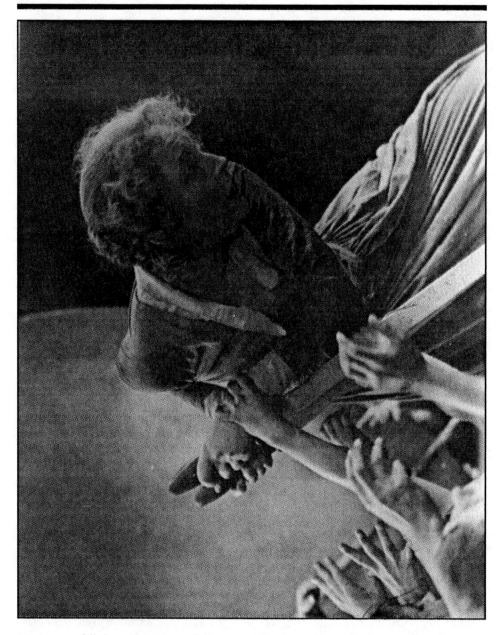

Maria scrambled up. She counted the steps. Like the rushing of a thousand wings came the sound of the children's feet behind her, in the narrow spiral. She did not know how long she had been climbing up. Innumerable hands were clutching her damp dress. She dragged her burdens upward, praying, moaning the while—praying only for strength for another hour.

"Don't cry, little brothers!" she stammered. "My little sisters, please don't cry."

[Brigitte Helm (Maria)]

one, single lamp, remaining undamaged, threw the shaft of its sharp, corrosive light over the chaos, from the steel breast of the hindmost engine.

But Maria knew nothing of all this. She did not need to know. Sufficient for her that the door, which was the only means of deliverance for her and the children she wanted to save, remained inexorable, immovable, and finally, with bleeding hands and shoulders, with battered head, and feet crippled with numbness, she was obliged to resign herself to the incomprehensible, to the murderous.

She raised her face to the ray of light which fell upon her. The words of a little, childish prayer, now no longer intelligible, ran through her head. She dropped her head and sat down on the stairs.

The children stood in silence, crowded closely together, under the curse of something which, though they could not understand it, was very close above them.

"Little brothers, little sisters," said Maria's voice, very affectionately, "can you all understand what I am saying?"

"Yes," floated up from the children.

"The door is closed . . . We must wait a little . . . Someone is sure to come and open it for us. Will you be patient and not be frightened?"

"Yes," came an answer, as a sigh.

"Sit down as well as you can . . ."

The children obeyed.

"I am going to tell you a story," said Maria.

The film version of METROPOLIS treats the sequence with Maria and the children escaping the flood somewhat differently from that of the novel. When the flood waters begin to rise Maria gathers the children left behind and climbs onto the pedestal of the great gong in the central square of the "Lower City" to send a call for help (above). Freder and Josephat hear the gong and return to the "Lower City" where they find and help rescue Maria and the children (page 189) by locating and climbing up through the air shafts and (as in the novel) come to a dead end—a locked grille! [Brigitte Helm (Maria) and (page 189) with Gustav Fröhlich (Freder)]

A black and white reproduction of the Dust Wrapper from an early edition of METROPOLIS, The Readers Publishing Co., Ltd., London.

CHAPTER XVIII

THAT WOMAN MURDERED MY MACHINE!

"LITTLE SISTER . . ."

"Yes?"

"I am so hungry, sister . . .!"

"Hungry . . .!" echoed out of the depths.

"Don't you want to hear the end of my story?"

"Yes . . . But sister, when you've finished, can't we go out and have dinner?"

"Of course . . . as soon as my story's finished . . . Just think: Foxy Fox went for a walk—went for a walk through the beautiful flowery meadows; he had his Sunday coat on, and he held his bushy red tail bolt upright, and he was smoking his little pipe and singing all the while . . . Do you know what Foxy Fox sang?—

I am the cheerful Fox—Hurray!
I am the cheerful Fox—Hurray!

And then he hopped for joy! And little Mr. Hedgehog was sitting on his hillock and he was so glad that his radishes were coming on so nicely, and his wife was standing by the hedge, gossiping with Mrs. Mole, who had just got a new fur for the Autumn . . ."

"Sister . . ."

"Yes?"

"Can the water from down there be coming up after us?"

"Why, little brother?"

"I can hear it gurgling . . ."

"Don't listen to the water, little brother . . . just listen to what Mrs. Hedgehog has to chatter about!"

"Yes, sister, but the water is chattering so loud . . . I think it chatters much louder than Mrs. Mole . . ."

"Come away from the stupid water, little brother . . . Come here to me! You can't hear the water here!"

"I can't come to you sister! I can't move, sister . . . Can't you come and fetch me?"

"Me too, sister—yes, me too!—me too!"

"I can't do that, little brothers, little sisters! Your youngest brothers and sisters are on my lap. They have gone to sleep and I mustn't wake them!"

"Oh sister, are we sure to get out?"

"Why do you ask as if you were frightened, little brother?"

"The floor is shaking so and stones are tumbling down from the ceiling!"

"Have those silly stones hurt you?"

"No, but my little sister's lying down and she's not moving any more."

Don't disturb her, little brother. Your sister's asleep!"

"Yes, but she was crying just now . . .!"

"Don't be sorry little brother that she had gone where she need not cry any more . . ."

"Where has she gone to, then, sister?"

"To heaven, I think."

"Is heaven so near, then?"

"Oh yes, quite near. I can even see the door from here! And if I'm not wrong, Saint Peter is standing there, in front of it, with a large golden key, waiting until he can let us in . . ."

"Oh, sister . . . sister!! Now the water's coming up—! Now it's got hold of my feet! Now it's lifting me up—!"

"Sister!! Help me, sister.—The water has come—!!"

"God can help you—Almighty God!"

"Sister, I'm frightened!"

"Are you frightened of going into the lovely heaven?"

"Is it lovely in heaven?"

"Oh—glorious—glorious!"

"Is Foxy Fox in heaven, too—and little Mr. Hedgehog?"

"I don't know! Shall I ask Saint Peter about it?"

"Yes, sister . . . Are you crying?"

"No, why should I be crying?—Saint Peter—! Saint Peter—!"

"Did he hear?"

"Dear God, how cold the water is . . ."

"Saint Peter—! Saint Peter—!!"

"Sister . . . I think he answered, just now . . ."

"Really, little brother?"

"Yes . . . somebody was calling . . ."

"Yes, I heard it, too!"

" . . . So did I . . ."

" . . . So did I . . ."

"Hush, children, hush . . ."

"Oh, sister, sister—!"

"Hush, please—please—!"

" . . . Maria—!"

"Freder—!!!"

"Maria—are you there—?"

"Freder—Freder—here I am! Here I am, Freder—!!"

"On the stairs?"

"Yes!"

"Why don't you come up?"

"I can't raise the door!"

"Ten trains have run together . . . I can't come to you! I must go and get help!"

"Oh, Freder, the water's already close behind us!"

"The water—?"

"Yes!—And the walls are falling in!"

"Are you hurt—?"

"No, no . . . Oh, Freder, if you could only force open the door wide enough for me to push the little children's bodies through . . ."

The man above her did not give her an answer.

When steeling his muscles and sinews in the "Club of the Sons," playfully wrestling with his friends, he surely never guessed that he would need them one day to force a path through ruined cables, upright pistons and out-spread wheels of fallen machines to the woman he loved. He thrust the pistons aside like human arms, clutched into steel as into soft, yielding flesh. He worked his way nearer the door and threw himself on the ground.

"Maria—?"

"Freder?"

193

"Where are you? Why does your voice sound so far away?"

"I want to be the last whom you save, Freder! I am carrying the tiniest ones on my shoulders and arms . . ."

"Is the water still rising?"

"Yes."

"Is it rising fast or slowly?"

"Fast."

"My God, my God . . . I can't get the door loose! The machines are piled up on top of it like mountains! I must explode the ruins, Maria!"

"Very well." Maria's voice sounded as though she were smiling. "Meanwhile I can finish telling my story . . ."

Freder dashed away. He did not know where his feet should carry him. He thought vaguely of God . . . "Thy will be done . . . Deliver us from evil . . . For Thine is the . . . power . . ."

From the sooty black sky a frightful gleam, of the colour of spilt blood, fell upon the city, which appeared as a silhouette of tattered velvet in the painful scarcity of light. There was not a soul to be seen and yet the air throbbed under the unbearable knife-edge of shrieks of women from the vicinity of Yoshiwara, and, while the organ of the cathedral was shrilling and whistling, as though its mighty body were wounded unto death, the windows of the cathedral, lighted from within, began, phantom-like to glow.

Freder staggered along to the tower-house in which the heart of the great machine-city of Metropolis had lived, and which it had torn open from top to bottom, when racing itself to death, in the fever of the "12," so that the house now looked like a ripped open, gaping gate.

A lump of humanity was crawling about the ruins, seeming, from the sounds it emitted, to be nothing but a single curse, on two legs. The horror which lay over Metropolis was Paradise compared with the last, cruel destruction which the lump of humanity was invoking from the lowest and hottest of hells upon the city and its inhabitants.

He found something among the ruins, raised it to his face, recognised it and broke out into howls, similar to the howls of a kicked dog. He rubbed his sobbing mouth upon the little piece of steel.

"May the stinking plague gnaw you, you lice—! May you sit in muck up to your eyes—! May you swill gas instead of water and burst every day—for ten thousand years—over and over again—!"

"Grot!"

"Filth—!"

"Grot!!—Thank God . . . Grot, come here!"

"Who's that—"

"I am Joh Fredersen's son—"

"Aaah—Hell and the devil—I wanted you—! Come here, you toad—! I must have you between my fists. I'd much rather have had your father, but you're a bit of him and better than nothing! Come along here, if you've got the guts. Ah—my lad, wouldn't I like to get hold of you! I'd like to smear you from top toe in mustard and eat you! D'you know what your father's done—?"

"Grot—!"

"Let me finish—I tell you! Do you know what he did—? He made me give up . . . he made me give up my machine . . ."

And once more the miserable howling of a kicked dog.

"My machine . . . my—my machine—! That devil up there! That God-damned devil! . . ."

"Grot, listen to me—"

"I won't listen to anything!—"

"Grot, in the underground city, the water has broken in . . ."

Seconds of silence. Then—roars of laughter, and, on the heap of ruins, the dance of a four-legged lump, which kicked its stumps amid wild yells, clapping its hands the while.

"That's right—! Hallelujah Amen—!"

"Grot—!" Freder laid fast hold of the dancing lump and shook it so that its teeth rattled. "The water has flooded the city! The lights lie in ruins! The water has risen up the steps! And upon the door—upon the only door, there lie tons upon tons of trains which collided with each other there!"

"Let the rats drown—!"

"The children, Grot—!!"

Grot stood as if paralysed.

"A girl," continued Freder, clutching his hand into the man's shoulder, "a girl," he said sobbingly, bending his head as if to bury it in the man's breast, "a girl has tried to save the children and is now shut in with them and can't get out—"

Grot began to run.

"We must explode the ruins, Grot!"

Grot stumbled, turned about and went on running, Freder behind him, closer than his shadow . . .

" . . . But Foxy Fox knew very well that Mr. Hedgehog would come to help him out of the trap, and he wasn't a bit frightened and waited quite cheer-fully, although it was a good long time before Mr. Hedgehog—gallant Mr. Hedgehog! came back . . ."

"Maria—!"

"Oh Christ . . . Freder?"

"Don't be startled, do you hear?"

"Freder, you're not in danger?"

No answer. Silence. A crackling sound. Then a childish voice:

And did Mr. Hedgehog come, sister?"

"Yes—"

But the "yes" was drowned by the tearing of thousands of steel cables, the roar of tens of thousands of rocks which were hurled up to the dome of heaven, to burst the dome and to sink, to hurtle downwards, causing the earth to sway under their fall.

Supplementary crackling. Grey, leisurely clouds. Distant rumbling. And steps. Childish crying. And, up above, the door which was hauled upwards:

"Maria—!"

A blackened face bent downwards; filthy hands stretched out, gropingly.

"Maria—!"

"Here I am, Freder!"

"I can hardly hear you . . ."

"Get the children out first, Freder . . . The wall's sinking . . ."

Grot came lumbering along and threw himself on the ground by Freder's side, clutching down into the pit from which the children were scrambling out, screaming. He grabbed the children by the hair, by the neck, by the head, and hauled them up, as one pulls up radishes. His eyes were popping out of his head with fear. He hurled the children over his body, so that they tumbled over, shrieking miserably. He cursed like a hundred devils.

"Isn't that nearly all of them—?"

He bawled down two names . . .

"Father, father—!" sobbed two little voices in the depths.

"The devil take you, you couple of Jackanapes!" roared the man. He rum-maged the children aside with his fists, as if he were shovelling rubbish on the dustheap. Then he gulped, snorted, clutched out, and had two children hanging around his neck, wet and shivering piteously, but alive—and their limbs stood more in danger of his fumbling fists than previously of the water and the tumbling stones.

With the children in both arms, Grot rolled over on his side. He sat up and planted the couple before him.

"Maria—!"
"Here I am, Freder!"
"I can hardly hear you . . . "
"Get the children out first, Freder . . . The wall's sinking . . . "
[Brigitte Helm (Maria) and Gustav Fröhlich (Freder)]

"You God-damned pair of ragamuffins!" he said, amidst sobs. He wiped the tears from his eyes. And sprang up, hurling the children aside, like two little hay-stooks. With the furious roar of a lion, he ran to the door, from the depths of which Maria was emerging, with closed eyes, supported by Freder's arm.

"You bloody—!" he howled out. He dragged Freder aside, shoved the girl back into the depths, slammed the trap-door to, and slung his entire weight upon it, drumming the rhythm of his laughter upon it with clenched fists.

A grim effort had kept Freder on his feet. Beside himself, he fell upon the maniac to tug him from the trap-door, fell over him and rolled with him, in furious embrace, among the ruins of the machines.

"Let me go, you dog, you mangy dog!" howled Gort, trying to bite at the angry fist which held him. "That woman murdered my machine—That dam' woman led the rabble—! That woman alone turned the lever to "12"—! I saw it when they were trampling on me—! The woman can drown down there—! I'm going to kill that woman—!"

With marvellous tension of all his muscles Grot drew himself up and heaved himself, with a jerk, away from the raving man—with such infuriated strength that he, Grot, shot, describing a curve, amidst the children.

Cursing ardently, he gathered himself up again; but, though he was uninjured, he could not move a limb. He stuck, an impotent spoon, in a porridge of children, which adhered to his arms, legs and fists. No steel fetters could have condemned him so effectually to helplessness, as did the little cold, wet hands, which were defending her who had rescued them all. Yes, his own children were standing before him, pommelling angrily upon his clenched fists, unscared by the blood-shot eyes with which the giant glared at the dwarves, cudgelling him.

"That woman murdered my machine—!" he howled out at last, more complainingly than angrily, looking at the girl, who was resting upon Freder's arm, as though expecting her to bear him out.

"What does he mean?" asked Maria. "And what has happened?"

And she looked with eyes, the horror in which was only modified by the deepest of exhaustion, at the destruction round about, and at the snorting Grot.

Freder did not answer.

"Come," he said. And he raised her up in his arms and carried her out. The children followed them like a flock of little lambs, and Grot had no alternative than to run along in the tracks of the tiny feet, whither the little, tugging hands drew him.

CHAPTER XIX

KILL THE WITCH!

THEY HAD TAKEN the children into the house and Freder's eyes sought Maria, who was kneeling in the street, among the last remaining children, consoling them, and bestowing her loving smile upon weeping and bewildered eyes.

Freder ran across to them and carried Maria into the house. "Don't forget," he said, letting her down upon a couch before the blazing fire in the entrance hall, and holding captive in his longing arms her half-lying, half-sitting, gently resisting form, "that Death and madness and something very like destruction of the world have passed very close by us—and that, after all that has happened, I do not even know the colour of your eyes—and that you have not yet kissed me once by your own free will . . ."

"Dearest," said Maria, leaning towards him, so that her pure eyes, bathed in painless tears, were quite near to him, while, at the same time, a great, concentrated gravity kept her lips away from his, "are you sure that Death and madness have already passed by?"

"By us, beloved—yes!"

"And all the others—?"

"Are you sending me away, Maria?" he asked, lovingly. She did not answer, at least not in words. But, with a gesture which was at once frank and touching, she put her arms about his neck and kissed him on the mouth.

"Go along," she said, stroking his bewildered face with her virginal, motherly hands. "Go to your father. That is the most hallowed way . . . I shall go to the children as soon as my clothes are a little dryer. For I'm afraid," she added with a smile which made Freder blush to his eyes, "numerous as the women

199

are who live in the 'House of the Sons,' and willing and eager as they may be, not one of them has a dress she could lend me . . .!"

Freder stood bending over her with lowered eyes. The flames of the huge fire glowed upon his handsome, open face, which wore an expression of shame and sadness. But when he raised his glance to meet Maria's eyes, which were silently fixed upon him, without saying a word he took her hands and pressed them against his eyelids, remaining thus for a long time.

And all this while they both forgot that, on the other side of the wall which was protecting them, a city was throbbing in grisly conflict, and that among the ruins thousands of beings, themselves but ruins, hurled hither and thither, were losing their reason, and perishing, tortured by deadly fear.

The voice of the Archangel Michael, coming from the cathedral, recalled them to consciousness of the hour, and they parted hurriedly, as if caught neglecting their duty.

Maria listened to the man's retreating step . . .

Then she turned and looked about her.

What a strange sound the Michael bell had . . . The bell was calling so furiously—so agitatedly, as though to tumble over at every peal . . .

Maria's heart became an echo of the bell. It fluttered in its piteous fear, which had no source other than the general vibration of terror above the town. Even the warming flames of the fire frightened her, as if they had some knowledge of secrets of Horror.

She sat up and put her feet to the ground. She felt the hem of her dress. It was still rather wet but she would go now. She took a few steps through the dimly-lighted room. How brown the air was outside the windows . . . She hesitatingly opened the nearest door and listened . . .

She was standing in the room in which she had stood on the day when she saw Freder for the first time, when she had led the train of little, grey child-spectres to those who were care-free and joyous—when she had called to Freder's heart with her gentle:

"Look, these are your brothers!"

But of all the dearly beloved sons of boundlessly wealthy fathers, to whom this house belonged, not one was to be seen. They must have left the tottering town long ago.

Sparsely distributed candles were burning, giving the room an inward cosiness and a warm air of comfort. The room was filled with the tender twittering of sleepy child-voices, chattering like swallows before they fly to their nests.

Answering them in tones which were but little darker, came the voices of the beautiful, brocaded, painted women, who had once been the playthings of the sons. Equally frightened at the thought of flight as of remaining where they were, they eventually stayed in the "House of the Sons," being still undecided; and Maria had brought the children to them, because they could have found no better refuge; for, by the beautiful and dreadful chance of all that had taken place, the troupe of loving little harlots became a troupe of loving little mothers, burning with a new fire in the execution of their new duties.

Not far from Maria the little drink-mixer was kneeling, washing the skinny slender-limbed body of Grot's daughter, who was standing in front of her. But the child had taken the sponge from her hand, and, without saying a word, proceeding with intense gravity, was thoughtfully and untiringly washing the beautiful, painted face of the drink-mixer.

The girl knelt quite still, her eyes closed, neither did she move when the child's hands began to dry her face with the rough towel. But Grot's daughter was not quite successful in this undertaking; for, whenever she dried the girl's cheeks, again and again did the swift, bright drops run over them. Until Grot's daughter dropped the towel to look at the girl who was kneeling before her inquiringly, and not without reproach. Upon which the girl caught the child in her arms, pressing her forehead to the heart of the silent creature, uttering to this heart words of love which she had never found before.

Maria passed by with soundless step.

But when the door to the hall, into which no noise from the noisy Metropolis could penetrate, closed behind her, the ore-voice of the angel of the cathedral struck at her breast like a fist of steel, that she stood still, stunned, raising her hands to her head.

Why was Saint Michael crying out so angrily and wildly? Why was the roar of Azrael, the angel of Death joining in so alarmingly?

She stepped into the street. Darkness, like a thick layer of soot, lay over the town, and only the cathedral shimmered, ghost-like, a wonder of light, but not of grace.

The air was filled with a spectral battle of discordant voices. Howling, laughing, whistling, were to be heard. It was as though a gang of murderers and robbers were passing by—in the unrecognisable depths of the street. Mingled with them, shrieks of women, wild with excitement . . .

Maria's eyes sought the New Tower of Babel. She had only one way in her mind: to Joh Fredersen. She would go there. But she never went.

For suddenly the air was a blood-red stream, which poured itself forth, flickering, formed by a thousand torches. And the torches were dancing in the hands of beings who were crowding out of Yoshiwara. The faces of the beings shone with insanity, every mouth parted in a gasp, yet the eyes which blazed above them were the bursting eyes of men choking. Each was dancing the dance of Death with his own torch, whirling madly about, and the whirl of the dancers formed a train, revolving in itself.

"Maohee—!" flew the shrill cries above it. "Dance—dance—dance—Maohee—!"

But the flaming procession was led by a girl. The girl was Maria. And the girl was screaming with Maria's voice:

"Dance—dance—dance—Maohee!"

She crossed the torches like swords above her head. She swung them right and left, brandishing them so that showers of sparks fell about the way. Sometimes it seemed as if she were riding on the torches. She raised her knees to her breast, with laughter which brought a moan from the dancers of the procession.

But one of the dancers ran along at the girl's feet, like a dog, crying incessantly:

"I am Jan! I am Jan! I am the faithful Jan! Hear me, at last, Maria!"

But the girl struck him in the face with her sparkling torch.

His clothes caught fire. He ran for some time, a living torch, along by the girl. His voice sounded as if from the blaze:

"Maria—! Maria—!"

Then he swung himself up on to the parapet of the street and hurled, a streak of fire, into the blackness of the depths.

"Maohee—! Maohee—!" called the girl, shaking her torch. The procession was endless. The procession was endless. The street was already covered, as far as the eye could see, with circling torches. The shrieks of the dancers mixed themselves sharply and shrilly with the angry voices of the archangels of the cathedral. And behind the train, as though tugged along by invisible, unbreakable cords, there reeled a girl, the damp hem of the hose dress lashed about her ankles, whose hair was falling loose under the clawing fingers which she pressed to her head, whose lips babbled a name in ineffectual entreaty: "Freder . . . Freder . . ."

The smoke-swathes from the torches hovered like the grey wings of phantom birds above the dancing train.

Then the door of the cathedral was opened wide. From the depths of the cathedral came the rushing of the organ. There mixed itself in the fourfold

For suddenly the air was a blood-red stream, which poured itself forth, flickering, formed by a thousand torches. And the torches were dancing in the hands of beings who were crowding out of Yoshiwara. The faces of the beings shone with insanity, every mouth parted in a gasp, yet the eyes which blazed above them were the bursting eyes of men choking. . . .

But the flaming procession was led by a girl. The girl was Maria. And the girl was screaming with Maria's voice:
"Dance—dance—dance—Maohee!" [Brigitte Helm (Futura/Maria)]

tone of the archangel bells, in the rushing of the organ, in the shrieks of the dancers, an iron-tramping, mighty choir.

The hour of the monk Desertus had come. The monk Desertus was leading on his own.

Two by two walked those who were his disciples. They walked on bare feet, in black cowls. They had thrown their cowls back from their shoulders. They carried the heavy scourges in both hands. They swung the heavy scourges in both hands, right and left, right and left, upon the bare shoulders. Blood trickled down from the scourged backs. The Gothics sang. They sang to the time of their feet. To the time of their scourge strokes did they sing.

The monk Desertus was leading the Gothics on.

The Gothics bore a black cross before them. It was so heavy that twelve men had to carry it, pantingly. It swayed, held up by dark cords.

And on the cross hung the monk Desertus.

The black flames of the eyes in the flame-white face were fixed upon the procession of dancers. The head was raised. The pale mouth was opened.

"See!" shouted the monk Desertus in a voice which all-powerfully outrang, the fourfold tone of the archangel bells, the rushing of the organ, the choir of scourge-swingers and the shrieks of the dancers: "See—! Babylon, the great—! The Mother of Abominations—! Doomsday is breaking—! The destruction of the world—!"

"Doomsday is breaking—! The destruction of the world—!" chanted the choir of his followers after him.

"Dance—dance—dance—Maohee—!" shrieked the voice of the girl leading the dancers. And she swung her torches over her shoulders, and hurled them far from her. She tore her gown from shoulders and breasts, standing, a white torch, stretching up her arms and laughing, shaking her hair; "Dance with me, Desertus—dance with me—!"

Then the girl, dragging herself along at the end of the train, felt that the cord, the invisible cord upon which she was hanging, snapped. She turned around and began, not knowing, whither, to run—only to get away—only to get away—no matter where to—only to get away—!

The streets flashed by in a whirl. She ran and ran, down, and down, and at last she saw, running along the bottom of the street and towards her, a wild mob of people, saw, too, that the men wore the blue linen uniform and sobbed in relief:

"Brothers—brothers—!"

And stretched out her hands.

But a furious roar answered her. Like a collapsing wall, the mass hurled itself forward, shook itself loose and began to tear along, roaring loudly.

"There she is—! There she is—! The bitch, who is to blame for it all—! Take her—! Take her—!"

The women's voices shrieked:

"The witch—! Kill the witch—! Burn her before we all drown!"

And the trampling of running feet filled the dead street, through which the girl fled, with the din of hell broken loose. The houses flashed by in a whirl. She did not know the way in the dark. She sped on, running aimlessly, in a blind horror, which was the deeper for her not knowing its origin. Stones, cudgels, fragments of steel, flew at her from behind. The mob roared in a voice which was no longer human:

"After her—! After her—! She'll escape us—! Quicker—!! Quicker—!!"

Maria could no longer feel her feet. She did not know if she was running on stones or water. Her panting breath came through lips which stood apart as those of one drowning. Up streets, down streets . . . A twirling dance of lights was staggering across the way, far ahead of her . . . Far away, at the end of the enormous square, in which Rotwang's house also lay, the mass of the cathedral rested upon the earth, weighty and dark, yet showing a tender, reassuring shimmer, which fell through cheerful stained-glass windows and through open portal, out into the darkness.

Suddenly breaking out into sobs, Maria threw herself forward with her last, entirely despairing strength. She stumbled up the cathedral steps, stumbled through the portal, perceived the odour of incense, saw little, pious candles of intercession before the image of a gentle saint who was suffering smilingly, and collapsed on to the flags.

She no longer saw how, at the double opening of the street which led to the cathedral, the stream of dancers from Yoshiwara coincided with the roaring stream of workmen and women, did not hear the bestial shriek of the women at the sight of the girl who was riding along on the shoulders of a dancer—who was torn down, overtaken, captured and stamped to earth—did not see the short, ghastly hopeless conflict of the men in evening dress with the men in blue linen—nor the ridiculous fight of the half naked woman before the claws and fists of the workmen's wives.

She lay in deep oblivion, in the great, mild solemnity of death, and from the depths of her unconsciousness she was not awakened even by the roaring voice of the mob which was erecting a bonfire for the witch, before the cathedral.

205

CHAPTER XX
DANCE WITH ME—!

"FREDER—!!! GROT—!!! Freder—!!!"

Josaphat shouted so that his voice cracked, and raced with the bounds of a harried wolf, through passages, across steps of the great pump-works. His shouts were not heard. In the machine rooms were wounded machines in agony, wanting to obey and not being able. The door was closed. Josaphat hammered against it with his fists, with his feet. It was Grot who opened it to him, revolver in hand.

"What in the name of seething hell . . ."

"Get out of the way—! Where's Freder—?"

"Here! What's the matter?"

"Freder, they've taken Maria captive—"

"What?"

"They've taken Maria captive and they're killing her—!"

Freder reeled. Josaphat dragged him towards the door. Like a log, Grot stood in his way, his lips mumbling, his eyes glaring.

"The woman who killed my machine—!"

"Shut up, you fool—get out of the way—!"

"Grot!" A sound born half of madness . . .

"Yes, Mr. Freder!"

"You stop with the machines!"

"Yes, Mr. Freder!"

"Come on, Josaphat—!"

The sound of running, running, retreating, ghostlike. Grot turned round. He saw the paralysed machines, He lifted his arm and struck the machine with the full of his fist, as one strikes a stubborn horse between the eyes.

"The woman," he shouted with a howl, "who saved my little children—!"

And he flung himself upon the machine with grinding teeth . . .

"Tell me—!" said Freder, almost softly. It was as if he did not want to waste an atom of strength. His face was a white stone in which his two eyes flamed like jewels. He jumped to the wheel of the little car in which Josaphat had come. For the pump works lay at the extreme end of the great Metropolis.

It was still night.

The car started.

"We must go terribly out of our way," said Josaphat, fixing the flashlight. "Many bridges between the houseblocks are blown up . . ."

"Tell me," said Freder. His teeth met, chattering, as if he were cold.

"I don't know who found it out . . . Probably the women, who were thinking of their children and wanted to get home. You can't get anything out of the raving multitude. But anyway: When they saw the black water running towards them from the shafts of the underground railway, and when they realised that the pump-works, the safe-guard of their city, had been destroyed by the stopping of the machines, then they went mad with despair. They say that some mothers, blind and deaf to all remonstrance, tried, as if possessed, to dive down through the flooded shafts, and just the terrible absoluteness of the futility of any attempt at rescue has turned them into beasts and they lust for revenge . . ."

"Revenge . . . on whom?"

"On the girl who seduced them . . ."

"On the girl . . .?"

"Go on . . ."

"Freder, the engine can't keep up that speed . . ."

"Go on . . ."

"I do not know how it happened that the girl ran into their hands. I was on my way to you when I saw a woman running across the cathedral square, with her hair flying, the roaring rabble behind her. There has been the very hell of a night anyway. The Gothics are parading through the town scourging themselves, and they have put the monk Desertus on the cross. They are preaching: Doomsday had come, and it seems that they have converted a good many already, for September is crouching before the smoking ruins of Yoshiwara. A troop of torch dancers joined itself to the flagellants and, with frothing curses upon the Mother of Abominations, the great whore of Babylon, they burned Yoshiwara down to the ground . . ."

"The girl, Josaphat—"

208

"She did not reach the cathedral, Freder, where she wanted to take refuge. They overtook her on the steps because she fell on the steps—her gown hung down in ribbons from her body. A woman, whose white eyes were glowing with insanity shrieked out, as one inspired with the gift of prophecy . . ."
"And—"
"Before the cathedral they are erecting a bonfire on which to burn the witch . . . "
[Brigitte Helm (Futura/Maria)]

"She did not reach the cathedral, Freder, where she wanted to take refuge. They overtook her on the steps because she fell on the steps—her gown hung down in ribbons from her body. A woman, whose white eyes were glowing with insanity shrieked out, as one inspired with the gift of prophecy:

" 'Look—! Look—! The saints have climbed down from their pedestals and will not let the witch into the cathedral.' "

"And—"

"Before the cathedral they are erecting a bonfire on which to burn the witch . . ."

Freder said nothing. He bent down lower. The car groaned and leapt.

Josaphat buried his hand in Freder's arm.

"Stop—for God's sake!!!"

The car stopped.

"We must go to the left—don't you see? The bridge has gone!"

"The next bridge?"

"Is impassable!"

"Listen . . ."

"What is there to hear—"

"Don't you hear anything?"

"No . . ."

"You *must* hear it—!"

"But what, Freder—?"

"Shrieks . . . distant shrieks . . ."

"I can't hear anything . . ."

"But you *must* be able to hear it—!!"

"Won't you drive on, Freder?"

"And don't you see that the air over there is getting bright red?"

"From the torches, Freder . . ."

"They don't burn so brightly . . ."

"Freder, we're losing time here—!"

Freder did not answer. He was staring at the tatters of the iron bridge which were dangling down into the ravine of the street. He must cross over, yes, he must cross over, to get to the cathedral by a short cut . . .

The frame-support of a ripped-open tower had fallen over from this side of the street to the other, gleaming metallically in the uncertain light of the fading night.

"Get out," said Freder.

"Why?"

"Get out, I tell you . . ."

"I want to know why?"

"Because I'm going across there . . ."

"Across where?"

"Across the frame-support."

"Going to drive across—?"

"Yes."

"It's suicide, Freder!"

"I didn't ask you to accompany me. Get out!"

"I won't permit it—it's blazing lunacy!"

"The fire over there is blazing, man—!"

The words seemed not to come from Freder's mouth.

Every wound of the dying city seemed to be roaring out of him.

"Drive on!" said Josaphat through clenched teeth.

The car gave a jump. It climbed. The narrow irons received the sucking, skidding wheels, with an evil, maliciously hypocritical sound.

Blood was trickling from Freder's lips.

"Don't—don't put the brake on—for God's sake don't put the brake on!" shouted the man beside him making a clutch of madness at Freder's hand. The car, already half-slipping, shot forward again. A split in the frame-work—over, onwards. Behind them the dead frame-work crashed into space amid shrieks.

They reached the other side with an impetus which was no longer to be checked. The wheels rushed into blackness and nothing. The car overturned. Freder fell and got up again. The other remained lying.

"Josaphat—!!"

"Run! It's nothing!—I swear to God it's nothing" a distorted smile upon the white face. "Think of Maria—and run!"

And Freder raced off.

Josaphat turned his head. He saw the blackness of the street flashing bright red. He heard the screams of the thousands. He thought dully, with a thrust of his fist in the air: "Shouldn't I like to be Grot now, to be able to swear properly . . ."

Then his head fell back into the filth of the street, and every consciousness faded but that of pain . . .

But Freder ran as he had never run. It was not his feet which carried him. It was his wild heart—it was his thoughts. Streets and stairs and streets and at last the cathedral square. Black in the background, the cathedral, ungodded, unlighted, the place before the broad steps swarming with human beings—and

A wild, red gleam caught his eyes. The pyre flamed up in long flames. The men, the women, seized hands and tore around the bonfire, faster, faster and faster, in rings growing ever wider and wider, laughing, screaming with stamping feet, "Witch—! Witch!" [Brigitte Helm (Futura/Maria)]

amid them, surrounded by gasps of madly despairing laughter, the howling of songs of fury, the smouldering of torches and brands, high up on the pyre . . .

"*Maria*—!"

Freder fell on his knees as though his sinews were sawn through.

"*Maria*—!"

The girl whom he took to be Maria raised her head. She sought him. Her glance found him. She smiled—laughed.

"Dance with me, my dearest—!" flew her voice, sharp as a flashing knife, through uproar.

Freder got up. The mob recognised him. The mob lurched towards him, shrieking and yelling.

"Jooooo—oh! Joh Fredersen's son—! Joh Fredersen's son—"

They made to seize him. He dodged them wildly. He threw himself with his back against the parapet of the street.

"Why do you want to kill her, you devils—? She has saved your children!"

Roars of laughter answered him. Women sobbed with laughter, biting into their own hands.

"Yes—yes—she has saved our children—! She saved our children with the song of the dead machines! She saved our children with the ice cold water—! High let her live—high and three times high!"

"Go to the 'House of the Sons'—! Your children are there!"

"*Our* children are not in the 'House of the Sons!' There lives the brood, hatched out by money. Sons of your kind, you dog in white-silken skin!"

"Listen, for God's sake—do listen to me—!!!"

"We don't want to hear anything—!"

"Maria—beloved!!!—Beloved!!!"

"Don't bawl so, son of Joh Fredersen! Or we'll stop your mouth!"

"Kill me, if you must kill—*but let her live*—!"

"Each in his turn, son of Joh Fredersen! First you shall see how your beloved dies a beautiful, hot magnificent death!"

A woman—Grot's woman—tore a strip off her skirt and bound Freder's hands. He was bound fast to the parapet with cords: He struggled like a wild beast, shouting that the veins of this throat were in danger of bursting. Bound, impotent; he threw back his head and saw the sky over Metropolis, pure, tender, greenish-blue, for morning would soon follow after this night.

"God—!" he shouted, trying to throw himself on his knees, in his bonds. "God—! Where art thou—?"

A wild, red gleam caught his eyes. The pyre flamed up in long flames. The

213

men, the women, seized hands and tore around the bonfire, faster, faster and faster, in rings growing ever wider and wider, laughing, screaming with stamping feet, "Witch—! Witch!"

Freder's bonds broke. He fell over on his face among the feet of the dancers.

And the last he saw of the girl, while her gown and hair stood blazing around her as a mantle of fire, was the loving smile and the wonder of her eyes—and her mouth of deadly sin, which lured among the flames:

"Dance with me, my dearest! Dance with me—!"

CHAPTER XXI

TRAPPED!

ROTWANG AWOKE; but he knew quite well he was dead. And this consciousness filled him with the deepest satisfaction. His aching body no longer had anything to do with him. That was perhaps the last remains of life. But something worried him deeply, as he raised himself up and looked around in all directions: Hel was not there.

Hel must be found . . .

An existence without Hel was over at last. A second one?—No! Better than to stay dead.

He got up on his feet. That was very difficult. He must have been lying as a corpse for a good long time. It was night, too. A fire was raging out there, and it was all very noisy . . . Shrieking of human beings . . .

Hm . . .

He had hoped to have been rid of them. But, apparently the Almighty Creator could not get along without them. Now—but one purpose. He just wanted his Hel. When he had found Hel, he would—he promised himself this!—never again quarrel with the father of all things, about anything at all . . .

So now he went . . . The door leading to the street was open and hanging crookedly on its hinges. Strange. He stepped in front of the house and looked deliberatingly around. What he saw seemed to be a kind of Metropolis; but a rather insane kind of Metropolis. The houses seemed as though struck still in St. Vitus' dance. And an uncommonly rough and impolite sort of people was ramping around a flaming bonfire, upon which a creature of rare beauty was standing, seeming, to Rotwang, to be wondrously at ease.

Ah—it was that, ah yes—that, in the existence which, thank the Lord, lay far behind him, he had tried to create, to replace his lost Hel—just to make the handiwork of the Creator of the world look rather silly . . . Not bad for a beginning . . . hm . . . but, good God, compared with Hel; what an object; what a bungle . . .

The shrieking individuals down there were quite right to burn the thing. Though it appeared to him to be rather a show of idiocy to destroy his test-work. But perhaps that was the custom of the people in this existence, and he certainly did not want to argue with them. He wanted to find Hel—his Hel—and nothing else . . .

He knew exactly where to look for her. She loved the cathedral so dearly, did his pious Hel. And, if the flickering light of the bonfire did not deceive him,—for the greenish sky gave no glimmer—Hel was standing, like a frightened child in the blackness of the cathedral door, her slender hands clasped firmly upon her breast, looking more saint-like than ever.

Past those who were raving around the bonfire—always politely avoiding getting in their way—Rotwang quietly groped his way to the cathedral.

Yes, it was his Hel . . . She receded into the cathedral. He groped his way up the steps. How high the door looked . . . Coolness and hovering incense received him . . . All the saints in the pillar niches had pious and lovely faces, smiling gently, as though they rejoiced with him that he was now, at last, to find Hel, his Hel, again.

She was standing at the foot of the belfry steps. She seemed to him to be very pale and indescribably pathetic. Through a narrow window the first pale light of the morning fell upon her hair and brow.

"Hel," said Rotwang, his heart streaming over; he stretched out his hands. "Come to me, my Hel . . . How long, how long I had to live without you!"

But she did not come. She started back from him. Her face full of horror, she started back from him.

"Hel," begged the man, "why are you afraid of me? I am no ghost, although I am dead. I had to die, to come to you. I have always, always longed for you. You have no right to leave me alone now! I want your hands! Give them to me!"

But his groping fingers snatched into space. Footsteps were hurrying up the steps of the stone-staircase which led to the belfry.

Something like anger came over Rotwang's heart. Deep in his dulled and tortured soul reposed the memory of a day upon which Hel had likewise fled from him—to another . . . No, don't think, don't think of it . . . That was a part of his first existence, and it would be quite senseless to go through the same again—in the other, and, as humanity in general hoped, better world.

Why was Hel fleeing from him? He groped along after her. Climbed up stairs upon stairs. The hastening, frightened footsteps remained constantly before him. And the higher the woman before him fled, the more wildly did his heart beat in this mighty ascent, the redder did Rotwang's eyes become filled with blood, the more furiously did his anger boil up within him. She should not run away from him—she should not! If only he could catch her by the hand he would never, never let her go again! He would forge a ring about her wrist with his metal hand—and then she should never try to escape him again . . . to another!

They had both reached the belfry. They raced along under the bells. He blocked the way to the stairs. He laughed, sadly and evilly.

"Hel, my Hel, you can no longer escape me!"

She made a swift, despairing leap, and hung on the rope of the bell which was called Saint Michael. Saint Michael raised his ore voice, but it sounded as though broken, complaining wildly. Rotwang's laughter mingled with the sound of the bell. His metal arm, the marvellous achievement of a genius, stretched, like the phantom arm of a skeleton, far out on the sleeve of his coat, and snatched at the bell-rope.

"Hel, my Hel, you can no longer escape me!"

The girl staggered back against the breastwork. She looked around. She was trembling like a bird. She could not go down the stairs. Neither could she go any higher. She was trapped. She saw Rotwang's eyes and saw his hands. And, without hesitation, without reflection, with a ferocity which swept a blaze of scarlet across the pallor of her face, she swung herself out of the belfry window, to hang upon the steel cord of the lightning conductor.

"Freder—!!" she screamed. "Help me—!!"

Below—far below, near the flaming pyre, lay a trampled creature, his forehead in the dust. But the scream from above smote him so unexpectedly that he shot up, as if under the lash, be sought and he saw—

And all those who had been dancing in wild rings around the bonfire of the witch saw, as he—stiffened—petrified: The girl who hung, swallowlike, clinging to the tower of the cathedral, with Rotwang's hands stretching out towards her.

And they all heard how, in the shouted answer: "I am coming, Maria, I am coming—!" there cried out all the relief and all the despair which can fill the heart of a man to whom Heaven and Hell are equally near.

CHAPTER XXII
THEY LUST FOR REVENGE

JOH FREDERSEN stood in the dome-room of the New Tower of Babel, waiting for Slim. He was to bring him news of his son.

A ghostly darkness lay upon the New Tower of Babel. The light had gone completely out, gone out as though it had been killed—at the moment when the gigantic wheel of the Heart-machine of Metropolis came free from its structure with a roar as from the throats of a thousand wounded beasts, and, still whirling around, was hurled straight up at the ceiling, to strike it with a shattering crash, to bound back, booming the while like a gong as large as the heavens and to crash down upon the splintered ruins of the erstwhile masterpiece of steel, to remain lying there.

Joh Fredersen stood long on the same spot, not daring to move.

It seemed to him that an eternity had passed since he sent Slim out for news of his son. And Slim wouldn't and wouldn't come back.

Joh Fredersen felt that his whole body was frozen to an icy coldness. His hands, hanging helplessly downwards, were clasped around the pocket-torch.

He waited . . . waited . . .

Joh Fredersen threw a glance at the clock. But the hands of the giantness stood at an impossible time. The New Tower of Babel had indeed lost itself. Whereas, every day, the throbbing of the streets which tunnelled their course below it, the roar of the traffic of fifty million, the magic madness of speed, had raged its way up to him, there now crouched a calm of penetrating terror.

Stumbling steps were hastening towards the door of the outer room.

Joh Fredersen turned the beam of his pocket-torch, upon this door. It flew wide open. Slim stood upon the threshold. He staggered. He closed his

219

eyes dazzled. In the excessively glaring light of the powerful torch his face, right down to his neck, shone a greenish white.

Joh Fredersen wanted to ask a question. But not the least sound passed his lips. A terrible dryness burnt his throat. The lamp in his hand began to tremble and to dance. Up to the ceiling, down to the floor, along the walls, reeled the beam of light . . .

Slim ran up to Joh Fredersen. Slim's wide, staring eyes bore an inextinguishable horror.

"Your son," he stammered, almost babbling, "your son, Mr. Fredersen—"

Joh Fredersen remained silent. He made no movement, but that he stooped a little—just a very little, forward.

"I have not found your son . . ." said Slim. He did not wait for Joh Fredersen to answer him. His tall body, with the impression it gave of asceticism and cruelty, the movements of which had, in Joh Fredersen's service, gradually gained the disinterested accuracy of a machine, seemed quite out of joint, shaken out of control. His voice inquired shrilly, in the grip of a deep innermost frenzy: "Do you know, Mr. Fredersen, what is going on around you, in Metropolis—?"

"What I will," answered Joh Fredersen. The words sounded mechanical, and as though they had been read before they were spoken: "What does that mean: You have not found my son—?"

"It means what it means," answered Slim in his shrill voice. His eyes bore an awful hatred. He stood, leaning far forward, as if ready to pounce upon Joh Fredersen, and his hands became claws. "It means that Freder, your son is not to be found—it means that he, perhaps, wanted to look on with his own eyes at what becomes of Metropolis by his father's will and the hands of a few lunatics—it means, as the now half-witted servants told me, that your son left the safety of his home, setting out in company with a man who was wearing the uniform of a workman of Metropolis, and that it might well be difficult to seek your son in this city, in which, by your will, madness has broken out—the madness to destroy, Mr. Fredersen, the madness to ruin!—and which has not even light to lighten its madness—!"

Slim wanted to continue, but he did not do so.

Joh Fredersen's right hand made a senseless, fumbling gesture through the air. The torch fell from his hand, continuing to burn on the floor. The mightiest man of Metropolis swung half around, as though he had been shot, and collapsed empty-eyed, back into the chair by the writing-table.

Slim stooped forward, to look Joh Fredersen in the face. Before these eyes he was struck silent.

Ten—twenty—thirty seconds long he did not dare to draw a breath. His horrified gaze followed the aimless movements of Joh Fredersen's fingers, which were fumbling about as though seeking for some lever of rescue, which they could not find. Then, suddenly, the hand rose a little from the table-top. The forefinger straightened as though admonishing to attention. Joh Fredersen murmured something. Then he laughed. It was a tired, sad little laugh, at the sound of which Slim thought he felt the hair of his head begin to bristle.

Joh Fredersen was talking to himself. What was he saying? Slim bent over him. He saw the forefinger of Joh Fredersen's right hand gliding slowly across the shiny table-top, as though he were following and spelling out the lines of a book.

Joh Fredersen's soft voice said:

"Whatsoever a man soweth, that shall he reap . . ."

Then Joh Fredersen's forehead fell on to the smooth wood, and, unceasingly, in a tone which, except for a dead woman, no one had ever heard from Joh Fredersen, his soft voice cried the name of his son . . .

But the cries remained unanswered . . .

Up the steps of the New Tower of Babel there crept a man. It seldom happened in the great Metropolis, Joh Fredersen's time-saving city, that anyone used the stairs. They were reserved in case of all the lifts and the Pater-noster being overcrowded, of the cessation of all means of transit, of the outbreak of fire and similar accidents—improbable occurrences in this perfect settlement of human beings. But the improbable had happened. Piled up, one above the other, the lifts, which came hurtling down, blocked up their shafts, and the cells of the Pater-noster seemed to have been bent and charred by a hellish heat, smouldering up from the depths.

Up the stairs of the New Tower of Babel did Josaphat drag himself. He had learnt to swear in that quarter of an hour, even as Grot used to swear, and he made full use of his newly acquired art. He roared at the pain which racked his limbs. He spat out an excess of hatred and contempt at the agony in his knees. Wild and ingenious were the execrations which he hurled at every landing, every new bend in the staircase. But he conquered them all—one hundred and six flights of stairs, each consisting of thirty steps. He reached the semicircle where the lifts had their opening. In the corners before the door to Joh Fredersen's rooms there crouched knots of human beings, pressed together by the common pressure of a terrible fear.

They turned their heads to stare at the man who was crawling up the stairs, dragging himself up by aid of the walls. His wild eyes swept over them.

"What is it?" he asked breathlessly. "What are you all doing here?" Agi-

221

tated voices whispered. Nobody knew who was speaking. Words tumbled over each other.

"He drove us out into the town, where death is running as though amok . . . He sent us out to look for his son, Freder. We couldn't find him . . . None of us . . . We daren't go in to Joh Fredersen . . . Nobody dares take him the news that we haven't been able to find his son . . ."

A voice swung out, high and sharp from out the knot:

"Who can find one single damned soul in this hell—?"

"Hush . . . hush . . .!"

"Listen—!"

"He is talking to Slim."

And in the tension of listening, which smothered every sound, the heads bent towards the door.

Behind the door a voice spoke, as were the wood rattling: "Where is my son . . .?"

Josaphat made for the door, staggering. The panting cry of many men tried to stop him. Hands were stretched out towards him.

"Don't—don't—!!"

But he had already pushed open the door. He looked about him. Through the enormous windows the first glow of the youthful day was flowing, lying on the shining floor like pools of blood. By the wall, near the door, stood Slim. And just before him stood Joh Fredersen. His fists were pressed against the wall, right and left of the man, holding him fast, as though they had been drilled through him, crucifying him.

"Where is my son—?" said Joh Fredersen. He asked—and his voice cracked as if in suffocation:

"Where is my child?"

Slim's head flung back against the wall. From his ashen lips came the toneless words:

"To-morrow there will be many in Metropolis who will ask:

" 'Joh Fredersen, where is my child?' "

Joh Fredersen's fists relaxed. His whole body twisted around. Then the man who had been the Master over Metropolis saw that another man was standing in the room. He stared at him. The sweat trickled down his face in cold, slow, burdensome drops. The face twitched in a terrible impotence.

"Where is my son—?" asked Joh Fredersen, babblingly. He stretched out his hand. The hand shot through the air, groping aimlessly. "Do you know, where my son is—?"

Josaphat did not answer. Yes, the answer shouted in his throat. But he could not form the words. There was a fist at his throat, strangling him . . . God—Almighty God in highest heaven, was it Joh Fredersen who was standing before him?

Joh Fredersen made an uncertain step towards him. He bent his head low to look at him the more closely. He nodded again.

"I know you," he said tonelessly. "You are Josaphat and you were my first secretary. I sent you away. I treated you cruelly. I did you wrong and I ruined you . . . I beg your forgiveness . . . I am sorry that I was ever cruel to you or to anyone else . . . Forgive me . . . Forgive me, Josaphat, for ten hours I have not known where my son is . . . For ten hours, Josaphat, I have been sending all the men I could get hold of, down into that damned city to look for my son, and I know it is senseless, and I know it is quite pointless, the day is breaking, and I am talking and talking and I know that I am a fool but perhaps, perhaps you know where my son is . . .?"

"Captured," said Josaphat, and it was as though he ripped the word from his gullet, and feared to bleed to death therefrom. "Captured . . ."

A stupid smile hovered over Joh Fredersen's face. "What does that mean . . . captured . . .?"

"The mob has captured him, Joh Fredersen!"

"Captured—?"

"Yes."

"My son—?"

"Yes!—Freder, your son—!"

A senseless, pitiable, animal sound broke from Joh Fredersen's mouth. His mouth stood open, distorted—his hands rose as in childish defence, to ward off a blow which had already fallen. His voice said, quite high and piteously:

"My son . . .?"

"They took him prisoner, "—Josaphat tore the words out—"because they sought a victim for their despair, and for the fury of their immeasurable, inconceivable agony. When they saw the black water running towards them from the shafts of the underground railway, and when they realised that, as the result of the stopping of the pumps, the whole workmen's town had been flooded out, then they went mad with despair. They say that some mothers, blind and deaf to all remonstrance, tried, as if possessed, to dive down through the flooded shafts, and just the terrible absoluteness of the futility of any attempt at rescue has turned them into beasts and they lust for revenge . . ."

223

"Revenge . . . on whom?"

"On the girl who seduced them . . ."

"On the girl . . ."

"Yes . . ."

Go on . . ."

"They have taken captive the girl, on whom they put the blame of all this horror . . . Freder wanted to save her, for he loves the girl . . . They have taken him captive and are forcing him to look on and see how his beloved dies . . . They have built the bonfire before the cathedral . . . They are dancing round the bonfire . . . They are yelling: 'We have captured the son of Joh Fredersen and his beloved' . . . and I know—I know: He'll never get away from them alive . . .!"

For the space of some seconds there was so deep and perfect a silence that the golden glow of the morning, breaking forth, strong and radiant had the effect of a powerful roar. Then Joh Fredersen turned around, breaking into a run. He flung himself at the door. So forceful and irresistible was this movement that it seemed as if the closed door itself were not able to withstand it.

Past the knots of human being ran Joh Fredersen—across to the stair-case and down the steps. His course was as a pauseless series of leaps. He did not notice the height. With hands stretched forward he ran, in bounds, his hair rearing up like a flame above his brow. His mouth was wide open and between his parted lips there hovered--a soundless scream—the unscreamed name: "Freder!"

An infinity of stairs . . . clefts . . . rents in walls . . . smashed stone blocks . . . twisted iron . . . destruction . . . ruin . . .

The street.

The day was streaming down, red, upon the street . . .

Howls in the air. And the gleam of flame. And smoke . . .

Voices . . . shouts—and no exultant shouting . . . shouts of fear, of horror, of terribly strained tension . . .

At last the cathedral square . . .

The bonfire. The mob . . . men, woman, immeasurable masses . . . but they were not gazing at the bonfire, on the smoking fireiness of which smouldered a creature of metal and glass, with the head and body of a woman.

All eyes were turned upwards, towards the heights of the cathedral, the roof of which sparkled in the morning sunshine.

Joh Fredersen stopped, as though a blow had been struck at his knees.

"What . . ." he stammered. He raised his eyes, he raised his hands quite slowly to the level of his head . . . his hands rested upon his hair.

Soundlessly, as though mown down, he fell upon his knees.

Upon the heights of the cathedral roof, entwined about each other, clawed to each other, wrestled Freder and Rotwang, gleaming in the sunlight.

They fought, breast pressed to breast, knee to knee. One did not need very sharp eyes to see that Rotwang was by far the stronger. The slender form of the boy, in white silken tatters, bent under the throttling grip of the great inventor, farther and farther backwards. In a fearfully wonderful arch the slender, white form was extended, head back, knees bent forward. And the blackness which was Rotwang stood out, massy, mountain-like, above the silken whiteness, forcing it downwards. In the narrow gallery of the spire Freder crumpled up like a sack and lay in the corner, stirring no more. Above him, straightened up, yet bent forward—Rotwang, staring at him, then turning . . .

Along the narrow roof ridge, towards him—no, towards the dullish bundle of white silk, staggered Maria. In the light of the morning, risen glorious and imperious, her voice fluttered out like the mourning of a poor bird:

"Freder—Freder—!"

Whispers broke out in the cathedral square. Heads turned and hands pointed.

"Look—Joh Fredersen! Look over there—Joh Fredersen!"

A woman's voice yelled out:

"Now you see for yourself, don't you, Joh Fredersen, what it's like when someone's only child is murdered—?"

Josaphat leaped before the man who was on his knees, hearing nothing of what was going on around him.

"What's the matter—?" he shouted. "What's the matter with you all—? Your children have been saved! In the 'House of the Sons!' Maria and Joh Fredersen's son—they saved your children—!"

Joh Fredersen heard nothing. He did not hear the scream, which, like a bellowed prayer to God, suddenly leaped from the one mouth of the multitude.

He did not hear the shuffling with which the multitude near him, far around him, threw itself on its knees. He did not hear the weeping of the women, the panting of the men, nor prayer, nor thanks, nor groans, nor praises.

Only his eyes remained alive. His eyes which seemed to be lidless, clung to the roof of the cathedral.

Maria had reached the white bundle, which lay, crumpled up in the corner, between the spire and the roof. She slid along to it on her knees, stretching her hands out towards it, blinded with misery:

He pushed himself up and flung himself across to the ladder. He climbed up the ladder almost at a run, with the blindly certain speed born of fear for his beloved. He reached Rotwang, who let Maria fall. She fell. [Brigitte Helm (Maria), Rudolf Klein-Rogge (Rotwang), Gustav Fröhlich (Freder)]

"Freder . . . Freder . . ."

With a savage snarl, like the snarl of a beast of pray, Rotwang clutched at her. She struggled amid screams. He held her lips closed. With an expression of despairing incomprehension he stared into the girl's tear-wet face.

"Hel . . . my Hel . . . why do you struggle against me?"

He held her in his ironlike arms, as prey which, now, nothing and no one could tear away from him. Close to the spire a ladder led upwards to the cathedral coping. With the bestial snarl of one unjustly pursued he climbed up the ladder, dragging the girl with him, in his arms.

This was the sight which met Freder's eyes when he opened them and tore himself free from the half-unconscious state he was in. He pushed himself up and flung himself across to the ladder. He climbed up the ladder almost at a run, with the blindly certain speed born of fear for his beloved. He reached Rotwang, who let Maria fall. She fell. She fell, but in falling she saved herself, pulling herself up and reaching the golden sickle of the moon on which rested the star-crowned Virgin. She stretched out her hand to clutch at Freder. But at the same moment Rotwang threw himself down upon the man who was standing below him, and clasped tightly together, they rolled along, down the roof of the cathedral, rebounding violently against the narrow railing of the gallery.

The yell of fear from the multitude came shrieking up from the depths. Neither Rotwang nor Freder heard it. With a terrible oath Rotwang gathered himself up. He saw above him, sharp against the blue of the sky, the gargoyle of a waterspout. It grinned in his face. The long tongue leered mockingly at him. He drew himself up and struck, with clenched fist, at the grinning gargoyle . . .

The gargoyle broke . . .

In the weight of the blow he lost his balance—and fell—and saved himself, hanging with one hand to the Gothic ornamentation of the cathedral.

And, looking upwards, into the infinite blue of the morning sky, he saw Hel's countenance, which he had loved, and it was like the countenance of the beautiful angel of Death, smiling at him, its lips inclining towards his brow.

Great black wings spread themselves out, strong enough to carry a lost world up to heaven.

"Hel . . ."said the man. "My Hel . . . at last . . ."

And his fingers lost their hold, voluntarily . . .

Joh Fredersen did not see the fall, neither did he hear the cry of the multitude as it stared back. He saw but one thing: the white-gleaming figure of the man, who, upright and uninjured, was walking along the roof of the cathedral

227

with the even step of one fearing nothing, carrying the girl in his arms.

Then Joh Fredersen bent down, so low that his forehead touched the stones of the cathedral square. And those near enough to him heard the weeping which welled up from his heart, as water from a rock.

As his hands loosened from his head, all who stood around him saw that Joh Fredersen's hair had turned snow-white.

Color lithograph by Boris Blinsky, Paris, 224 x 303.5 cm.

CHAPTER XXIII
THE WINE OF SUFFERING

"BELOVED—!" SAID Freder, Joh Fredersen's son.

It was the softest, the most cautious call of which a human voice is capable. But Maria answered it just as little as she had answered the shouts of despair with which the man who loved her had wished to re-awaken her to consciousness of herself.

She lay couched upon the steps of the high altar, stretched out in her slenderness, her head in Freder's arm, her hands in Freder's hand, and the gentle fire of the lofty church-windows burnt upon her quite white face and upon her quite white hands. Her heart beat, slowly, barely, perceptibly. She did not breathe. She lay sunken in the depths of an exhaustion from which no shout, no entreaty, no cry of despair could have dragged her. She was as though dead.

A hand was laid upon Freder's shoulder.

He turned his head. He looked into the face of his father. Was that his father? Was that Joh Fredersen, the master over the great Metropolis? Had his father such white hair? And so tormented a brow? And such tortured eyes?

Was there, in this world, after this night of madness, nothing but horror and death and destruction and agony—without end—?

"What do you want here?" asked Freder, Joh Fredersen's son. "Do you want to take her away from me? Have you made plans to part her and me? Is there some mighty undertaking in danger, to which she and I are to be sacrificed?"

"To whom are you speaking, Freder?" his father asked, very gently.

Freder did not answer. His eyes opened inquiringly, for he had heard a voice never heard before. He was silent.

"If you are speaking of Joh Fredersen," continued the very gentle voice, "then be informed that, this night, Joh Fredersen died a sevenfold death . . ."

Freder's eyes, burnt with suffering, were raised to the eyes which were above him. A piteously sobbing sound came from out his lips.

"Oh my God—Father—! Father . . . you—!"

Joh Fredersen stooped down above him and above the girl who lay in Freder's lap.

"She is dying, father . . . Can't you see she is dying—?"

Joh Fredersen shook his head.

"No, no!" said his gentle voice. "No, Freder. There was an hour in my life in which I knelt, as you, holding in my arms the woman I loved. But she died, indeed. I have studied the face of the dying to the full. I know it perfectly and shall never again forget it . . . The girl is but sleeping. Do not awaken her by force."

And, with a gesture of inexpressible tenderness, his hand slipped from Freder's shoulder to the hair of the sleeping girl.

"Dearest child!" he said. "Dearest child . . ."

And from out of the depth of her dream the sweetness of a smile responded to him, before which Joh Fredersen bowed himself, as before a revelation, not of this world.

Then he left his son and the girl and passed though the cathedral, made glorious and pleasant by the gay-coloured ribbons of sunshine.

Freder watched him go until his gaze grew misty. And all at once, with a sudden, violent, groaning fervour, he raised the girl's mouth to his mouth and kissed her, as though he wished to die of it. For, from out the marvel of light, spun into ribbons, the knowledge had come upon him that it was day, that the invulnerable transformation of darkness into light was becoming consummate, in its greatness, in its kindliness, over the world.

"Come to yourself, Maria, beloved!" he said, entreating her with his caresses, with his love. "Come to me, beloved! Come to me!"

The soft response of her heart-beat, of her breathing, caused a laugh to well up from his throat and the fervour of his whispered words died on her lips.

Joh Fredersen caught the sound of his son's laugh. He was already near the door of the cathedral. He stopped and looked at the stack of pillars, in the delicate, canopied niches of which stood the saintly men and women, smiling gently.

"You have suffered," thought his dream-filled brain. "You have been redeemed by suffering. You have attained to bliss . . . Is it worth while to suffer?—Yes."

And he walked out of the cathedral on feet which were still as though dead, tentatively, he stepped through the mighty door-way, stood dazzled in the light and swayed as though drunken.

For the wine of suffering which he had drunk, was very heavy, and intoxicating, and white-hot.

His soul spoke within him as he reeled along: "I will go home and look for my mother."

CHAPTER XXIV

GOD'S SMILING ON US, MARIA

"FREDER . . . ?" said the soft Madonna-voice.

"Yes, you beloved! Speak to me! Speak to me!"

"Where are we?"

"In the cathedral."

"Is it day or night?"

"It is day."

"Wasn't your father here, with us, just now?"

"Yes, you beloved."

"His hand was on my hair?"

"You felt it?"

"Oh Freder, while your father was standing here it seemed to me as though I heard a spring rushing within a rock. A spring, weighted with salt, and red with blood. But I knew too, when the spring is strong enough to break out through the rock, then it will be sweeter than the dew and whiter than the light."

"Bless you for your belief, Maria . . ."

She smiled. She fell silent.

"Why don't you open your eyes, you beloved?" asked Freder's longing mouth.

"I see," she answered. "I see, Freder . . . I see a city, standing in the light . . ."

"Shall I build it?"

"No, Freder. Not you. Your father."

"My father?"

"Yes . . ."

"Maria when you spoke of my father, before, this tone of love was not in your voice . . ."

"Since then much has taken place, Freder. Since then, within a rock, a spring has come to life, heavy with salt and red with blood. Since then Joh Fredersen's hair has turned snow-white with deadly fear for his son. Since then have those whom I called my brothers sinned from excessive suffering. Since then has Joh Fredersen suffered from excessive sin. Will you not allow them both, Freder—your father as well as my brothers—to pay for their sin, to atone, to become reconciled?"

"Yes, Maria."

"Will you help them, you mediator?"

"Yes, Maria."

She opened her eyes and turned the gentle wonder of their blue towards him. Bending low above her, he saw, in pious astonishment, how the gay-coloured heavenly kingdom of saintly legends, which looked down upon her from out the lofty, narrow church-windows, was reflected in her Madonna-eyes.

Involuntarily he raised his eyes to become aware, for the first time, of whither he had borne the girl whom he loved.

"God is looking at us!" he whispered, gathering her up to his heart, with longing arms. "God is smiling to us, Maria."

"Amen," said the girl at his heart.

CHAPTER XXV

UNTO THE END OF THE WORLD

JOH FREDERSEN came to his mother's house.

Death had passed over Metropolis. Destruction of the world and the Day of Judgment had shouted from out the roars of explosion, the clanging of the bells of the cathedral. But Joh Fredersen found his mother as he always found her: in the wide, soft chair, by the open window, the dark rug over the paralysed knees, the great Bible on the sloping table before her, in the beautiful old hands, the figured lace at which she was sewing.

She turned her eyes towards the door and perceived her son.

The expression of stern severity on her face became sterner and more severe.

She said nothing. But about her closed mouth was something which said: "You are in a bad way, Joh Fredersen . . ."

And as a judge did she regard him.

Joh Fredersen took his hat from his head. Then she saw the white hair above his brow . . .

"Child—!" she said quietly, stretching her hands out towards him.

Joh Fredersen fell on his knees by his mother's side. He threw his arms about her, pressing his head into the lap, which had borne him. He felt her hands on his hair—felt how she touched it, as though fearful of hurting him, as though this white hair was the mark of an unhealed wound, very near the heart, and heard her dear voice saying:

"Child . . . My child . . . My poor child . . ."

The rustling of the walnut tree before the window filled a long silence with longing and affection. Then Joh Fredersen began to speak. He spoke with

the eagerness of one bathing himself in Holy water, with the fervour of a conquered one, confessing, with the redemption of one ready to do any penance,
and who was pardoned. His voice was soft and sounded as though coming
from far away, from the farther bank of a wide river.

He spoke of Freder; then his voice failed him entirely. He raised himself
from his knees and walked through the room. When he turned around there
stood in his eyes a smiling loneliness and the realisation of a necessary giving-
up—of the tree's giving up of the ripe fruit.

"It seemed to me," he said, gazing into space, "as though I saw his face
for the first time . . . when he spoke to me this morning . . . It is a strange face,
mother. It is quite my face—and yet quite his own. It is the face of his beautiful,
dead mother and yet it is, at the same time, fashioned after Maria's features, as
though he were born for the second time of that young, virginal creature. But
it is, at the same time, the face of the masses—confident in her, related to her,
as near to her as brothers . . ."

"How do you come to know the face of the masses, Joh?" asked his
mother gently.

For a long time Joh Fredersen gave no answer.

"You are quite right to ask, mother," be said then. "From the heights of
the New Tower of Babel I could not distinguish it. And in the night of lunacy, in
which I perceived it for the first time it was so distorted in its own horror that it
no more resembled itself . . .

"When I came out of the cathedral door in the morning the masses were
standing as one man, looking towards me. Then the face of the masses was
turned towards me. Then I saw, it was not old, was not young, was sorrowless
and joyless.

"What do you want?" I asked. And one answered:

"We are waiting, Mr. Fredersen . . ."

"For what?" I asked him.

"We are waiting," continued the spokesman, "for someone to come, who
will tell us what way we should go . . ."

"And you want to be this one, Joh?"

"Yes, mother."

And will they trust in you?"

"I do not know, mother. If we had been living a thousand years earlier, I
should, perhaps, set out on the high road, with pilgrim's staff and cockle hat,
and seek the way to the Holy Land of my belief, not returning home until I had
cooled my feet, hot from wandering, in the Jordan, and, in the places of re-

demption, had prayed to the Redeemer. And, if I were not the man I am, it might come to pass that I should set out on a journey along the roads of those who walk in the shadow. I should, perhaps, sit with them in the corners of misery and learn to comprehend their groans and their curses into which a life of hell has transformed their prayers . . . For, from comprehension comes love, and I am longing to love mankind, mother . . . But I believe that acting is better than making pilgrimages, and that a good deed is worth more than the best of words. I believe, too, that I shall find the way to do so, for there are two standing by me, who wish to help me . . ."

"Three, Joh . . ."

The eyes of the son sought the gaze of the mother.

"Who is the third?"

"Hel . . ."

" . . . Hel—? . . ."

"Yes, child."

Joh Fredersen remained silent.

She turned over the pages of her Bible, until she found what she sought. It was a letter. She took it and said, still holding it lovingly:

"I received this letter from Hel before she died. She asked me to give it you, when, as she said, you had found your way home to me and to yourself . . ."

Soundlessly moving his lips, Joh Fredersen stretched out his hand for the letter.

The yellowish envelope contained but a thin sheet of paper. Upon it stood, in the handwriting of a girlish woman:

> *"I am going to God, and do not know when you will read these lines, Joh. But I know you will read them one day, and, until you come, I shall exhaust the eternal blissfulness in praying God to forgive me for making use of two Sayings from His Holy Book, in order to give you my heart, Joh.*
>
> *"One is: 'I have loved thee with an everlasting love.' The other: 'Lo, I am with you always, even unto the end of the world!'"*
>
> *"Hel."*

It took Joh Fredersen a long time before be succeeded in replacing the thin sheet of note-paper in the envelope. His eyes gazed through the open window by which his mother sat. He saw, drawing across the soft, blue sky, great, white clouds, which were like ships, laden with treasures from a far-off world.

"Of what are you thinking, child?" asked his mother's voice, with care.

But Joh Fredersen gave her no answer. His heart, utterly redeemed, spoke stilly within him:

"Unto the end of the world . . . Unto the end of the world."

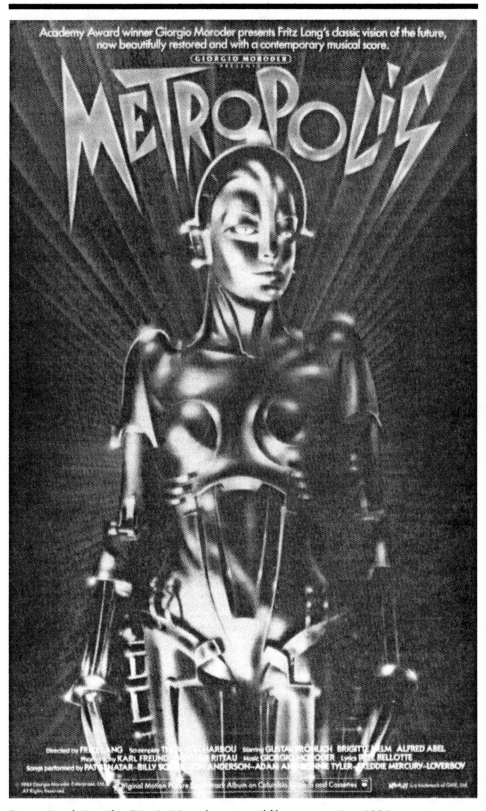

Promotional piece for Giorgio Moroder restored film presentation, 1984 .

This book was typeset in 10-point Optima.
Book and cover design by Lynne Rock.